THE ETHICS OF VIOLENCE

The Study of A Fractured World

George H. Faust

History Professor Emeritus, Lecturer on World Affairs,
and Chairperson on Law and Ethics in
The International Society for the Study of
Multiple Personality & Dissociation

UNIVERSITY
PRESS OF
AMERICA

Lanham • New York • London

Copyright © 1994 by
University Press of America®, Inc.
4720 Boston Way
Lanham, Maryland 20706

3 Henrietta Street
London WC2E 8LU England

Library of Congress Cataloging-in-Publication Data

Faust, George H.
The ethics of violence : the study of a fractured world /
George H. Faust.
p.   cm.
Includes bibliographical references and index.
1. Violence—History.   2. Violence—Moral and ethical aspects.
HM283.F38   1993   303.6'09—dc20   93–8800 CIP

ISBN 0–8191–9228–7 (cloth : alk. paper)

 The paper used in this publication meets the minimum requirements of
American National Standard for Information Sciences—Permanence
of Paper for Printed Library Materials, ANSI Z39.48–1984.

To my wife and partner, Betty

AUTHOR'S ACKNOWLEDGEMENTS

This book is the result of many hours spent in the study of world history, a subject wherein I find the chain which links what was, what is, and what ultimately will be.

I want to thank all those who share my interest and concern for the world. For encouraging me in this effort and giving of your time, physical help, and moral support. I hope I have earned your trust.

Immeasurable gratitude to Roshi Philip Kapleau, my teacher and long time friend, for his wise counsel, encouragement, and advice in this endeavor. I am grateful, also, for his time and patience.

I gratefully acknowledge my devoted wife and partner, Betty, for her constant faith in this pursuit. Her total commitment to countless hours of typing, editing, and copying has brought this book to fruition.

My sincere appreciation to Mary Hovanic, my long time friend and colleague in the teaching profession, whose help and expertise on this subject was invaluable to me.

I am deeply indebtedness to Cary and Marcia Lawson whose proficiency in personal computers greatly eased the task of turning a jumble of information into a book, and for sharing with us those wonderful Chinese meals.

George H. Faust, PhD, JD
Shaker Heights, OH
May 11, 1993

CONTENTS

FOREWORD

There are macroscopic and microscopic perspectives on the impact of violence on the individual.

It is indeed an honor to write the foreword for Dr. Faust's important analysis in the field of Ethics, a book which will serve as an aid in cultural recontextualization, and in this commentary I hope to do justice to his work. I want to emphasize that understanding his contribution in the field of ethics, culture, cultural history and violence is a *sine qua non* in changing for the better, a world gone awry. Disjointed commentaries, disjointed interventions, and disjointed programs, where all parts are isolated one from another and separate from a common core, will only continue to foster an atmosphere of disintegration and personal/social cultural dissociation. Dr. Faust's work shines as a beacon and points us toward a more integrative way of thinking and understanding.

As a clinical psychologist and a university professor in the department of psychiatry, the importance of the impact and *sequelae* of violence stands at the forefront of my concern at both the societal and individual level. I will take what may appear at first blush to be a somewhat mechanistic perspective, trying to create a microcosm about violence at the level of the individual, and begin to consider what Dr. Faust describes in more global ways at the level of the person proper. The overlap and parallels between general and specific concerns should seem obvious.

In her new chapter on the aftermath of victimization, Janoff-Bulman (1985) cites Epstein (1980), who says that "whether we like it or not, each of us, because he has a human brain, forms a theory of reality which brings order into what otherwise would be a chaotic world of experience. We need a theory to make sense of the world (p.34)." Epstein (1973, 1979, 1980) has suggested that theories of reality are actually divided into two sub-theories based on experience surrounding oneself and views surrounding the world. The functions of world and self reality are of course intertwined and reciprocally influence one another. Chaos or attack in any aspect of these two interconnected views will de-stabilize not only the aspect of reality under direct attack but also the other, by proxy. Violence to the individual is just this kind of attack; being a victim of violent interpersonal crime affects the individual's perception of self and the world around him/her in profound ways. Nowhere is this better expressed or more profoundly understood than in the field of Trauma and Dissociation where researchers and clinicians face on a day to day, moment to moment basis, the impact of violence on the mind of a human being. The younger the person, the longer the duration of the attack (years versus days), as well as the nature of the relationship between abuser and victim, the more the person's mind will stop its normal integrative processes and attempt to understand, explain and incorporate the assault. Regardless of the best efforts of the mind, the results are temporary and lean toward pathological rather than a healthy homeostasis.

The field of Multiple Personality Disorder (MPD) is one in which psychiatry/psychology has come to the forefront fairly recently because of MPD's pleiomorphic and puzzling presentations. Within the last ten years, therapists have come to understand MPD as an adaptation originating in childhood to violence sustained over a long period of time, emotionally strangulating the child's negotiating the normal Piagetian stages of development, thus hindering the child's step-wise socioemotional growth, and producing an individual who is not only disintegrated from society, but one who may be so separate from parts of himself/herself that he/she does not even know how little he/she really knows. The incidence of self-generated and self induced violence is extreme in this group.

Multiple Personality Disorder, a chronic dissociative psychopathology with problems in identity and memory, is increasingly recognized as one of the possible sequelae to child abuse. Ninety eight per cent of MPD sufferers report such a history. It is supposed that for MPD to develop, the intensity of abuse is such that the traditional and less handicapping defenses available to the child are overridden, and that the victimized child needs to mobilize ad hoc defenses rather than ex post facto defenses.

Dr. Braun (1988) has proposed a model of dissociation for the mind which suggests that when in a non-dissociated state the mind is able to incorporate and understand the world according to the acronym, BASK. This means that an individual experiences an event along the Behavioral dimension, the Affective dimension, the level of the Sensations, as well as Knowing, that the event happened. Someone who dissociates can separate any or all of the four BASK dimensions one from another; therefore, a dissociating person can decontextualize an event from its respective parts. Semiotic theory would predict that this modification at the descriptive level of understanding and communication of information would have serious consequences on the semantic and pragmatic levels. The meaning of the event is changed by the absence or presence of certain core components. Consolidation of core conflicting themes, whether affectively or cognitively based, is at the origin of the formation of personalities in MPD individuals. The above example represents what happens to **one** event. In actuality, repeated violent intrusions on the child's mind not only segregates aspects of events, one from another, but also the events themselves, each from the other. Events and meanings are decontextualized, one from another. Order and organization loses its consensually understood meaning at the level of the individual, and there is a reduction from the perspective of the whole mind to that of the personality, or ego-state structure, an attempt to gain predictability and consistency. This reductionistic view of functioning and relating carries with it grave consequences for the person who subscribes to it, whether intentionally or not, whether consciously or not. The personalities may co-exist in a democratic, federated, oriented way. These individuals are rarely seen in therapy. More often though, the level of communication between the parts and cooperation between the parts is nihil and there are rival wars between personalities who have no idea that the war they subscribe to is actually a civil war where the conquering of one part or one group of personalities actually means everybody loses. The goal of treatment for the MPD patient becomes the unification of the mind through appropriate communication between the parts of the mind. The communication is intended to lead to empathy and identification for all parts of the mind where as a whole they can work in peace towards growth, each learning from the other in the moment, and from those of the past.

Dr. Faust's book, for me, carries the message that somehow world cultures have not only maintained their separateness from one another, they have also ignored or forgotten their origins within themselves, their goals and their purposes. They have all too often subscribed to the politics of violence, sometimes based on religion, at other times based on economics —to the loss of everyone. They seem not to know, or they do not care.

Dr Faust's expertise takes us through culture after culture with an exacting study of the proposed origins of violence and its perpetuation as well. Violence lends itself to more violence and to lame attempts at finding solutions through strong leadership. People who have been victims of violence are subject to mind control. Cultures who have lived under the reign of violence are equally vulnerable to the control of a few. Is it not interesting how conveniently human nature leaves in the dark those parts of the mind which are child-like and ignorant of powerful control (through destructive means)? Parallel processing also is alive and well at a cultural level. Those who assume control of major decisions often leave the people who elected them ignorant of their true motives. The decisions often surround the need of the few, rather than the need of the many. Dr. Faust presents to us in a vivid and exciting way what we really would rather not see. This book is not for the weak at heart.

FOREWORD

In the same way that we as a culture would rather see ourselves as dutifully protecting our children, well intended individuals who, regardless of political and religious affiliation, subscribe to the betterment of mankind. Dr. Faust systematically shows us how we are lacking: As a culture we neither protect our children nor are we so well intended, nor are we more selfless than Attila the Hun's troops or Hitler's armies. Why do we balk when other countries mock us for our naivete surrounding our economy, our education, etc..? Do they know something about us that we choose to either ignore or rationalize with the help of our "chosen few" politicians? How are we to understand the growing statistics on abuse and violence in the home and on the streets? The first thing we need to do is face it outright. I believe that we can learn from others and from the mistakes of others. We can also learn from our own mistakes if we have the courage to begin to acknowledge our contribution to the problem and begin to recognize our responsibility in the process of change and solution. Dr. Faust's book, I believe, will help us do that.

Each of us as a member of the human race can choose to enter into the change process at a different point. Each will impact the process and influence one another. Dr. Faust may choose to intervene at a historical/legal level. I may choose to engage in modification at the level of the individual. And a sociologist responsible for organization of programs for social policy may intervene at a group or community level.

Again, each bit of change will feed the wholeness of the evolutionary process of change at a sociocultural level. If this does not happen, we will have to contend with our own neglect of ourselves, and with the neglect of others as well. However grim this reality may appear, it is very likely to happen if the "me generation" (otherwise stated, the cultural narcissists) does not develop a larger sense of responsibility and community awareness. Experts like Dr. Faust are warning us. Do we have the courage to listen?

Catherine G. Fine, PhD
Institute of Pennsylvia Hospital

INTRODUCTION

Violence, commonly referred to as terrorism, has been traced back to ancient Mesopotamia and Egypt (through oral and written tradition) some five or six thousand years. The seeds of greed, hatred, and repression have long been scattered throughout our planet to germinate and propagate, and sequentially issue forth into violence. The purpose of this analysis is to reexamine the evidence and consider its effect from the onset of civilization, to modern day society. Leaders of the world community today search for ways to extinguish those fires which are fueled by hatred and prejudice.

A careful analysis of the past may show how the struggle for religious status and class recognition is inherent with violence. While examining economic imbalances which dominate both strong and weak governments, violence accelerates and nations become more complex as rivalry for world power becomes more acute. Perhaps a keener understanding of twentieth century acts of violence can be attained by a closer evaluation of terrorist activities from the past, and the psycho-spiritual dynamics from which they have been motivated. It should be understood that in principal the use of violence is approved; however, to make it an issue of ethics depends on how and to what objective it is being used.

In the definition of violence/terrorism some measure of comprehension is required in order to conceive of its use. Are there universal standards of social conduct in peace and war? What is war? How are violence and terrorism defined in relation to war, civil disobedience, and armed or unarmed revolt? The following evidence shall verify that violence in all its manifestations is an integral part of our past. Disparities over religious, cultural, and ideological beliefs continue to provoke violence. However, modern technology has aided greatly in the magnitude of its use by the rapid inventions of destructive weapons, thus presenting an even greater threat to our present day world society.

One also may come to realize that among the most frustrating global problems in the twentieth century are the myriad reasons to justify violence. That which has been our legacy is now being foisted on future generations.

Let us examine some definitions of terrorism and see how they conform to the configuration of the past as well as the present. The United States

Introduction

Department of State has defined terrorism as follows:

> The threat or use of violence for political purposes by individuals or groups whether acting for or in opposition to established governmental authority, when such actions are intended to influence a target group wider than the immediate victim or victims.

Here one can see how the definition of *terrorism is* defined by the word *violence.* The word terrorism dates from the Reign of Terror during the French Revolution (1793-1794). It traditionally refers to organized acts of violence, the purpose of which is to intimidate opponents and publicize grievances. The use of terrorism often involves bombing, kidnaping, various forms of hijacking, assassinations and the taking of hostages. These kinds of techniques are employed by those on the left as well as those on the right of the political spectrum. They also may be part of a state operation against an opposition, or a revolutionary group in guerrilla warfare for the overthrow of a government.

Though terrorism dates from the French Revolutionary period, the question remains: Is twentieth century terrorism essentially any different from our historical counterparts? Are its advocates criminals, revolutionaries, or realists? Are the death squads of Central America and the Near East examples of twentieth century government terror, or a carryover from the past? A review of our past provides countless incidents of terror, carried out by fanatics obsessed with a zeal and belief that their actions would earn them great rewards, while others pursued martyrdom. The word assassin derives from Hashishism, which describes a band of Hashish hit men (directed by an eleventh century Persian Hassan, Ibn Al Sabbath), who often risked their lives for their religious cause.

The type of violence described here is currently being carried out in Lebanon by suicide bombers more deadly than those who seize embassies, highjack airplanes, or kidnap officials. Each succeeding group is becoming more violent. The same may be said of our present day street gangs. Today, as in the past, terrorism is a means of gaining ideological, religious or material goals and the power, and identification associated with its use.

Our world society faces increased religious, ideological and cultural confrontation. Terror is a common weapon which, when put to use, can cause deep and enduring suffering. None of the world organizations appear to know how to begin to resolve or alleviate the pain, or its causes.

Introduction

A fundamental problem is the difficulty which humankind has in accepting the reality of impermanence. Unfortunately, we live our lives as though the self and its concomitant cultures and institutions will forever endure. Failing to recognize the law of impermanence, we create a reality based upon delusion, the consequence of which can only bring suffering, conflict, and violence. As world societies, institutions, ideologies, and religions change, we cling to notions and constructs of them until their reality crumbles, creating confusion, fear and fragmentation that is evident in our everyday lives. In the face of these conditions, the desirable endeavors of most proclaimed universal religions are lacking in fulfillment. On further examination we shall see how the situation has been exacerbated by the failure of religions in the main to respond to this basic human condition. None of the world religions or philosophies has become universal; and the only three theocentric (God centered) religions are Judaism, Islam, and Christianity.

Communism is a philosophy and a Judeo-Christian heresy of the West which was put in place after about one thousand years of Russian Orthodoxy, and some five thousand years of Chinese culture. The dynastic system of China ran from about 1800 B.C. up to the early hours of the twentieth century. And during that time from Confucius (6th and 5th centuries B.C.), until the twentieth century, Confucianism had been a powerful force in Chinese society.

Shintoism, if considered as a religion is not in any way theo-centric but primarily the ethnic and animistic faith of Japan.

Western and Eastern Orthodox Christianity are in many ways not only divided against themselves, but they also have a long and bitter history of unresolved war grievances.

Until the collapse of the Soviet Union in 1991, it challenged The People's Republic of China. Each government professed to be the fountainhead of true Communism.

Islam is spiritually and physically at war with itself. It also has a long history of violence against Hinduism, Judaism and the Christian world as well.

The People's Republic of China has a powerful substrata of Confucianism which is yet to be absorbed. Soviet Communism failed to absorb Russian Orthodox Christianity and its many ethnic and nationalistic subjects.

Introduction

Buddhism is a non-theocentric religion which has divisions within it but is absent of warfare, either against itself or other faiths. There are no sutras or koans that justify the use of violence in the name of Buddhism.[1] The Buddhists have fought in wars; however, they have not fought as a result of the teachings of The Buddha, or with the approval of the patriarchs.

Hinduism has been confined almost entirely to India. There are many faces to Hinduism, peaceful and violent. Currently, in the ongoing violence within India there is great difficulty with Islam, and with Sikhism as well.

When the present world situation is examined, it becomes obvious that society is presented with a fractured world, and there is considerable evidence to show it has come about as a result of ones own thinking. In other words: it arises from ones own perception of the world, and the alienation which one feels surging from within. One fails to see the *whole* world as a social order of human beings joined in a common bond, and not detached from it, with all sentient and non-sentient aspects of the earth and cosmos.

Although the fragmentation of human thought is not new in its appearance in human activity, it did not appear as part of our thought process during the earlier stages of human development. Neither did it appear when we were in the pastoral/nomadic stage of development, nor at the beginning of domestic agriculture, urban life, and the division of labor. Not even at the emergence of universal religions had this thought process appeared.

The people of early social groups saw themselves intermixed and interdependent with all they surveyed, including the sentient and non-sentient. They were neither separate nor distinct from all their surroundings. The breaking up of the unity of sentient and non-sentient bonding in human thought reaches as far back as the beginning of recorded history, to the early days of ancient Sumer some 4,000 years B. C. Here, and in the subsequent evolvement of the Babylonian civilization, are the earliest records of the classification of plants, rocks, animals and crops. The Sumerian people had rank within their sizeable city (temple) communities and a highly developed division of labor.

There were, at the apex of the Sumer temple communities, priests and gods. Sumerian temple communities began to engage in warfare among themselves for water and land at the delta of the Tigris-Euphrates rivers where water poured into the Arabian Persian Gulf. In conjunction with warfare

---

[1] *Zen Dawn In The West, Roshi Philip Kapleau, Doubleday Press, 1979*

among the Sumerian people, another conflict arose as the result of a tribal people crowding upon their frontier with population pressure from the north.

The oral and written traditions of our ancient forebearers are replete with instances of a change of thought and even with a change of consciousness. Humans began to alienate themselves from members within their own community as the division of labor became more and more complex. The Sumerians separated themselves from other communities within their own society by organized warfare and, in turn, against the tribal people of Mesopotamia -now modern day Iraq- who were attracted to their more highly developed social order.

From the time of ancient Sumer to this very hour, in moving from temple communities to super powers, we have created larger and larger units in which to live, yet we remain fragmented. In this long process we have attempted to conquer nature and nature now is fighting back. It is entirely possible that as humans we may one day realize that we cannot separate ourselves from the flow of nature throughout the universe.

Classification must be seen as part of a greater whole rather than a constraint that has its own reality. Perhaps the best way to illustrate the point is to contrast the views of two renowned theoretical physicists, Stephen Hawking and David Bohm.

In Steven Hawking's book "*A Brief History of Time*", his discussion of time begins with Aristotle (340 B.C.): "My position here is not one regarding any theory of physics, but as an historian." Hawking would have one believe that Aristotle was in the vanguard in determining that the earth was round. George Sarton's "*History of Science, Volume One*" makes clear that the people of Sumer reached this conclusion with amazing accuracy long before the Greeks appeared on the scene. They were able to determine the size of the earth and the distance from the earth to most of the visible stars. Moreover, Hawking makes no reference to the conclusion of Hindu scholars regarding the atom.

Yet another study shows that Buddhists found the following: [1]

> The atom was generally thought to be eternal, but some Buddhist conceived of it not only as the minutest object capable of occupying space, but also as occupying the minutest possible

---

[1] *The Wonder That Was India, pg. 197, A.L. Basham, The Grove Press, Inc.*

duration of time, coming into being and vanishing almost in an instant, only to be succeeded by another atom, caused by the first. Thus, the atom of Buddhism in some measure resembles the quantum of Planck. The atom was quite invisible to the human eye; the Orthodox Vaisesrika School believed the single atom to be a mere point in space, completely without magnitude.

These ideas were clearly independent of Greek thought and in existence at the time of The Buddha (C. 563- C. 483).

Hawking makes no reference to the works of Chinese scholars, such as Joseph Neidham, in referring to the history of time. [1] Nor does he make reference to the scientific discoveries of the ancient Mayan Indians of Mexico and Central America. [2] The knowledge of time contained in the Solar and Lunar Calendar of ancient Mexico far surpassed the measure of time in Western Europe until fairly recently.

Did philosophy begin only with Aristotle and end with Immanuel Kant and Ludwig Wittgenstein? Hawking seems to think so. He makes no reference to science or philosophy aside from the Greek and Western World of Europe and England. Is there no purpose in knowing the Praja Paramita Hridaya from India which existed long before Aristotle, or to The Hua-Yen School of China that also has its origin in India? [3]

Fragmentation in thought is further evident in a statement Hawking attributes to Einstein's attitude toward politics. "Equations are more important to me, because politics is for the present, but an equation is something for eternity." If atomic and hydrogen weapons are not put under control by politics, will there in fact be an eternity whereby the equations for these weapons are produced? How does one separate the equations from life?

---

[1] *Science And Civilization In China, Joseph Neidham, Cambridge, England, 1954. These volumes deal with far reaching developments in science.*

[2] *Mexico Mystique, Frank Waters, Sage Books, 1975. This book deals with the calculations of time into the past and future and astronomy as well. See, also, Distant Neighbors, Alan Riding, Vintage Press, 1986.*

[3] *Hau-Yen Buddhism, The Jewel Net Of India, Francis H. Cook, The Pennsylvania State Press, 1977.*

Introduction

Hawking, also fails to make reference to Eastern philosophy, as described in Masao Abe's book *"Zen and Western Thought."* Again, Hawking, in his book does not refer to David Bohm's notable work *"Wholeness and The Implicate Order."* Bohm, drawing upon the world of science and philosophy, comes to contrary conclusions: [1]

> It is proposed that the widespread and pervasive distinctions between people (race, nation, family, profession, etc.) which are now preventing mankind from working together for the common good and indeed, even for survival, have one of the key factors of their origin in a kind of thought that treats things as inherently divided, disconnected, and 'broken up' into yet smaller constituent parts. It is considered to be essentially independent and self-existent.
>
> When man thinks of himself in this way, he will inevitably tend to defend the needs of his own 'Ego' against others. Or if he identifies with a group of people of the same kind, he will defend this group in a similar way. He cannot seriously think of mankind as the basic reality, whose claims come first . . . What I am proposing here is that man's general way of thinking of the totality is crucial for the overall order of the human mind itself. If he thinks of the totality as constituted of independent fragment, then that is how his mind will tend to operate, but if he can include everything coherently and harmoniously in an overall whole that is undivided, unbroken, and without a border, then his mind will tend to move in a similar way, and from this will flow an orderly action with the whole . . .

The difference in the position of Hawking and Bohm is astonishing.

The religious and ideological forces of the world contain the hopes as well as the horrors of the future. It is therefore imperative that the universal objectives of religious and ideological forces come together in an attempt to overcome their fragmented practices. If the leaders of a divided world fail to look beyond the scope of their own self-centeredness, the future may well be written in the past, which ultimately could lead to total destruction.

---

[1] *"Wholeness And The Implicate Order", David Bohm, p. xi, p. 7. Ark Paperback, London and New York, 1980. See, also, The Holographic Paradigm, Edited by Ken Wilbur, New Science Library, Boston and London, 1985.*

LATIN CHRISTENDOM THROUGH THE AMERICAN REVOLUTION

The ethics of violence, religious and philosophical, are buried deep in the oral and written history of human society. The practice of violence and the myriad excuses to sanction and defend it is accelerating to such proportions that it now threatens to annihilate the entire universe.

Latin Christendom through the Reformation, and the rise of Protestantism through the American Revolution of 1776, is defined in this chapter. One discovers that the theological justification for violence in Sumer and Egypt was integrated with Judaism, and then with Christianity. It includes Latin Christian Society and all branches of Eastern Orthodox Christianity.

Long before Russian Orthodox Christianity took its form in Kievan Rus, and before the Reformation and Counter-Reformation fractured Latin Christendom, a third powerful religious movement was rising from the sands of Saudi Arabia. That religious movement was Islam. Each religion proclaimed universality —direct authority from God— and fashioned itself as the one true faith to the exclusion of all others. However, they all descended from the same root, exercising violence to gain and hold vast geographic spheres populated by massive numbers of people. Each religious movement employed violence and terror against other faiths. They even applied violence and terror against their own believers, as divergent views circulated against the main body of religious thought. Consequently, the rebellious members of each faith used tactics of terror against the established order. They also used theological arguments, as did the established order, to support counter-terrorism. For the justification of violence, each quoted from either the early Christian Fathers, the Old Testament, the New Testament, or The Holy Koran.

Latin Christendom fell in the West in a similar manner as did the Greco-Roman Empire in 476 A.D. After having governed much of the same area for approximately one thousand years, the internal and external problems of Latin Christendom paralleled those of the Greco-Roman Empire.

The changes which brought about the fall of the Church of Rome would coincide with the rise of the nation-state system, the expansion of Europe, and with international law. The most dominant factor would be the age old theory of divine rights of monarchs. This theory would be challenged in England by the Glorious Revolution, 1688-89, and it would be challenged in the New World by the revolt of the British colonies in 1776.

What was the structure of Latin Christendom? In 312 A.D., the Church and State merged by an agreement between Emperor Constantine and Pope Sylvester. After the fall of the Greco Roman Empire, the Church of Rome imperceptibly took over most of the area in Europe and England which had been held by the Empire. However, the Church State, under Rome, had a strong similarity of administrative structure to the former Greco-Roman Empire. The papacy was the primary law-giver. Below the papacy were the college of cardinals and arch-bishops, The parish priest was at the bottom. There were the far reaching canon laws, the church courts, the enforcement branch of the administration, and a tax system. A common Latin language was used throughout the realm. The power of the Church was supported further by writings of the early Christian Fathers,and used to suppress dissent and expand the domain of the Church against all theological enemies.

All subjects of Latin Christendom were considered members of a common Christian Society over which the Church held sway. In time, the expanse of the Church became so great that it failed to adjust to the demands of its far reaching domain. The emerging nation-state system of Divine Monarchs and the Renaissance began to weaken Church authority. Failing to adjust to demands for internal change in the West, the Reformation and the Counter-Reformation brought to an end the domination of Latin Christendom.

Latin Christendom has never fully recovered from its fracture by the religious wars of the 16th and 17th centuries. The same is true of the theory of the state, which is the authority of God, deemed an institution to which humankind must become subservient. While contested by the theory that the state is the servant of the people,it is that which is now the parent of the authoritarian state. The violence inflicted throughout the world by the contest between the two is yet to be resolved.

With this brief overview, let us examine *"the ethics of violence"* in Latin Christian Society through to the American Revolution of 1776.

People have pondered the question of human existence since the beginning of oral and written history. Who am I? What is the nature of humankind? What is my relation to the society of which I am a part? What is my relation to the unknown? These questions and the threat to human existence which confront humanity are as important today as in the past.

The earliest higher civilizations appeared in ancient Sumer and Egypt. The society of Sumer began to emerge around 4000 B.C. and the Egyptian Society began to emerge around 3100 B.C. Sumer was located in the delta of the Tigris-Euphrates Rivers in what is now modern-day Iraq. Later it extended along the Nile Valley in Northeast Egypt. In Arnold J. Toynbee's *"A Study of History,"* higher civilization is defined as those that developed domestic agriculture, urban centers, a division of labor, and a universal religion. To this was added a style of formal writing which appeared at approxmately the same dates as above. [1]

Both Sumer and Egypt believed they were creating an earthly society based upon a divine model. For many centuries, life was promulgated and obeyed by people in these societies who believed they were following the laws of their gods. They were all understood in terms of their religious beliefs for whatever reasons given: by success or failure, by war or peace, by floods or droughts, or by feast or famine.

From the earliest oral history and from written material, we find that the people of Mesopotamia, a land where Sumer was located, thought that their gods were jealous, arbitrary, capricious and wrathful in nature. However, the Egyptians along the Nile considered their gods to be compassionate, benevolent, kind and just. The reason for such contrast in their convictions seems to emanate from their respective views about the forces of nature as they perceived them.

The Sumerian world and subsequent societies of Mesopotamia were approachable from all sides by war-like tribes attracted to domestic agriculture. The people who settled in this area depended upon water from the Tigris-Euphrates Rivers and their source in the mountains far to the north in modern day Turkey. The water supply, at best, was unpredictable, depending on the melting of the snow upon the high mountains. Floods, droughts, feast or famine, consequently followed in an unpredictable fashion, thereby dominating all life in and around the delta and the Persian Gulf.

---

[1] *A Study of History, Arnold J. Toynbee, Oxford University Press. All twelve volumes have been combed thoroughly for this work. In addition, the same has been done to his following works: Experiences, Oxford University Press, 1969. Surviving The Future, Oxford University Press, 1971. Change and Habit, Oxford University Press, 1966. America And The World Revolution, Oxford University Press, 1961. Christianity Among The Religions of The World, Scribner, 1957. An Historian's Approach To Religion, Oxford University Press, 1978. Extensive use has been made from these works, too numerous to list separately.*

The Summerians accepted the theory that the gods controlled the forces of nature on earth and in the heavens. The temple communities were managed by a hierarchy of priests who had dominion over all manifestations of life. The theological premise was that humans should perform all common labor in order to free the gods from such lowly tasks. The people performed the work, hoping to appease the gods whom they feared. They feared that if the gods were displeased they would have to be punished. Punishment would be in the form of floods, droughts, war among the temple communities, or war with tribal people who would attempt to conquer their land. And the priests were the mediators between the people and the gods who often acted capriciously —beyond human understanding. The vulnerability of the people to natural forces had a profound influence on the religious ideas attributed to the gods.

When particular areas of Mesopotamia came under the control of kings rather than priests, annual ceremonies were held in order to sanctify the authority of the ruler.

Hammurabi, the great law-giver (1792-1750 B.C.), conquered the entire area of Mesopotamia. In Babylon, Hammurabi convinced the people that all the gods of the realm had chosen him king of gods. Therefore, under Hammurabi, Babylonia became the religious center of all Mesopotamian territory. The law of the realm was the code of Hammurabi; it was that which had come from God. Coming from God, the belief was that the law would not die but endure. Accordingly, the law of God endures, and not man. [1]

The Nile, a navigable river from both the north and south —contrary to the Tigris-Euphrates— was a fundamental factor in the early unification of Egypt for it was protected from outside interference for many centuries due to its geographical location. Vast desert expanses to the east and west, the unknown source of the Nile to the south and the Mediterranean Sea to the north gave the river-bound people in each location a higher sense of security, permitting them to unify the valley into one large community under one ruler. Aside from occasional minor conflicts with outside intruders, Egyptian life remained relatively unified and intact for just under one thousand years.

Along a ribbon of land known as the Valley of the Nile, the concept of a god was fundamentally different. Not unlike a large temple community, it

---

[1] *History of Science, Volume 1, George Sarton, The Norton Library, 1952, deals with Mesopotamia, p. 57-100. The Rise of The West, William H. McNeill, The University of Chicago Press, 1963 p. 135. Extensive use is made of this valuable work.*

was ruled by a god embodied in a human. The Pharaoh was given divine status in Egypt, creating a stability that Mesopotamia never knew. An additional security was a conviction that the Pharaoh would enjoy immortality, maintaining that no person could achieve such coveted status except through the ruler. The desire for eternal life therefore enticed all to try to assuage the ruler, in return for faithful service. In later days the hope for immortality was thought possible if proper spells, rituals and like ceremonies were carried out.

Egyptian gods, as gods of the Nile, could be depended on for they brought water and rich soil, giving rise to the testimony that to Egypt, "the Nile is the gift of the gods." The Pharaoh, Horus, as the chief god in human form, was a guarantee to the Egyptians that the gods of Egypt cared for their people. This was striking in contrast to the gods of Mesopotamia.

The Mesopotamians moved up the valley from the Tigris-Euphrates delta toward the eastern shores of the Mediterranean Sea, to what is modern day Lebanon, Palestine and Israel. Egyptian society moved out from the Nile Valley and became inter mixed with other cultures having diverse social systems then emerging on the eastern shores. Egypt and Mesopotamia, the two dominant forces of the past, developed fundamental components of Judaism from which Christianity and Islam became a major force. Consequently, Christianity and Islam contain strong elements of Egyptian and Mesopotamian thought. [1]

All ancient people believed floods, droughts, wars and famines —which today are attributed to natural causes— were the direct result of a supernatural force. This had a much deeper historical significance, coming from Egypt and Mesopotamia.

Monotheism, the focal point of Judaism and the law of Yahweh (God), was handed down to the Jews through Moses. The Hebrew people theorized that God was the ruler of history. If they were defeated in war, it was that which God had willed because of past failings. Monarchs were subject to the law of Yahweh in governing their affairs. Monotheism, combined with the influence of Egyptian and Mesopotamian theology, was the motivating factor to the future of the Hebrew people, and the subsequent evolution of Christianity and Islam. As trained warriors, the people of Israel were lawfully unified by King David, himself a warrior king.

---

[1] *Islam is professed to be as deep or its roots as ancient and historical as Judaism, according to The Holy Koran.*

Monotheism carried over into Christianity. Christian monarchs must be governed by the word of God through the Church or directly from God under the theory of the divine rights of monarchs. Spiritual force, the additional thesis that humankind had fallen from grace and therefore needed redemption could come only through the Church, as the mystic body of Christ. The Christians judged this thesis to be Judaic in origin. Christianity also took over two divergent views of man. In the Book of Job 25:6, man is referred to as a "maggot and a worm." In Psalms 8:6, man is spoken of as the being whom God hath "crowned with glory and honor." Further in Psalms 51:5, a man is revealed as a sinner, "For I was shaped in iniquity and in sin did my mother conceive me." This open contradiction about the nature of man is not resolved either in Christianity or in Judaism. The concept of sin seems to be the one point upon which the two religions seem to agree.

The root word of "sin" means "to miss the mark." One failing to conform to the laws of Judaism as revealed by Yahweh was doomed to sin. [1] Not only did this law apply to Jews as a body, but if the kings were to be considered just in their domains, it was enforced upon them, as well. Many of the kings were warrior kings, as was David. It must be recognized that King David succeeded where King Saul failed in defeating the Philistines when he captured the City of Jehusites (Jerusalem) and made it his capital. [2]

Great demands were placed on the rulers of Judaic law in domestic and foreign affairs. Wars were deemed just only when aligned with the law of Yahweh. The same was true relative to the domestic affairs of a given kingdom. When tensions escalated between ruler and subjects, it was concluded that the ruler was at variance with the law. There is a factor in Hebrew history that prophets appeared in the time of Judges, around 1000 B.C. A prophet in Judaic terms means "to speak for another" (Exodus 7). Judaic prophets spoke for Yahweh. Among them were Nathan (in the time of David), Elijah, Amos, Hosea, Isaiah, Micah, and many others. All prophets brought to public notice the personal conduct of the kings, when in conflict with the will of Yahweh. They also brought attention to the failure of the kings, when their rule did not conform to the law of social order. When the rule of the king and the law did not coincide, revolution could be expected.

For instance, when Naboth, a land owner, refused to turn over his vineyard to Ahab, the king of Israel, he was framed on fake charges of

---

[1] *The Interpreters Bible, Abington Press, Volume 3, p. 120.*

[2] *The Holy Bible, King James Version*

blaspheme against Yahweh. As a result of this, Naboth was stoned to death and King Ahab proceeded to take over his vineyard. When the prophet, Elijah, learned of this, he immediately heard the words of the Lord. He was told to speak to Ahab: "Arise, go down to meet Ahab, King of Israel . . . and you shall say to him, 'Thus says the Lord, in the place where dogs licked the blood of Naboth shall dogs lick thy blood, even thine.' I Kings, Chapter 21: 19.

Deuteronomy 13 says: "If a prophet arises that attempts to lead people to another God, that person shall be put to death even if it be brother, son, daughter, wife or friend. One is to show no pity, nor to spare them, nor conceal thee, thou shalt surely kill him; thine hand shall be first upon him to put him to death and afterwards the hand of all the people stone him that he die."

And, again, in Kings 18, a dispute arises between the prophets of Baal and Elijah as to which is the true God, the one of Baal or the Lord God of the prophet Elijah. The contest resulted in the God of Elijah being victorious. Elijah, therefore, killed all the prophets of Baal with his sword.

The wholesale and ruthless slaughter of the prophets of Baal was considered to be a righteous deed by the oppressed Yahwehistic worshipers. [1]

In Kings 20, the conflict between Ahab, the King of Israel, and the Syrians is described. In verse 26, the Syrians stated that the God of Israel is the God of the hills, 'but he is not God of the valleys.' A man of God spake to the King of Israel, "Thus saith the Lord . . . therefore will I deliver all this great multitude unto thine hand, and ye shall know that I am the Lord." (II Kings 19:20-34).

Quoting from II Kings 20:35, "And it came to pass that night, that the angel of the Lord went out, and smote in the camp of the Assyrians a hundred fourscore and five thousand; and when they arose early in the morning, behold, they were all dead corpses." This story is an account of the punishment of the impious attitude of the Assyrians.

The following principles of the ethics of violence are clearly stated or implied as evidenced in Judaism:

1. The king's rule is subject to the law of Yahweh. Violence or the threat, thereof, is permissible to sustain social order within the king's

---

[1] *The Interpreters Bible, op. cit., Vol. 9, p. 150.*

jurisdiction. The threat of violence, in itself, is a form of its use in that it is shown to be available.

2. The king is subject to the law of Yahweh if he is to maintain the correct social order in his collective responsibility. Failing to maintain the proper order could result in some form of revolution. Violence, divinely sanctioned, is invoked against a king who fails in his responsibility to the social order.

3. One is encouraged to kill anyone who seeks to persuade another person from the true God to a false one. This is violence of person against person. It is not the king who acts.

4. A king may use violence to support the thesis of the superiority of the God of Israel (the true God) over the Syrian God (deemed to be a false God).

5. There is an insistence upon obedience to the word of the prophet. The prophet is sent under compulsion of the word of God; this word has the power to get itself spoken, and when it has been spoken, to bring to pass that which has been expressed. [1]

In accordance with Christian thought, the coming of Christ was the conclusion of the Old Testament and the beginning of the New Testament. Although it was thought that the old was concluded, many of the ideas would be carried forward by the rapid expansion of the Christian movement. This is evident from the early days of Christianity. [2]

MacMullen concludes that for the first two and one-half centuries of the Christian era the Church was devoted to spiritual matters. The purpose of the Church was to establish on earth "the Kingdom of Heaven" or "Kingdom of God." It was during this time that respect for constituted authority became deeply rooted in Christian thought. The basis for conflict between the Christian community and Roman authority already existed, however. Christ was not a Roman citizen and some Pharisees wanted to find where the loyalty of Christ lay, with Caesar or with God. His answer was ambiguous, "Render therefore,

---

[1] *Ibid, p. 120*

[2] *Christianization of The Roman Empire, Ramsey MacMullen, Yale University Press, 1964. This work details the carrying forward of Old Testament ideas into the New Testament.*

unto Caesar the things that are Caesar's, and unto God the things that are God's." (Matthew 22:21; Mark 12: 17; Luke 20: 25). No clear line of loyalty is stated. The problem is stated again in Romans 13. Here St. Paul admonishes all to obey authority. The powers that are ordained of God, "Whosoever, therefore, resisteth the power, resisteth the ordinance of God; for rulers are not a terror to good works, but to the evil."

There are different points of view, relative to the positions of Christ and St. Paul that invite further study. In reference to Matthew 22: 21 and Mark 12: 17, biblical scholars state that had Jesus denied paying tribute he could have been arrested as a revolutionary. But at the same time he counseled the Pharisee to be as observant in obligations to God as to the emperor. The Jews, a conquered people, were to pay duty to the lawful civic leaders. In brief, the question was, in a theocracy, (a state under God's leadership) should Jews be required to pay tax to an intruding pagan overlord? When God is Lord of all, one must give to Caesar his due in the political sphere without denying the Lordship of God. When showing loyalty to God, there could be no compromise for God is supreme, even in Caesar's realm.

Under Roman law, Herod Antipas, of the Herodian family, levied a poll tax upon all adult males. The Jews resented having to pay the tax. And the question arose, should the Jews pay the tax or demand their independence on the theorem that God alone is the King of Israel? The Pharisees had resolutely invited Romans into the land of Judea. As a consequence, those who compromised with Rome had to pay the price, which is to say, pay the tax. Still another view was that the tax symbolized subjection to Roman authority. The coin was stamped with the relief of the head of the Caesar. It was believed that if Christ had said to pay the tax, he could lose his influence. But should Christ show disapproval for the taxing of Jews, he could be denounced by Pontius Pilate as a revolutionary. Still there were others who stated that since the coin belonged to Caesar, he had a right to recover the currency of the State. See Luke 20: 19-26. The coin containing the likeness of a deified emperor was objectionable to the Jews. Yet the tax had to be paid. This position was repudiated by extremists who held that they must not obey the Roman State. They could only serve God.

A contrary view is stated by St. Paul in Romans 13: 1-7, ". . . the powers that are ordained of God." He urged all to obey the ordinance of God and added that those who "resisteth shall receive to themselves damnation." The position of Christ, a Jew in territory conquered by the Romans, was clearly not the same as that of St. Paul, a Roman citizen holding legal status under Roman law. If one accepts St. Paul's thesis that government is of divine order, then it would be serious to set oneself against it. Both sources, Roman Catholic and

Protestant, which deal with the Biblical quotations, state that nothing in the material attributed to Christ gave a basis for a theory of politics or justified medieval theory of two empires, one secular, the other divine. [1]

However, it may be that the Church scholars of the middle ages drew that conclusion from Christ's statement. In short, no man can serve two masters. Can one be loyal to God and, at the same time, be loyal to the State?

From the inception of the Christian movement, especially 100 A.D. to 400 A.D., the Church followers were from the rural community, as well as those of urban centers. By 312 A.D., the Church membership would become so numerous that its role and status would undergo a change. The determining factors were the declining position of the empire in the west. This decline precipitated Emperor Constantine's conversion to Christianity. The consolidation of the empire with religion would give the Emperor a broader base from which to rule. From this strength the growing rural community would be incorporated, taking it from a weakened position of urban aristocracy, thus securing the emperor's base in town and countryside.

Although Christianity was still a minority religion, Constantine was impressed with the morality of its faithful. The Christians were worth a dozen legions to him, in his conflict with enemies within and without his empire. The hierarchical structure and discipline, with far reaching authority of the Church, gave him a spiritual correlate for the absolute monarchy that he wished to establish. The Emperor, in order to serve both ends, suppressed heretical sects and ordered the destruction of their assembly. Constantine was highly praised by the Church for these acts.

When Christianity became the religion of the empire, it converted the world. However, it would come to pass that Christianity would also be converted by the world. Constantine gave the authority of judges to the bishops in their dioceses, freed the Church of taxation, allowed the Church to own land, and gave money to needy congregations.

Pope Sylvester (314-335) and Constantine set the pattern of the future

---

[1] *Collegeville Bible Commentary, Robert J. Karris, OFM, Imprimatur, George H. Spoltz, D.D., Bishop of St. Cloud, July 22, 1982. Data from Philip Van Luiden, C.M., Jerome Kodell, O.S.B., Roman Catholic. The subjects are discussed under scripture headings in sections of the work as are the services below. The Jerome Biblical Commentary, Printice Hall, Roman Catholic, 1968. The Interpreter's Bible, Abington Press, Vol. VII, VIII, 1951, Protestant.*

when Christianity was made the religion of the Roman Empire. Following the example of previous Roman rulers who had used the supreme Roman College of Pontiffs, Constantine and his successors would use the Bishop of Rome as supreme Pontiff under the theory that all authority comes from God. In the progression of time, civil and Church authority would come under the control of the Church in the West. This was especially true after the collapse of the western empire in 476 A.D.

In setting the pattern for the future of the Church, Constantine entangled spiritual power with secular power. No pope since Sylvester has worn a different cloak, even to these last hours of the twentieth century. While Constantine cared little for the theological disputes of the day, he never hesitated in crushing dissent for imperial unity. Christian teachers taught submission to civil authority, and rarely revolted, building upon ancient pre-Christian thought, they taught the divine right of kings. Inasmuch as Constantine aspired to absolute authority, he nonetheless believed that government and religion could work together. Within a relatively short period the Church became the richest religious organization in the empire.

Although the emperor was stationed in Constantinople before 476 A.D., with the passing of time his authority declined appreciably in the west. The Church became heir to the same problems as those of the Roman Empire. It had to establish power, firmly guarding itself against all internal and external threats.

The Church had to maintain peace against all forces, expanding its organization into the area over which the empire had ruled in the west. In brief, the church-state took over the territory, the legal structure, the social problems, and the political theory of the previously fallen order.

Western Christian Society had been centralized within the papacy by the twelfth and thirteenth centuries. The pope professed to be a monarch, head of the Roman Church, with supreme authority from God, the mystical body of Christ.

The avowal to monarchy did not exist at the beginning of church history. The Pope of Rome was, in fact, only one of many popes, none of which had authority over the other. All bishops were called popes, equally subject to the authority of the emperor who determined and confirmed their election. The clergy was successful in declaring that the Church be ruled by a papal monarchy, and not by a senate of bishops. To emphasize this requirement, it was ordered that no bishop other than the Bishop of Rome could call himself pope. Peter received the position of the Vicar of Christ on earth by the teachings of the Church. He and subsequent popes were deemed to have the authority of Christ. To suppose there was more than one pope would foster the idea that there could be more than one God.

With the emergence of Islam from Arabia and its expansion in the seventh and eighth centuries A.D., a dramatic challenge was presented to the Roman Church. Islam would swoop down like a swarm of locusts, seizing all of the territories in the Near East, North Africa and Spain. The result would bring all the patriarchs of Antioch, Constantinople and Jerusalem, and the bishops of North Africa and Spain, under Islamic rule. The only one left in Latin Christendom was either the Roman bishop or the pope. Thus, the Vicar of the Church of Rome could ignore the Eastern emperor. This later became true also in the West.

At the pinnacle of the Roman Church was the Vicar of Christ, head of His Mystic Body, whose authority came from God, and who forbade other bishops from using the title of Pope in reference to themselves. In this administrative organization, the clergy was superior to the laity in spiritual matters and clerical magistrates were above lay magistrates.

Much of this structure rested upon "false decretals." From the fourth century for almost a thousand years it was believed that the Emperor Constantine had granted temporal authority to the Bishop of Rome. This so called grant was discovered to be a forgery. Hence, the name, "false decretals." Despite the discovery of the forgery, the span of nearly a thousand years could not be erased.

In addition to the monarchial structure established from previous models in Roman history, the Church had a theology that fit into an earlier philosophy, that of Lucius Annaes Seneca (4 B.C.- 65 A.D.), a stoic philosopher. [1] As later scholars would contend, Seneca believed humankind at one period had been innocent, kind, peaceful and devoid of greed. Hence, there was no need for government. However, with the development of the concept of property, the

---

[1] *A History of Political Theory, George Sabine, Henry Holt, 1958, p. 174. See A History of Medieval Thought in the West, R.W. and A.J. Carlyle, 6 Volumes, London, 1903-36. The Growth of Political Thought in the West From the Greeks to the End of the Middle Ages. C.H. McIlwain, New York, 1935. These works deal extensively with all early Christian thought covered through the Middle ages. The Age of Reform, 1250-1550, Steven Ozment, Yale University Press, 1980. Augustine, Great Books of the Western World, Vol. 35, 1952. Encyclopedia Britannica, New York.*

people became greedy. Wanting things for themselves, rulers of cities became tyrants. Government came into being as a remedy for the wickedness of people. Consequently, force was a necessary component of the law to control wickedness. Government, to Seneca, was divinely appointed, declaring complete obedience.

With the collapse of the Roman Empire in the West, 476 A.D., the Roman Church gradually took over the same territory formally held by the Empire. This was done, as previously described, when the Church and State united. Its theory coincided with Greco-Roman theory —the law of nature is the law of God. The Church held dominion over the land, the buildings, the courts and the people. There was, in addition, an administrative structure at the apex, the Vicar of Christ. Here were all the ingredients of a state that fit into the thesis of law of the Greco-Roman theory, with theological arguments to support it.

As the empire had enemies from within, and was threatened by enemies from without, so too did the Church that replaced it. The threat from within was heresy, which was considered to be a threat against the Estate-Church structure and its theology.

Heresy may be defined as a teaching contrary to that of the Church of Rome. This would not have to be necessarily theological in nature. It was often coupled with an attempt to free some area from imperial Roman power. The Monophysites wished to free Syria and Egypt from Constantinople. The Donatist wanted to free Africa from Rome. The Albi movement differed from Rome (basic points shall be explained, subsequently). Furthermore, acts or teachings involving heresy were considered to be crimes of man against God.

Perhaps the first great challenge to the new arrangement came by Donatus, Bishop of Carthage, immediately after the conversion of Constantine. The previous emperor, Diocletian, carried out extensive persecution of Christians and many bishops and lay people renounced the faith to avoid the terror. When Constantine ended the persecution, many of the bishops asked to be readmitted to the Church and Constantine consented. However, Donatus strongly objected, affirming that once having renounced the faith, there could be no readmittance. He therefore asserted that the sacraments administered after reacceptance to the faith would be void, otherwise the Church would not be pure. Subsequently, he organized an army to oppose the Emperor and called upon the people to rise up against Rome as the arm of the Lord. His objective was to cleanse the church in preparation for the Second Coming of Christ. If the empire could not be saved, therefore, it must be destroyed.

Meanwhile, he established his own Church structure and announced that only those priests associated with him could administer a valid sacrament. George Williams [1] states the following: "The Donatist of North Africa were the first considerable body of Christians to have resorted to belief-inspired violence against other Christians and in due course Christian imperial coercion, at first fiscal and then capital, and was used against the Donatists. The Donatists called themselves 'Soldiers (of Christ)' and their battle cry was 'praise be unto God.'" Williams continues: "St. Augustine, after tiring of debate and persuasion with Donatist, turned to Luke 14:15-24: 'Counsel them to come in that my house (the Church) may be filled,' and this was used as a Dominical warrant for the use of governmental power for the true religion. The violence used by Donatist against the forces was supported by no less a person than St. Augustine."

St. Augustine (354-430) believed that "the powers that be are ordained by God," and that force was necessary in government. Force was made necessary by sin, and was a divinely appointed remedy for sin. The church, to him, was the "march of God in the world." History is the successive unfolding of a divine salvation of the Christian Church. The state must be Christian, for no state can be just unless it is Christian.

Coinciding with these views were those of St. Gregory (c. 540-604). [2] In the age of anarchy in which he lived, St. Gregory believed rulers must be obeyed regardless of their wickedness. Their lives and conduct were not to be criticized. According to St. Gregory, the authority of the ruler was the authority of God and a ruler was subject only to God and could commit illegal acts if willing to risk damnation. His actions were between him and God.

It is clear that the actions and beliefs of the Donatists challenged the combined authority of Church and State under Constantine. In either case, the Donatist and Constantine used theological arguments to support violence, each against the other. The Donatist uprising is the first case of a ruling authority to use a Christian justification for violence.

Perhaps the best example of Church-State acts of violence against challenges is the Albigensian movement —also known as Cathars— in the 12th and 13th centuries. The Albigensian's greatest conflict arose in southwest

---

[1] *Four Modalities of Violence, George Huston Williams, Journal of Church And State, Vol. 16, Winter, 1974, Number 1, p. 11, Vol. 16, Spring, 1974, Number 2, p. 237.*

[2] *See The Rise of Christian Europe, Hugh Trevor-Roper, Harcourt Brace, 1964.*

France around the city of Albi. The movement had its origins in Persia early in the Christian era. Through the centuries, the Albigensian movement developed its own doctrines. It did not accept the divinity of Christ, believing he was only a priest. Nor did it believe Jesus was killed or crucified. However, the faithful did believe that Jesus married and had a family, as was the custom of rabbis at the time.

By the twelfth century, the Albigensian movement had its own laity, clergy, bishops and international councils. Clearly the Albigensians challenged Rome and the movement was declared heretical. By the end of the 13th century the Crusade brought death to its followers and put an end to the movement. The Crusade against the Albigensians, one of the bloodiest massacres of its kind in history, lasted nearly forty years, It has a close corollary, however, with the Crusade against the Turks of Islam. [1]

The Crusade, called by the Pope, promised forgiveness of all sins to all participants, assurance of heaven as a reward, and all the booty one could plunder. The Arc of Languedoc was reduced to barbarianism. The Crusade was carried out to rid the area of the Albigensian heresy —"the foul leprosy of the South." This was the case even though most of the victims were nonviolent. They were committed to attaining a union with the principle of love —Jesus was their prophet of love. The Albigensian movement was destroyed. Europe would not again witness a culture such as theirs until the Renaissance.

The movements against the Church of Rome arose within the Church itself. Those movements which could not be absorbed were rooted out and crushed. Both St. Dominic and St. Francis, together with his cult of Holy Poverty —originally against the Church— were ultimately absorbed by the Church.

The Inquisition was a religious organization established in the twelfth and thirteenth centuries to protect the doctrine of the Church and deal with the issue of heresy. Heresy may be defined as any belief opposed by the Church, especially those beliefs which are likely to cause schism. The term, Inquisition, came to mean "any judicial inquiry conducted with ruthless severity." The Inquisitors were given judicial authority over all Catholics, with sanction to

---

[1] *Williams, op. cit. For material on this conflict see Holy Blood, Holy Grail, Michael Baigent, Richard Leigh, Henry Lincoln, Dell Publishing Co. Inc., 1983. See The Messianic Legacy, same authors, Henry Holt, 1986. The Decline and Fall of The Roman Church, Malachi Martin, Bantam Books, 1983. The expansion of the Church and the Church Fathers are discussed at length in this work.*

arrest, imprison, and execute all those who were in opposition to them. It was considered necessary to root out all teachings which were judged contrary to the laws of God. Heresy was considered to be an act of man against God. The Inquisition was in force extensively throughout Spain and beyond, expanding to Poland, the northern fringes of Europe, England, and Ireland. This was the area which in the past had been occupied by Imperial Rome. The Inquisition extended even into Spanish and Portuguese America.

When the Crusades took place against the Islamic Turks, the crusaders justified it by denouncing them as "God's enemies and ours, accursed unbelievers." As the conquest proceeded, the Crusaders slaughtered all before them. When the army and the clergy marched into Africa and Latin America, it used Genesis 9: 25, to justify slavery, "And he said cursed be Canaan; a servant of servants shall be unto his brethren."

Monarchs were also opposing the Church. To whom did the laity owe obedience when there was a conflict between the two? When monarchs and emperors claimed authority directly from God, and not through the Church, the question of obedience was crucial.

Did the laity have a divided loyalty? By what premise could one make a choice between the two when his/her authority was from the same source? What was the laity to do when ruled by a tyrant? St. Paul stated that all authority came from God. Accordingly, the office was the issue —not the person in the office. A tyrant must be obeyed as a punishment for the sins of man. The tyrant's acts were between himself and God, subject to His judgment —not that of his subjects.

When Roman influence moved throughout Western Europe, the peasants had but one other recourse, aside from submitting to their command, to strike back with force. A similar condition existed when the monarchs began to resist the Pope and Emperor. Force became an issue of terror by the Pope, the Emperor, and the Monarch. Therefore, when the peasants chose to revolt, rather than submit, that became an issue of counter-terrorism. The Church and State assumed two positions. When constraints were used by the Church and State it was acclaimed for the good of the people. However, when the same constraints were implemented with equal force by the resisters, it was judged to be terrorism.

Royal authority had been obtained by three different theories by the middle ages: by inheritance, by choice of the people, and by the grace of God. Royal authority was the authority of God, by whatever means. Anyone who resisted authority was a "subject of the devil and an enemy of God." [1]

Resistance was possible under the nebulous idea of a higher law, despite these theories. Should the monarchs trample on fundamental moral law, regarded as a legal right; their subjects might resist. The resistance was not regarded to be contrary to legal authority.

Yet, in the middle of the twelfth century (1115-1180) John Salisbury was among the first to write a document on the justification of tyrannicide. He believed that kings should be bound by principles that have the magnitude of law among nations. St. Thomas Aquinas (1225-74) did not agree with Salisbury's point of view. He believed that before tyrannicide could be justified, it had to represent the public as a whole. Should one resist authority, before it could be absolved, it must be determined whether the remedy may be worse than the problem. St. Thomas held that "rendering to Caesar" did not apply when both secular and spiritual authority resided in one office. That office being that of the pope.

In England, John Wycliffe (1320-1384) believed that monarchs are the representatives of God and to resist the King is evil. He further held that bishops received their power from monarchs. If there are abuses within the Church, the King was obligated to correct them. Marsilius of Padua (1290-1343) held the highest regard for secular authority by exalting it over the Church. Therefore, his conception was that all coercive authority should be usurped from the pope and exclusively assigned to temporal authority.

A significant point to remember here is that the argument was *not against* the use of violence, but to whom should the authority be given for its theological justification? The Christian fathers did not oppose violence for they believed the use of violence was justified because of the sins of mankind. Violence was used by the pope as the Vicar of Christ. [2] All kings and popes approved in their use of violence —never against them, but by them. Those who opposed it, either secular or Church rulers, used arguments similar to John of Salisbury. As previously stated, St. Thomas believed in total obedience to the pope when both temporal and secular authority was his. Again, the question is, *who* shall use it and its theological justification?

---

[1] *Williams, op. cit.*

[2] *Feudal Society, Marc Bloc, Translated by L.A. Manyon, Vol. 2. Social Classes and Political Organization, The University of Chicago Press, 1961. Caesar and Christ, Will Durant, Simon and Schuster, 1944.*

The problem of maintaining social order and cohesion was constant in Latin Christendom. Compared to the violence since the Reformation, there was relative stability. Feudal war was in contrast to ancient and present day conflict. The social order that existed was due to a strict adherence to a common faith, to the canon law, to the common sacraments of the Church, and a universal language of the Church. People regarded themselves to be members of a common Christian community. There was, however, the threat of excommunication, penance and the inquisition. Equally strong was the factor of widespread social acceptance of the Church and the people's desire to be a part of the community.

The Church opposed any system that became a threat to its centralized authority. In the long-term growth of population and the gradual growth of cities, many social factors in the life of the people could not be controlled by the clergy.

There came a period from around 1066 to 1300 in which the bonds of feudal barons were gradually broken. It was the opening of trade in Europe, a limitation on feudal wars, robber barons, and pirates along the rivers and sea lanes. However, a great constraint was put on trade merchants and travelers who had to use the numerous toll bridges and toll roads. Shipbuilding and navigation surged forward on large rivers inland, as well as seaports. This encouraged the growth of banking institutions, development of currency, accounting, surcharge or interest on lending, and on insurance. It also encouraged industrial development, the worker's guilds, and the beginning of an agricultural revolution. Fairs became the fashion in many cities of industrial England and Europe.

Europe was at last recovering from the successive blows of the Goths, the Huns, the Vandals, the Moslems, the Magyars and the Norse. Clearly, this period marks the emergence of the present day Nation-State system. However, to gain this end, the fractured and chaotic conditions that came with the collapse of the Roman Catholic Empire had to take place.

Consequently, local civil authority began to sharply increase its degree of control because the Church could not deal with the social problems among its people. The Church opposed the gradual growth of civil authority in feudal lords and monarchs, and the warfare which broke out among them. The lords (master of an area) began to fight among themselves in order to increase their territory.

To use violence upon noncombatants subjected one to excommunication. The movement spread into areas of reconquered Spain, northern Italy and parts of the Carolingian area, which included all of continental Europe by 805, except Spain, Scandinavia, Southern Italy and the Slavic fringes to the east. The Church tried to promote peace in the greater part of Latin Christendom. Peace associations were organized among the bishops in France from about 989. The theory that cohesion existed in the world was because all were Christian. To kill a Christian was considered the same as shedding the blood of Christ. To keep the peace, decrees such as *Pax Dei*, or Peace of God, or the Truce of God, were declared. From about 1027, the French nobles outlawed violence during Lent and the harvest seasons. War was prohibited from August 15th through November 11th. War was also prohibited on special holidays and during the week from Wednesday evening to Monday morning. Finally, war was permitted only eighty days out of each year.

In the twelfth century, The Truce of God became part of civil law. The Second Lateran Council (1139) forbade the use of war machines. In the thirteenth century it was requested that all disputes be submitted to the pope for arbitration. As the unity of the Church began to fracture the monarchs opposed this request since they had already begun to extensively exert power for themselves.

It is significant to note that both the Church and the secular authority had the same aspiration to discard violence. The Church needed peace to secure itself. The lords, who later became kings, shared the same interest. They also wanted peace. However, their desire for peace was not to secure the Church, but for their own objectives. The ensuing kings became the future heads of the nation state system which was largely supported by the commercial class. *Pax Dei* and the Truce of God began to crumble as the Nation-States began to supersede the power of Rome. Nationalism and the Reformation would prove a greater doctrine than the moderately unified society out of which each ascended.

The religious revolts and wars of the Reformation in the sixteenth century brought an end to Latin Christian Society. And out of the old Society a new social order began to surface. The old customs of morality, spirituality, psychology and legal structure did not apply to the new emerging society.

In Matthew 9:17, it states "Neither do men put new wine into an old wineskin," which implies that the wine will spoil. When an old order falls away, a new age arises. However, the old order, clouded by suspicion and mistrust, carries over certain aspects into the new age. When old institutions and old habits of thought become altered, countless ideas remain as transfixed as though time has no place in human conduct. And when a social order fractures, there, consequently, can be no cohesion.

The old leaders had different objectives. Since no consensus existed in Western Society, this sequentially brought about the Reformation, and the religious wars and revolts of the sixteenth and seventeenth centuries.[1]

During the transition of the Reformation and the Counter-Reformation, and until the Treaty of Westphalia (1648), there was one great force at work with four different aspects. Certain leaders wanted to direct institutions into the future on the basis of the past, while other leaders wanted drastic modifications in the same institution. These are two aspects of the same issue and the other two are the elements of force and consent.

Let us put the following into context: When the universal structure of the Church of Rome began to collapse under the force of the Reformation, the Counter-Reformation was launched. The forces of the Reformation faced the future with one plan, the Church proposed another. Each movement appealed to force and consent. The result was violence on both sides, which sequentially produced the Nation-State system of today.

When both movements failed to gain control of the West, the result was a fractured society. Various members of the new order endeavored to fill the vacuum created by the collapse of the Church. This was made possible, in large measure, by the commercial and mercantile systems that paralleled the evolution of the Italian and Germanic city-states and the Nation-State system.

Violence predated the Reformation as made clear by Barbara Tuchman's "A Distant Mirror"[2] during the sixteenth and seventeenth centuries. Quincy Wright, in his "Study of War"[3] records nine battles between 1480-1499. Between 1500-1599, there were 81 battles. And between 1600-1699, 239 battles were fought. The acceleration of battles fought parallels the Reformation, the Counter-Reformation, the full emergence of the nation-state system, and the first great thrust of science as applied to the technology of war, agriculture and medicine.

How would the leaders of the new constellation justify the use of

---

[1] *Ozment, op. cit.   The transition in the Church at The Reformation is exceptional in its coverage.*

[2] *A Distant Mirror, Barbara Tuchman.*

[3] *A Study of War, Quincy Wright, The University of Chicago Press.*

violence? Martin Luther, at the forefront of the Reformation, stated his position in strong terms. During the Peasants Revolt of 1525, an appeal was made to higher divine law and the courts of ethics and equity to support the revolt. Luther believed the kingdom of God and the kingdom of the world would be in peril if the rebellion succeeded. Although he thought the cause of the peasants' complaints were just, he urged them to not use violence. According to Luther, worldly rulers were the only ones with the authority to punish (Romans 13:4 and Peter 2:17). He further stated that Christians could not rebel for such was contrary to divine and common law and condemned by the Bible. So Christians were to suffer wrong and to endure evil.

Thomas Muntzer, an ex-Lutheran priest, took an opposite view. As a theologian of the peasant revolt, he appealed to divine law against the legal sanctions of landholders. Muntzer became the strongest critic of Luther, the Church, the priests and the landowners, demanding far-reaching land reforms and [1] calling for an armed revolt by the peasants. But as the result of leading the revolt, he was tortured and beheaded.

On theological issues, Luther called upon the State to suppress heresy and its exhortations. His theory, more than likely, was that the Church could not correct the problem. What the Church could not do he, therefore, petitioned the State to do. He chose this position against the Church of Rome and subsequently, against anti-Lutherans. Luther and Calvin regarded passive obedience to the State as one's duty. Calvin proclaimed that armed revolt in the name of religion had no place in the Reformation. A careful study shows a contradiction on the various positions taken by leaders of the Reformation. Whatever the case may have been, Biblical approval was used for the promotion of whatever position might be taken.

Regardless of which alliance retained the power in this age of change, the Church, the State, or the opposing party, they all used force and theological arguments to sustain their own positions. During the years from 1517 to 1648, the monarchs increased in power. As Protestantism would aid the authority of monarchs, it would also augment opposition to monarchs. The opposition was based upon Christian belief. The hypothesis was predicated on the theory that all authority is derived from the people. The two opposing forces clearly faced each other on the issue of the authority to use violence and each predicated its own position upon the same authority. The authority of God.

From the same inclination of thought, there would come another of

---

[1] *21VV, op. cit.*

considerable difference. When *The Prince* appeared (circa 1513), it was clear that its author, Machiavelli, had no concern about the morality of the state. To him, the structure of the Church would be discarded, but the substance would be the same. His theories on violence would contain the basis for much of the thinking of the last two centuries. It was of no concern to him whether the state was cruel, faithless, or lawless. Machiavelli's purpose was to teach a prince how to rule.

Machiavelli believed that Christian character obviously made people servile. He proposed a double standard, one for the ruler and another for the people. The purpose of the ruler was to attain power and increase it. It was Machiavelli's theory that the ruler was above the morality of his people. Assuming that mankind is selfish, *government*, he concluded, is based upon the weakness of the individual and, therefore, mankind cannot operate without government.

It is also interesting to note here an analogous sixteenth century secular statement of St. Paul and Seneca: Mankind is aggressive and acquisitive. The limits of these traits can be controlled only by the power of the state. Without a strong state, there would be anarchy and the individual would have no security. Finally, corruption of the individual can be overcome by despotic rule.

Rulers, Machaivelli maintained, were to be judged by only one standard: They must remove the corruption of their subjects. That judgment was made on the ability to expand the power of the state, internally and externally. State-craft and the art of war were the interlocking means by which this was done. He discussed the use of morality to attain the ends desired by the prince. In personal conduct, the prince must always appear moral, but never if contrary conduct and appearance calls for it. As his model, Machiavelli used the Papacy and its control of Papal States over Austria, Spain, and the Italian City-States, even to preventing the unification of Italy, except under Papal control.

Looking into previous material and comparing it with Machiavelli, one can discern that the structure of the Church is absent but the substance is clear: mankind is greedy, corrupt, and grasping. An all powerful state is the only means by which these traits can be controlled.

Thomas Hobbes (1588-1679) had a theory of state and the justification of force and violence not dissimilar, in many ways, to that of Machiavelli. [1]

---

[1] *The Prince, The Leviathan, Great Books of the Western World, Vol. 23,* Encyclopedia Britannica, Inc., 1952.

Living in the seventeenth century during the time of England's civil wars, his chief work, Leviathan, has the same basic thought of Seneca and St. Paul. To him, mankind is "solitary, poor, nasty, brutish and short." Motivated for one's own security, mankind must have a Leviathan State, merely for private security. This structure can be attained only by the sword —for agreements among humankind by words alone are but words. Consequently, social order is held together only by fear of punishment. Living at a time of the decadence of institutions in Europe, his theories produced the Leviathan State to which he believed we owe obedience under immortal God. Machiavelli and Hobbes infrequently referred to Biblical and Christian fathers as references, however, their influence is clear. Although Hobbes was influenced by the development of physical science and looked upon mankind in the scientific emphasis of his time, fundamentally, he was a materialist.

As previously explained, the sixteenth and seventeenth centuries witnessed increased warfare. Contending European powers were trying to fill the vacuum created by the collapse of the universal structure of the Church of Rome. In the sixteenth century, Austria and Spain had been foremost in this conflict. Meanwhile, wars in the Germanies were under way, ending momentarily in the Peace of Augsburg, 1555. Under its terms, each ruler would determine the branch of Christianity that subjects would take. Subjects had no voice in the matter. Should their choice be contrary to the ruler in the area, subjects were required to move elsewhere. Peace was not to be endured for long. By 1618, a power struggle within the Germanies brought in Austria, France and a non-Christian power, the Ottoman Turks, who were Muslim. Virtually all the Western powers, plus the Ottoman Turks, were engulfed in the Thirty Years War which devastated major portions of the Germanies and its population.

However sharp the divisions of religion were at the inception of the Thirty Years War, 1618, by the end of the Conflict, 1648, the primary objective of all contenders was to fill the vacuum created by the collapse of the structure of the Roman Church. The religious issue of 1618 became secondary to a drive for power by 1648.

This long and bitter war fostered the development of the Nation-State system which remains in vogue today. The legal forces which kept the Church in power for centuries was no longer suited to the conditions brought about by the Reformation, the Counter-Reformation, and The Thirty Years War. A new force was emerging in Western Society and in Europe and England as well. The arising powers —motivated by a commercial and mercantile revolution— began to expand into the new world which began the colonization of Africa, the takeover of vast areas in India, and in Southeast Asia.

A new system, both legal and administrative, was needed to manage the complex and expanding new order in the West which was rapidly encompassing the entire world. That need was met by Hugo Grotius, "The Miracle of Holland." [1] From the seventeenth century viewpoint, it appeared that the world was bent on self destruction. Some one third of the European population was destroyed. This was the period when the thoughts of Machiavelli prevailed —much as it does today. Recognizing the nation-state system, Grotius produced ideas he hoped would be adjusted to the new position, while carrying forward the best ideas from the past. "In many respects, Hugo Grotius was an exemplary visionary of the shadow land, whose life coincided with the times of transition in Europe from the old feudal order to the new order of sovereign states." (See "Miracle of Holland."

The conflicts throughout the sixteenth and seventeenth centuries were times of absolute monarchy when authority was divine. The evidence was manifest that nothing could restore unity in the emerging order. Some kind of structure must be mounted to deal with events as they were, predicated upon the fact that all the monarchs professed Christianity and in nearly all cases the Church and State were united. The question posed was how to limit violence among members of the new order. Grotius grasped the problem in his work *De Jure Belli Ac Pacis*. Its substance was included in the Peace of Westphalia (1648). John of Salisbury stated as early as the conflict of Thomas A. Beckett (1118-1170) and Henry II of England that the monarchs of the arising Nation-States were bound by some higher law to preserve peace. Other scholars expressed similar thought through the unfolding time but not until the years of Grotius did the idea take root.

Grotius theorized that inasmuch as monarchs were Christian, they would restrain themselves in the use of warfare. Thus, peace could be attained, short of war. This is not dissimilar to the postulate the bishops of the Church, who in the tenth century, set forth the Peace of God and Truce of God. They announced that, as all were Christian, for one to kill another was the same as shedding the blood of Christ. In *De Jure Belli Ac Pacis*, Grotius merged two sets of laws, Roman law and Church law which, at the apex of the Roman Church had been operative in structure. This structure emerged from St. Auqustine, Pope Gelasius (492-496), and St. Gregory VII in the eleventh century (1073-85) and later from St. Thomas Aquinas. This structure which

---

[1] *Hugo Grotius, The Miracle of Holland, Charles S. Edwards, Nelson Hall, 1981. This fine work deals with legal and political thought to provide a new order in international society. The Age of Religious Wars, 1559-1689, Richard S. Dunn, Norton, 1970.*

operated under the papacy, cardinals, archbishops, bishops and parish priests was to be applied among the conflicting nations of the seventeenth century through the scope of Latin Christian Society. The difference was notable. The administration was relatively unified under the papacy and the faith of the society was more highly unified by common rites, customs, traditions and common language. The people held themselves in a remarkable manner to be members of a common Christian society. During the early days of the Thirty Years War this, however, was not the case. The Church was split by the Reformation, the Counter-Reformation and the Lutherans. The so called reformers split into many segments, concurrently with the augmentation of the arising monarchs. They all became more powerful as a consequence of the commercial and mercantile revolutions. Where universal values had superseded parochial interests in the past, the situation was now reversed. It was as Machiavelli and Hobbes had asserted: each against all.

This was the point precisely at issue by Grotius. He believed there was a law that bound all nations, and that rulers should be obligated to observe it. This law was reason bound in custom. For war to be legal, hence moral, formalities were required. Conflict could only be waged among those who had secular authority and, in addition, certain formalities had to be observed. The conclusion of peace had to be engaged in a certain fashion. Regulations had to be followed relative to combatants, non-combatants, prisoners of war, and neutrals as well. Grotius did not include any protection for the individual against the State. The individual was secured from social disorder within the State and protection from invasion by other monarchs. To Grotius, the prime purpose of his system was to moderate, if not abolish, violence among states. Concurrently, in the sixteenth and seventeenth centuries there was constant upheaval against the tyrants of the time. It is this body of law that spread throughout the world, and set forth the basis of what became international law.

However, Western Society was still burdened by the hand of the past. Science as applied to agriculture, medicine, and technology combined to increase the propensity of war. The new legal system did not control violence as it spread throughout the world. For example: in the seventeenth century the number of European battles (1600-99) was 239, from 1700-1799, 181, from 1800-99, 651 and from 1900-40, 892. This does not include the battles from 1940 to the present nor does it include acts of terrorism.

England was undergoing fundamental changes in the sixteenth and seventeenth centuries. While royal absolutism and authority from God was astride the European scene, a parliamentary change was under way in England. Sovereignty saddled up the English subjects and the monarchs were in the saddles. Authority came from the top down. Henry VIII, in his struggle to secure a male heir to the throne, began to fatuously undercut his legal-spiritual position by requesting Parliament to contrive a series of basic policy decisions, legally-customarily confined to the sovereign. His activities, as well as those of Elizabeth I and the Stuarts of the next century, gradually set the stage for the Glorious Revolution of 1688-89, whereby Parliament and not the Crown determined policy. This was declared as the Bloodless Revolution of 1688-89.

John Locke had written a manuscript on civil government some twenty years prior to the Glorious Revolution. With the abdication of King James II (1685-1688) Locke's treatise on government was published and parliamentary supremacy was established. King James II, according to Locke, planned to reestablish Catholicism against the Church of England and therefore had broken a social contract with the English people. James II was prepared to impose the Church of Rome upon England by force, against the will of the of English people. Locke theorized that since the social contract had been broken between the English people and the Crown, James II could be justly dethroned. The nucleus of his thesis was that civil government was established to defend property. The purpose of government is to protect life, liberty and property. Locke believed the traditional rights of Englishmen were being destroyed by a willful monarch. Contrary to Hobbes, Locke believed man to be basically good. Therefore, mankind could rule itself.

William and Mary of the House of Orange inherited the throne in 1689 and ruled according to conditions set forth by Parliament. A new rider sat astride the sovereign saddle. The new monarch promised to observe the fundamental laws that became the Bill of Rights.

To summarize the events, James II planned to reestablish the Church of Rome in England with the aid of the English Army. When he realized the army would not support him, but instead supported and welcomed William and Mary of Orange, he fled to Ireland and eventually went to France. To James II, the crucial factor was, when he lost control of the agents of violence, he failed to enforce his will. The theory was now being changed. Instead of the people being the servant of the state, the state was to become the servant of the people. This theory became a hallmark in the world of human history.

The ideas which Locke expressed: that monarchs have obligations to their subjects by social contract, had been in vogue by the Puritans for many years. The subjects and the monarchs had mutual obligations. Subjects could ultimately rebel if monarchs over-stepped their position, thereby violating basic rights of Englishmen. The rights were life, liberty and estate. Consequently, these specific ideas set the stage for the Thirteen Colonies revolt against George III —thus legislating the Declaration of Independence by Thomas

Jefferson. The colonies believed George III violated their rights as Englishmen upon the theory propounded by John Locke. [1]

Locke and Jefferson agreed and disagreed. They agreed that man was basically good and that government existed by contract between the people and the state. Locke thought this contract covered life, liberty and estate. Jefferson went further, however. He asserted that government rested upon the consent of the governed. Its purpose, he declared, was to promote life, liberty and the pursuit of happiness.

The Declaration of Independence best describes his view:

> We hold these truths to be self evident, that all men are created equal; that they are endowed by their creator with certain inalienable rights; that among these are life, liberty and the pursuit of happiness; that, to secure these rights, governments are instituted among them, deriving their powers from the consent of the governed, that whenever any form of government becomes destructive of these ends, it is the right of the people to alter or abolish it, and to institute a new government.

The theory that the equality of all men was founded on the belief that *all men are created equal*, without rank or status. There is a theological implication here which is not necessarily Christian. Equal rights exist for all, and government cannot take them away. The government must rest on the consent of the governed. Whenever any government violates the rights of its subjects, that government may be altered or abolished and another instituted to replace it. Notice must be drawn to the fact that no concept of property was to abridge those without estate. These brief words of Jefferson brought terror to those who ruled or aspired to rule without the consent of the governed. It continues to frighten many contemporary rulers.

In Arnold J. Toynbee's eloquent volume "America and The World Revolution," he vividly shows the impact of a philosophy which abolishes the ethics of a government that rules without consent. From the Americas, The Shot Heard Round The World resounded in France before the eighteenth century was over. Early in the nineteenth century it was heard in Spanish America, and in Greece. By mid-century, the whole of Europe felt its impact. It was the leading force in the unification in Italy. In France, the commune

---

[1] *Locke, Berkeley, Hume, Great Books of the Western World, Vol. 35, 1952, Encyclopedia Britannica.*

responded. It influenced the Russian and Persian revolts of 1905 and 1906. Its influence was clearly on the founding of the Indian National Congress. The latter movement went far to influence the independence movements of European dominated colonial Asia and Africa. The revolt and subsequent end of China's Manchu Dynasty in 1911 was without doubt the result of Thomas Jefferson's words. And the same holds true for the Mexicans revolt the year before. Similar events occurred in Turkey (1919-28), and again in 1948. China would again react in 1948, as did the Cubans in 1960, when its people became fervently aroused. Drawing from Toynbee, here is one of the most cogent comments which he takes from Jefferson: "The disease of liberty is catching."

These revolutions of which we speak were inspired, in part, by Jefferson exhibiting violence against the established legal system where peaceful means of change had failed. The law of nations promulgated in 1648 provided for no means of peaceful change within the state structure. Where diplomacy and means short of war might work among nations, there was no procedure within a nation, or within its colonies, or against its own constituted authority. If, as Jefferson theorized, men were inherently good, then the State is the servant of the people. Although Locke and The Glorious Revolution set the stage for the British Colonial Revolution, it was perfected by Thomas Jefferson.

The absence of Christian theology, which appealed to those who considered revolt their only recourse, was, perhaps, one of the major reasons that the Declaration of Independence was lauded with such worldwide enthusiasm. And it sprang from roots deeply embedded in the Western, Islamic, African, Indian and Chinese soil.

The Eastern Orthodox Society of Czarist Russian which fashioned the former Soviet Union had the same basic theological concept of violence as did Latin Christian Society in the West. The concept of each society springs from the same root.

Emperor Constantine and Pope Sylvester, in 321 A.D., brought church and state together. Constantine established Constantinople, in 330 A.D., as the primary capital of the East —and he named it after himself. Holding to theories of the past, that the state is the authority of God, Constantinople became an even more powerful state. In the East the Emperor transmitted and set in motion the same precepts as those which the papacy had implemented in the West. Thus, Constantine was able to wield the authority to crush all religious opposition. Despite repeated attempts, the emperors of the Greco-Roman Empire, failed to regain the West and around 476 A.D. it began to wane and ultimately collapse. Inspired by these theological events, the emperors of Constantinople were able to expand the Byzantine Empire, the domain of the East.

However, the Eastern Empire of Christendom would come under attack and fall before the forces of Islam, as we shall see. In the early years of Christianity, missionaries moved into the Ukraine, north of the Black sea. The city of Kiev became a vital point of military and political activity. In time, Kiev became the Center of the Orthodox Church under Prince Vladimir, Grand Duke of Kiev (980-1015). Vladimir sanctioned the Orthodox interpretation of Christian doctrine; (the same as Emperor Constantine) that the authority of the state is the authority of God. And by this act Vladimir became head of the Church and state.

From the time of Vladimir to the end of the Russian dynasty, all rulers held to the belief that their authority came from God. Consequently, the state could and did administer that authority to expand its domain against all external and internal non-Christians forces, and demanded all subjects to accept the Orthodox version of Christianity. Rebellion was an act against God, as His authority was the authority of the state. Therefore, the consequence of contradiction was a perilous road to travel. The Orthodox Society of Czarist Russia set the stage for the turbulence which occured within the former Soviet Union.

The former Soviet Union is the successor to the Russian Empire. To grasp the physical dimensions of this colossal territory, consider: it was roughly seven thousand miles from east to West, and 28,000 to 3,000 miles from north to south. The territory in the sixth century was about one five-hundredth of the area as that of today, currently, some 8,649,489 square miles. Its population today is approximately 267,697,000. However, in the sixth century its population was about one four-hundredth of that. This would be about 669,217 people. Viewing it another way: If the eastern edge of the former Soviet Union were geographically placed over England, the western edge would rest in the Pacific Ocean —having reached across the Atlantic, the United States and beyond its western shores.

The historical, psychological and ethical distinction professed by the former Soviet Union is an outgrowth of the primary theme of Czarist Russia. The Russian Orthodox Society proclaimed to the world that their translation of Christianity was indeed *the only repository* of the one true faith. All other faiths were considered false; even other segments of Christianity were regarded as incorrect. The former Soviet Union is a direct product of Czarist, Orthodox Russia in the same way that Western Society, since the Reformation, is an outgrowth of Latin Christian Society. Czarist Russia, the former Soviet Union, and the contemporary West each affirm their religion to be unique.

The religious prominence of Czarist Russia was the foundation upon which a similar assertion was made by the former Soviet Union. While the Russian revolution merely substituted Orthodox Christendom for Marxism, one might say that Marxism arose as a Judeo-Christian heresy, and Lenin, the Soviet Czar, imposed the heresy upon the Russian people. Arnold Toynbee, in his book "*The Study of History*" greatly expands this thesis. Marxism-Leninism, aside from portending that their religion was unique, had a sense of fatalism similar to that of Calvinism. Lenin and his associates considered themselves humble servants of the class struggle and the dialectic process. Calvin postulated that the forces of history were predetermined, or foreordained, by some cosmic force to which humankind must submit. Marxism-Leninism, also propounded, in the same manner, the thesis of class struggle and the dialectic process.

Marxism-Leninism conforms to a deeply set Orthodox Christian idea originating from the Greco-Roman Empire. Taking an example from Peter the Great, Lenin adopted Western technology and applied it to Soviet needs. This application was a twentieth century reaction to nearly four hundred and fifty years of confrontation with Western powers in Russian territory. Where Peter the Great failed in his efforts to roll back Western encroachment, Soviet communism was to carry out the purpose of Peter the Great. That purpose was to take the struggle into the Western homeland. [1]

Lenin chose communism as the faith of the former Soviet Union in roughly the same way that Peter the Great fashioned the Orthodox Church into a part of the state. The Orthodox priests served as agents of the state, dutifully reporting to the Czar the people whose acts were questionable. In a similar fashion, members of the K.G.B. —secret agents in the Kremlin of the former Soviet Union— probed into the lives of those citizens whose acts were suspect and reported them to the state.

While proposing to be materialistic, communism belies this thesis by proposing its own sense of spiritual destiny. Russian Orthodoxy affirming to be the one true faith, also believes its faith contained the correct answer to human purpose, in a world of humanity's relation to the unknown. In no less fashion, Marxism-Leninism proposes the same.

Russian Orthodoxy believed it had taken over the mantle of the Jews as the Chosen People of God, and Soviet communists believed they were the elect of human history, the one repository to the knowledge of human history and its destiny. Orthodox Christendom obtained its knowledge from the Bible, while Marxism-Leninism obtained its knowledge from Das Kapital. Both espouse an idealized future for humanity. Marx, through his dialectic process and class struggle theories, believed the evils of society would be removed by violent uprisings of the industrial proletariat. Orthodox Christianity, in common with other Christian thought, stakes its theorem upon graphically described violence in the Book of Revelation. In both cases a millennium is promised for the church.

The following is taken from Revelation 20: 1-5:

---

[1] *The European powers, Austria, Prussia, Sweden, Poland, and Lithuania, had been encroaching on Russian territory for centuries. Although they failed to overthrow Russia, at times the encroaches had been serious. In Arnold Toynbee's works, he describes these raids extensively, and shows how it influenced Ivan the Terrible, Peter the Great, on through to Catherine the Great. One should also examine the works of Sir Bernard Pares, A History of Russia, Alfred A. Knopf, 1964.*

1. And I saw an angel come down from heaven, having the key of the bottomless pit and a great chain in his hand.

2. And he laid hold on the dragon, that old serpent, which is the Devil, and Satan, and bound him a thousand years.

3. And cast him into the bottomless pit, and shut him up, that he should deceive the nations no more, till the thousand years should be fulfilled; and after that he must be loosed a little season.

4. And I saw thrones, and they sat upon them, and judgment was given unto them; and, I saw the souls of them that were beheaded for the witness of Jesus, and for the word of God, and which had not worshipped the beast, neither his image, neither had received his mark upon their foreheads, or in their hands; and they lived and reigned with Christ a thousand years.

5. But the rest of the dead lived not again until the thousand years were finished. This is the first resurrection.

In a similar fashion, Marx foresaw a classless/stateless society for those who survived the violence necessitated in bringing to an end the evils of a capitalist nation state society. The center of the struggle in both cases was the same. In Orthodox Russia, the internal struggle was against Jews, Muslims, Latin Christians, Protestants, and dissenters within the Church as well. The external enemies were the same in terms of faith. Additionally, in the West and the South, these various faiths were connected with expanding nation states systems where faith and armed force were united.

The ideology is the only change here. One prepared the way for the other. Moscow, advocating that it was the only reservoir of the one true faith in Orthodoxy stood as the only fountain for the flow of unfolding laws of history.

When we examine Soviet communism and find that it sprang from the well of Czarist history, we also see Kiev, an ancient municipality bordered by the Dnieper River and the great forest areas to the north and west. And to the south and east, we see the Black Sea and Ural Mountains, over which tribal people have migrated since pre-history. Unfortunately, access to Kiev has always caused unavoidable conflict for Kievan Rus, and therefore made the future of a Kievan city-state confederation precarious. Fighting to protect its development would create a pattern for life from the earliest days to the present.

The two main cities of trade in the ninth century were Novgorod around 862, and Kiev, established somewhat earlier. By the end of the ninth century, however, Kiev had overshadowed Novgorod and trade was established with Byzantium —Constantinople, early in the tenth century. Because Kiev was located along the Dnieper River and had easy access to Constantinople, it became the point from whence Russia evolved. Roman Christianity had been in and around Kiev even before Prince Vladimir (987/88). Roman Christianity seems to go back to St. Ol'has, Prince Vladimir's grandmother. She appears to have been baptized around 955 A.D. There is considerable evidence, however, that she was converted to the universal church at a time when the East and West branches of the church recognized the primacy of the Roman See.

The Rurikide Church was isolated from the West because of its geographical location. [1] Therefore, it developed its own characteristics which formed the culture of the people. The forceful administration of the church by St. Ol'has set the basis for supremacy in the area. Her work, with that of her grandson, Vladimir, merits the title, "Equal to the Apostles."

During the reign of Vladimir, (980-1015), Kiev was the center when the first state was established. Vladimir was far ahead of his time as his state stretched northeast to Moskva, north to Lake Byelo, west to Novgorod, and south to the Dnieper River. Long before this time, the many city states had engaged in internal rivalry. With war or the threat of war among the city-states, there was always an invasion or threat of invasion from surrounding tribal people. However, if in reverse, peace prevailed among the city-states and a threat ensued from outside, an outbreak of war between at least two or more city-states was assured.

What was clearly needed in Kiev was a means to bring about a cohesive government to this far flung state. The Jews had migrated to the area prior to this time, as the result of various Diaspora. Latin Christians were already in the area and the last prominent arrivals were the Muslims. From these various faiths, Vladimir was to choose one as a state religion, hoping to bring about some degree of stability to a long-term troubled area. The adoption of a state religion would enlarge his position and connect the people to a common religion. Judaism was rejected for Vladimir did not wish his state identified

---

[1] *According to the first Russian Chronicle, in relating the origin of this family and its followers, Rurik was the first Varanger Prince to rule in Russia. Varangers were Vikings who came from the far north in 806 and settled in Novgorod at the invitation of the people of that city. A History of Russia, Sir Bernard Pares, op. cit. p. 35.*

with a religion whose God had failed His followers in a time of war. Latin Christianity was unacceptable for it required its followers, including priests, hierarchy and the Prince, himself, to render fidelity to the papacy, whose offices were far from Kiev. He rejected Islam also because there was no hierarchy over whom he could gain control and all sacred areas were outside his domain. The Greek Orthodox position was different, however. Roman emperors were regarded as both human and divine, prior to the Christian era. Constantine became a convert and was the first emperor to recognize Christianity as the legal religion of the Greco-Roman Empire. A succeeding emperor made Christianity the state religion of the Greco-Roman Empire. The emperor could decree the state religion which complied with Roman law. Thus, the emperor became head of church and state. Vladimir, quick to follow the lead, in nine hundred and eighty nine commanded that his people accept the Greek Orthodox form of Christianity. This now put Vladimir in conformity with Roman law and the Byzantine concept of absolute ruler, head of church and state with divine authority instituted by God. But the difference in liturgy, faith and geography would cause the Orthodox Church to break from Rome in 1054, and contribute to Russia's isolation from Latin Christianity.

Let us recall the papacy's assertion to primacy that, if accepted by Prince Vladimir, would make, not only the clergy subject to Rome under Kievan reign, but the Grand Prince, himself. This Papal claim as sole agent of God on earth, aside from the members of the clergy, would consequently make the people of Kievan Rus subject to Rome. This would preclude any continuous accord with Rome which was already separated by great geographical differences, not to mention the language, customs and tradition, which in time produce a preference for that which is near at hand rather than that which was distant. In essence, time produced a dedication to local Kievan authority rather than to that afar in Rome.

The isolation of Kiev from the west, as previously stated, became a decisive issue in the development of the Church in conformity with the culture of the area. This became firmly established and was integrated with the future of the Rurikide Church and subsequent Orthodox Church history. Vladimir set the course of subsequent history when he accepted the Greek Orthodox Christianity. He was the agent of God on earth subject to no legal restraint. He was charged to protect the one true faith from all opponents within and without his domain. Russia and its rulers came to believe in the unique destiny of Russia under the concept of orthodox supremacy. Believing Christianity was betrayed when Constantinople submitted to the rule of Islam (for they believed Islamic people to be infidels), Moscow would later be proclaimed the only area free from foreign domination. Hence, the indestructible Third Rome.

Constantinople was overrun by Islam in 1452. Therefore, the Church of Byzantium was no longer independent. In 1472, Russian Czarism took the theory of imperial authority from Constantinople and its Byzantine past. The two-headed eagle was adopted in 1480, when the area was freed from Mongol control. Later, Ivan IV, dubbed "Ivan the Terrible," was crowned emperor in 1547. Shortly thereafter the council of the Russian Church proclaimed its superiority over all other Orthodox Churches. And to them this was in line with the theories set forth in the Book of Daniel, 7:1-28. The following is taken from Verse 14, Chapter 7 of the Book of Daniel:

> And there was given him dominion, and glory, and a kingdom, that all people, nations, languages, should serve him: his dominion shall not pass away, and his kingdom shall not be destroyed.

When Grand Duke Basil III (1505-33) was installed in office, part of the statement in his inauguration was: "Thy Christian kingdom shall not be given to another." The doctrine of Moscow as the Third Rome was proclaimed. Rome had fallen to the barbarians. Constantinople was taken over by the infidels, the Islamic religion. The Third Rome now was Moscow and it was to be eternal. Thus, fulfilled is the quotation from the Book of Daniel.

By 1589, the first Patriarch of Moscow proclaimed the Czar to be the only Christian sovereign of the world, the master of all faithful Christians. The permanence and enduring nature of Rome was now seen to reside in Moscow. It was now the sole repository of Orthodox Christianity. Carried to its logical conclusion, the one true faith was required to preserve itself from all contaminants within; and spread it to the rest of the world. This was the mission undertaken by Peter the Great when he attempted to put his thesis of Russia in affirmative western relations.

The area encompassed by the Kievan city-state confederation was too extensive not to undergo complications after the death of Vladimir. Even the best of his efforts, which extend some thirty-five years, could not resolve the long turmoil which had existed prior to his time. In time, it would suffer the same fate as the worlds of Alexander the Great and Charlemagne.

Alexander the Great (356-323 B.C.) was crowned King of Macedonia in 336 B.C., after which he conquered all of Greece. He took over Persia in 334-3, then Egypt in 332, Mesopotamia in 331, and on through to India in 326. However, after his death in 323 B.C., his far flung empire collapsed in spite of his many conquests because he failed to wear down the long sustained provincialism into an administrative unit. [1]

The fate of Charlemagne (Charles the Great 800-814), whose reign was much the same as that of Alexander. He consequently laid the basis for the Holy Roman Empire. As Emperor he conquered a major section of Italy, northeast Spain, Bavaria and finally Saxony. But his realm would also collapse after his death in 814.

In the Kievan Confederation's city-states, the ruling prince was in some way related to the Grand Prince of Kiev. An oath of allegiance was owed the Grand Prince in helping to suppress internal wars and invasions as well. There was an assembly in all cities which seized every occasion to encourage the local prince to take advantage of any eventuality which might enhance himself, at the expense of the Grand Prince. In later years when Moskva, a military outpost without a city council, was established; it would become a vital point.

After the death of Vladimir Monomah who ruled from (1113-25), the ensuing years would evidence brother against brother in warfare for control of Kievan Rus. Each prince concluded that by inheritance the city-state was his personal property. The Grand Prince of Kiev rarely held power long enough to control the entire area, despite the efforts of Yaroslav (1015-54) and Vladimir. Both rulers fought enemies from outside invasion and made strenuous efforts to govern in a fashion that would secure the area under Kiev control. Their efforts failed, however. In the thirteenth century, conflicts in concert with the invasion of the Khazars, the Pechenegs, and the Mongolians would end the predominance of Kiev. During the long occupation of Kievan Rus by the Golden Horde, one stronghold could not be brought under Mongol occupation —the military outpost of Moscow. The domination of Kiev by Mongols promoted an exodus of people from Kiev and the surrounding area to the north. Moscow would grow in population and strength. The Mongol Empire expanded from Mongolia to Canton, China, to Northern India, and to the outskirts of Moscow. Moscow was not captured and thus became the focal point of ultimate resistance to Mongol control. Moscow was the force to drive the outstretched Mongol Empire from their gain. Operating from Moscow, the final stage of resistance was directed by Ivan III, and lastly, by Ivan IV.

The Mongols ruled through princes during their occupation of Kievan Rus. They left the Church to its own operation. This would lead to the need for unification of administration and taxation which would be implemented

---

[1] *Sarton, op. cit . . . Discusses the experiences of Alexander the Great, as well as discussions by Arnold Toynbee.*

after the Mongols lost their area. The Church became a focal point of support for the various princes, as well as the center of spiritual support for the people against an alien ruler. This unique union of Church and state is clearly stated by Ivan III (1462-1505), who had finally broken Mongol power about 1480 and became the unique holder of princely power. In a letter to the Holy Roman Emperor, Frederick III (1440-1493), Ivan refused the offered title of king from Frederick, in return for marriage of his daughter to Ivan's nephew. He answered as follows:

> We by the Grace of God have been sovereign over our domains from the beginning, from our first forbearers...
>
> As in the past we have never needed appointments from anyone, so now do we not desire it.
>
> (I. Grey, Ivan III and the Unification of Russia, Collier *books, New York, 1967, p. 3)

When Constantinople fell in 1453, the clear concept of Caesaro-papism confirmed the position of the absolute rulers of Russian. All other Christian rulers were heretics. The Czar was the only rightful ruler. The Czar of Moscow was the king above all.

When liberated from the Mongols after 1505, in view of Vladimir of Kiev centuries earlier, the Czar proclaimed his God-given right over all princes and subjects on a larger scale. Under Ivan IV, the Terrible (1553-1584), this domination was complete. He proclaimed himself Czar and drove the Mongols to the East in 1552-56, adding greatly to Russia's geographic areas. He subjugated the Boyars to his complete control, fastened the peasants to the land, took over profitable business as governmental monopolies and finally created peasant serfdom. [1] At the end of the Ruirik Dynasty, Ivan the Terrible, was the foremost ruler of Russia. Having finally expelled the Mongols from all of Russia's surrounding area, the Orthodox clergy looked upon him as the one sent from God.

From the time of Grand Prince Vladimir and his conversion to Orthodox Christianity, descendants had professed to be the agents of God on earth, not subject to any constitutional restraint. This thesis was drawn from the asserted

---

[1] *Boyars were supposedly the Vikings of earlier days, warriors who fought for the princes of the realm. They became a disturbing factor in Czarist history and hence had to be brought under control by Ivan the Terrible.*

authority of Emperor Constantine. Even though there were parishes in which the Church of Rome had influence, it is clear that one of the prime reasons that Grand Prince Vladimir accepted Orthodox Christianity was to not be subject to any spiritual or secular ruler, but have all subordinate spiritual or secular rulers subject to him. After 1505, when the Grand Prince Ivan III, had driven back the Golden Horde, the theory became a reality. Russian Churchmen would no longer accept the primacy of the patriarch of Constantinople. This was especially true after Constantinople became subject to the Turks. Hence, as previously referred to, Moscow as the Third Rome was developed. This was the proclamation that went out in 1492. Consequently, Ivan the Terrible completed the work of Ivan III. No previous ruler has ever expanded or dominated the Russian realm as did he.

During the early years of The House of Romanov, around 1652,the Church accepted an enormous challenge. The Patriarch, Nikon, sought to reform the Church in accordance with early Byzantine practices for it was his belief that it had lost its liturgical form, and had become too Russian. He believed further that the Czar's authority came from God through the clergy, and not directly from God. He also considered the Church to be superior to the state. His desire to restore Byzantine practices to the Church caused a conflict among the clergy. When Nikon petitioned that a change of words and form be made in the liturgical books, the conservative clergy disagreed and a rift in the Church occurred which to this day has not completely healed. The Orthodox followers, who became known as "Old Believers," insisted on keeping the forms which Nikon sought to correct. This schism in 1654 subsequently caused the persecution of millions of Orthodox Russians. The devout peasantry, without any perception of Nikon's purpose, rebelled for they believed the true religion of Russia was being subverted. Their reward for devotion was slaughter. The official Church would not tolerate opposition and used violence to suppress it. And as a result, some twenty thousand "Old Believers" were hunted down and murdered for opposing the Patriarch's views. Various forms of persecution and terrorism indeed continued until the edict of toleration appeared in April 1905.

During the sixteenth and seventeenth centuries, many areas of Western Society were undergoing the commercial and mercantile revolution. The end result was an increase in military power by the acceleration of science as applied to agriculture, medicine and warfare. Ivan the Terrible, saw the difference in power between Czarist Russia and much of Western Europe, but internal problems prevented him from doing anything about it.

Peter the Great (1689-1725) was determined to face the challenge from the West and his greatest opponents were Sweden, Poland and Austria. Serious problems arose from within his realm when he looked to the West for a means to confront and push it back. His chief opposition within Russia was the community of "Old Believers." Affirming that Russia was the source of the one true faith which they had inherited from the Jews, that they were the Chosen People of God, the "Old Believers" firmly opposed acquiring anything from the West. They prayed that God might protect them from the incursions of Western power, and they therefore felt that the individuality of Russia could be preserved. Peter argued that faith nonetheless must be joined with action, consequently he began a program of westernizing Russia to meet the West with its own instruments and at the same time preserve its distinction. The program was in part to transform the Orthodox Church into an agency of the state. As to the controversy, neither side convinced the other of the correctness of the position. Peter would, however, set an example for the future of Russia until the end of the House of Romanov. In Riasanovsky's "A History of Russia," p 317, he made Peter the Great the key to the transition movement of the westernization of Russia, a transition which was in process long before his time. This movement, consisting of everything from artillery to philosophy, accelerated during the time of Peter the Great.

From the time of Ivan the Terrible, contact between Russia and the European powers had been increasing. The increase of monarchs in Europe and their centralization of power stood in stark contrast to that of the Russian czars. The shift of Western Europe from a primarily agricultural society to a commercial and mercantile order formed the basis of what has become nineteenth and twentieth century nationalism. The new evolving order was evident in France, Austria, Prussia, Sweden and England, where science as applied to agriculture, medicine and warfare was the force behind the accelerating power of the monarchs of these nations in Europe, and to their expansion into new areas. The expansion of Europe into Latin America by Spain and Portugal, England and France into Africa, India and Southeast Asia. These new forces in Europe posed not only a new order in the West and its domain, they also posed a more powerful threat to Russia, especially Austria, Prussia, Poland, and Sweden.

In order for Russia to build up a powerful army and navy, Peter the Great's first priority of business was to bring the most advanced techniques of war from France, the Lowlands and England. This he accomplished as the result of his trip to the West. Every rank of artisan craftsmen was brought to Russia to train the people in all aspects of warfare. This necessitated the restructuring of the Russian administrative organization from the old bureaucracy to one fashioned from Sweden. Men from the lowest ranks were brought into the new revolutionary administrative organization of Peter the Great and placed along-side European administrators and members of Russian nobility. This new organization, in many respects, was literally forced upon Russia, in order to adjust to the new emerging forces in Western society.

From the latter part of the fifteenth century, Moscow became the center of the Eastern Orthodox Christian struggle to preserve its independence against the encroachment of the West. Five hundred years after Grand Prince Vladimir's conversion, Russian Orthodox Christianity became unhappy in its experience with Latin Christianity and Protestantism when White Russia and Ukraine were subjugated to the Lithuanian-Polish conquest. Russian Orthodox Christendom was struck by the first wave of Latin Christian aggression in the thirteenth and fourteenth centuries. This would parallel the invasions of the Mongol Khans, the Turkish Beys, and the Swedish Lords. More recently, the French, British, Japanese, and Germans had defeated Russia. This was in addition to the pressure from the Nomads to the south and east in earlier days.

It was understood from the outset, when in 989 Prince Vladimir adopted Greek Orthodox Christianity, that the authority of the state was the authority of God. Centuries earlier St. Paul had promulgated that the office is the issuer and not the person. Although this idea had prevailed prior to the Christian era, St. Paul carved it even deeper into Christian thought. Consequently, when the two are integrated, no division of loyalty exists such as "rendering to Caesar the things that are Caesar's and to God the things that are God's."

When Constantinople and Pope Sylvester joined forces and the center of the empire moved from the "first Rome" to the "second Rome", there was no change in authority —merely a strategic shift in geopolitical location to Constantinople. When Vladimir proclaimed Greek Orthodox Christianity the state religion of Kievan Rus, the state was positioned for the future. When in 1472, Russian Czardom took over imperial rule from Constantinople as the third Rome, the form, the theory, and the practice was set in place for all the events leading to the revolution of 1917-18. The struggle of Vladimir and his most outstanding successors, Yaroslav and Vladimir Monomah (1113-25), to attain internal solidarity in Kievan Rus was done in the name of God. When the Mongols invaded and held the area for some 250 years, they ruled through the Grand Princes and subordinate princes in control of respective city-states. If one accepts the thesis that authority comes from God, then not only the Grand Prince, but all Mongol authority might be taken in the same light. Refusing to accept this thesis, the Orthodox Christians resisted, while cooperating with their conquerors. Time, the enemy of all empires, finally made it possible to drive out the Mongols. The cooperation, the resistance and the warfare in freeing the area of Mongol control, were all judged to be acts of God through the organized state that finally emerged free of alien control.

Holding fast that the Czar must spread the one true faith against all external enemies, war was waged against the Mongol Khans, the Turkish Beys, the Swedish lords, the Polish-Lithuanians, the British, the French, the Japanese, and lastly, the German empire of World War One. By the middle of the twentieth century, the conflict between Western Christian Society and Russian Orthodox Society had been an ongoing event since the thirteenth and fourteenth centuries. With the emergence of the commercial and mercantile revolutions and with the emergence of the nation-state system, supported by commercial and mercantile programs, Western Society would accelerate from the sixteenth century onward. And the Russian Orthodox Society would emerge with the advent of industrialization in the latter eighteenth century and beginning nineteenth century. The ideological and violent confrontation grew in direct proportion to the application of physical and natural science, to agriculture, medicine and technology. [1]

Until the House of Romanov's reign came to an end, the structure, operation, and expansion of Russian military control was carried out in the name of the Czar; whose authority came from God. The Czar authorized and carried out a successful expansion against Napoleon in France, Germany in World War One, the Ottoman Turks in Crimea, and the Russo-Japanese War. Had not events worked to the contrary, the Czar's plan was to expand to China and on to Tibet. With a diverse conversion to Christianity, the European powers felt the pressure from Russia and reacted to separate themselves from the Christian puissance of the East. To quote a phrase from a hymn intoned by Martin Luther —"A mighty fortress is our God."

The same religious ethics applied to both the internal and external enemies of Kievan Rus. It subsequently applied to the internal enemies of Greater Russia, as well. It is important to remember that the fundamental reason for Prince Vladimir's conversion to Eastern Orthodoxy was to enable him to establish a cohesive community within the Kievan city-state confederation. There were those beyond the horizon who were judged to be infidels other than the Islamic people. Until the Reformation in the sixteenth century, the enemy to the West was Latin Christendom. However, after the Reformation, the czars accused the Roman Catholics, Lutherans, and other branches of the Protestant movement of being heretics. These so-called heretics were fervently dedicated to organizing strong military city states. And eventually even the Jews were counted among the enemies for failing to accept Christ as the Messiah.

---

[1] *Arnold Toynbee greatly elaborates on this in The Study of History.*

The boyars were another group. They were the guards upon whom was placed the military supremacy of the rising princely power. However, Ivan IV envisaged a whole society of duty-bound sub-servants, a society with no rights. Inspired by the ideas of divine right and in 1564, his policy produced a violent reaction from the people which ignited a reign of terror that lasted some twenty years. Ivan's struggle for divine royal absolutism included the boyars and the members of the estates which he sought to destroy. The peasants also revolted. But the nobility, those in control of the estates, joined with the Czar against the peasants.

The reign of Ivan IV (1533-84) was the zenith of the House of Rurik. Following this period from (1584-1613) was a time of great difficulty during which the first great revolt took place against Boris Gudunov (1584-98, Czar until 1605). A false Dmitri claimed heir to the throne and a great number of peasants and borderland cossacks readily supported him. A social and agrarian revolt was mounted against Gudunov and boyars, and Dmitri became Czar after the sudden death of Gudunov. Although he had contact with Poland and Western Catholicism, he could neither keep peace nor maintain order. He was assassinated. The boyars played a major role in attempting to replace Ivan's absolutism with a government of the estates, and it set off a revolt. The National Assembly of all estates ultimately elected a new Czar in 1613, thus, the House of Romanov was inaugurated.

The early members of the House of Romanov became precursors of Peter the Great. As discussed previously, these rulers began a program of dealing with the West by the use of western techniques. Alexis Mikhalovich (1645-76) tried to make adjustments for new arms from the West and an armament industry, which created a terrible tax burden on the peasants. So heavy a tax burden that, after years of unrest, a peasant revolt erupted from 1668 to 1671. A Don Cossack, Stenka Razin, led the revolt with the peasants and cossacks in the Don and Volga River area. As one might have suspected, the revolt was ruthlessly put down and an estimated one hundred thousand fell victims to the repression. [1]

However, revolts and suppression were not confined only to peasants and cossacks. When reforms of the Church was attempted by Nikon, it produced the community of "Old Believers," and the split in the Church in 1654 would bring persecution to millions who would hold fast to their beliefs. Not until 1905 was a degree of peace attained in this division within the Church.

---

[1] "*A History of Russia, op. cit. . p. 161*".

The "Old Believers" posed a threat against the state in the same fashion as the revolts. Catherine the Great, (1772-1775) would add to the oppression of the peasants. Serfdom had spread to the White Russians and the people of the Ukraine. Arising from the horror of violence, revolt was the response that left a lasting impression on Russian nobility. A revolt was led by Emelyan Ivanovich Pugachev who had himself proclaimed Emperor Peter III, alleging that he had escaped a plot on his life by his wife, Catherine. But the revolt by peasants and cossacks was violently crushed by Catherine the Great and the leader, Pugachev, was executed in Moscow in 1775. Catherine's ultimate goal was to bring the best of Western culture to Russia in terms of literature, music, and architecture. In brief, what she wished to do in these fields, was what Peter the Great had done for Russian military forces, while at the same time following the European example of maintaining absolutism under God.

Prior to the uprising headed by Pugachev, Catherine the Great had spoken ill of the concept of serfdom. This came to a sharp end when the revolts called for a major part of the Russian army to crush the rebellion whereupon serfdom entered into its most oppressive days for the future. [1]

During the reign of Czar Nicholas (1825-55) virtually every form of social and philosophical thought was curtailed within Russia, although there were Western Europe socialist thoughts coming from France. Many of these theories were translated into acts of counter-terror against the Czarist regime. A prime example is the reign of Alexander II when an attempt was made on his life in 1866. Michael Bakunin made an appeal in 1866 for all-out violence against the Czar. He called upon Russians to free themselves, first from religion and then from the state. His ideas squared with those of Karl Marx.

Systematic warfare was waged against the police —and against those individuals who were agents of the state and lawless officials. The purpose of these concerted acts was to break down the prestige and respect of the state, and consequently raise the revolutionary spirit of the people. The answer of Czarist Russia was a violent put down, not a reprieve. This served to increase the revolutionary counter-terrorism, although not all revolutionaries accepted the philosophy of terror.

Individual acts of terror continued to the time of Alexander III, (1881-1894) and government terror virtually blocked organized counter terrorism against the state. To search and seize was the rule of law which was used extensively for indefinite periods; to arrest and hand over civilians to military

---

[1] *"Catherine the Great", Henry Troyat, Dutton, 1977.*

courts.

The same policy of repression continued under Nicholas II who insisted on maintaining the highest degree of autocracy without reform.

All modest demands for reform were violently rejected by the state. In January, 1905, a near crisis took place in St. Petersburg when a priest-double agent led a protest. Some 200,000 workers gathered to present their grievances to the Czar. Confronted by a cossack military force, a mass slaughter took place and more than a thousand workers were killed and an equal number injured. This execution went far in undercutting Russian peasant support for the Czar. [1]

Adam Ulman's Russia's Failed Revolutions, From the Decembrists to the Dissidents is an excellent account of the revolts from 1825 to the abortive revolt of 1917. It shows the internal repression of nineteenth century Russia until 1917. The Decembrists Revolt of 1825 is followed by the upheaval of the 1860's and 1870's which helped to lead to the major revolts of 1905 and 1917. [2]

From this historical analysis, one may see how Constanine's, Pope Sylvester's, and St. Paul's thesis (the authority of the state is the authority of God), greatly influenced the rulers of Czarist Russia and remained firmly correct to the end of the Romanov Dynasty. Thus, the Romanov's believed that their authority came from God to terrorize by military force, by censorship, by the secret police, by indefinite imperilment, and by terminating basic human rights whenever the Czar (the church and state) found it suitable, however indiscriminately, to further their own objectives.

---

[1] *"War In The Shadows", Volume 1, Robert B. Asprey, Double Day, 1975. See Chapter 22.*

[2] *For an excellent statement on Czarist Russia, one must consult McNeill's "The Rise of The West".*

CHAPTER THREE

ISLAM

In much the same fashion as Judaism, Western Christianity and the various branches of Orthodox Christianity, Islam affirms a mystique peculiar unto itself: a mystique that its relation to God is unique, and it is confident that its message will triumph over other religions in some undisclosed future. Islam and Christianity both hold themselves to be the fulfillment of the Judaic law. Each demands that all believers of other faiths forsake their own approach to God and accept their belief. Those of other faiths who refuse to accept this premise are considered enemies. At the time of St. Paul, the Christians saw themselves surrounded by the *Evil One* —working against God. And St. Paul therefore called upon the faithful to take up the shield and demolish the fiery dart of the Evil One. When Emperor Constantine converted to Christianity (312 A.D.), as head of the Roman Empire, the destruction of all other faiths became his quest. Islam took the same position as Emperor Constantine, maintaining that Islam superseded and predated both Judaism and Christianity.

There remains in back of these feelings a sense of superiority which is both theological and philosophical. The dominant element, when not openly opposed, is manifested in the common fact that each believes in faith, love and compassion. When this unique nature is opposed, however, violence is often used to uphold the promise that all means justify the end —in this case religion's dominion.

From the very outset, Islam chose to use violence as a means to convert others to its own religion, rather than a gentle approach. That kind of reasoning can be traced, in part, to Mohammed's flight from Mecca, which marked the turning point, or transition, in the path of Islam. It also marked the first date of the Islamic calendar.

Mohammed was born in the Arabian Peninsula around 560 A.D. The western division of the Greco-Roman Empire collapsed by the year 476 A.D., leaving the Byzantine-Eastern Roman Empire to border Arabia on the west, making it the center of Orthodox Christianity. To the east was Persia, the bastion of Zoroastors. Consequently, Islam leaders, like their Christian counterparts, were surrounded by hostile faiths even within their territorial borders. Islam had Christians and Jews to fear, as well as local tribal faiths.

Mohammed received his first revelation from Allah at the age of forty. However, fearing that it might create hostility among the oligarchy of Arabia, he kept this knowledge a secret for some three years, but then gave up his trade as a merchant and became a prophet. To the believers in Islam, Mohammed is proclaimed to be the successor of both Abraham and Christ, whose teachings he replaced with his own. His mission began as a teacher in Mecca; but the people refused to accept his word as revealed to him by Allah. So after a few years he withdrew from prophesying and became a conqueror. Thirteen years later he went to Medina. With much hostility toward him he was still able to establish an army of some 10,000 to 30,000 men, and in a matter of months fought battles, organized raids and was himself wounded. These acts were in conformity with his teachings. He warded off attackers by using war and diplomacy for a period of about ten years. Mohammed returned to Mecca as victor and ruler after having gained supremacy over other Arabian tribes. And at the time of his death in 632 A.D., with faith to champion his goals, he was prepared to strike at Syria and Iraq.

Much to his surprise, Mohammed found that Allah was not a local tribal God confined to one area, but the God of Abraham, a universal God. Consequently, Abraham was professed to be the first of the prophets and Mohammed was the last.

The belief in Islam set the stage for conflict within Arabia and within all branches of Christianity and Judaism as well. Mohammed and his successors saw themselves surrounded by hostile forces. Jews, most assuredly, would not accept Mohammed as the seal of the prophets anymore than they would accept Christ.   And the Christians could not believe Jesus was superseded by Mohammed anymore than the Jews could accept Christ as the Messiah.

Mohammed had proclaimed Allah to be the all-powerful creator of the world. A day of judgment would come at which time all would be rewarded according to their merit to heaven or hell. He demanded total obedience to himself as the messenger of Allah. The Jews and Christians who refused to accept him were ostensibly punished. But when the Jews were proclaimed "People of the Book" by Islam, the harsh treatment toward them subsequently discontinued. And as long as they paid a special tax they were protected by Islamic law.

In order to grasp Islam, it is important to note that in the Koran (the Holy Book of Islam) —hereafter referred to as "The Book—" there is no distinction between religious and political affairs. Islamic law is divided into two basic parts which refer to Dar al Islam: The House of Peace which covers all matters of the family, social community, commerce, trade and issues of crime. It covers also the relation of Islamic faithfuls with People of the Book, primarily Jews, Christians, and followers of Zoroaster in Persia. Dar al Harb, The House of War, deals with all aspects of Islam not included in the above. To Muslims, the prophet is believed to be perfect. However, they do not consider the prophet to be a divine being as Christians believe Christ to be. The faithful believe the Koran is the final word of Allah, to all humanity. Although the Koran is the prime source of Islamic law, there is also the Hadith Qudsi (Sacred Hadith). This work contains the maxims divinely communicated to Mohammed by Allah.

The successors of Mohammed, after his death in year 632 A.D., was Abu Bakr, Omar Osman, and Ali from the year 631 A.D. to 661 A.D. Their policy was to adhere as closely as possible to the practices of Mohammed. Consequently, great care was taken to record all sayings of Mohammed, especially the sayings which were revealed to him by Allah. Only by such practice as this could their problems of the future be faced. This short period comprised the golden age of Islam. Then between 767 and 855 A.D., Islamic Law became codified into four compartments: Hanifite, Sufism, Malikism and Hanbali which was the Sharia, otherwise know as Islamic law.

The purpose of Islam is to serve Allah. The translation of the word, Islam, is the submission to the will of Allah. The translation of the word, Muslim, is to resign oneself to Allah. From the outset, Islams' intense hostility, was directed toward the Persians to the east, and the Byzantines to the west. Thus, the internal tension kept the community of Islam unified for a long time.

In the one century after the death of Mohammed, 632 A.D.to 732 A.D., Islam had spread from Arabia to the west, across North Africa, to the City of Tours, some fifty miles from the city of Paris. To the north and to the east, it had extended to Asia Minor, the Iranian plateau, and into northwest India. By the middle of the thirteenth century, the northern two-thirds of India, China and Kievan Rus were under its sway. By the fourteenth and fifteenth centuries it had reached the Philippines, Southeast Asia and Sub-Sahara Africa, in the west. However, all of this was not gained by violence. Records indicate that many Christians and Jews became Muslim of their own will.

With the death of Ali (661 A.D.), a division occurred in the ranks of Islam, and continues to this day. Followers of the Sunnah, meaning the path, the Orthodox version of Islam, believe the faithful follow God directly. The other group, the Shiite, adhere to the view that Ali, the son of Mohammed's daughter, Fatima, possessed the divine illumination required to lead the faithful.

Others believed that Ali's descendants, by whatever method, could make the correct claim to lead, and there were those who stated that only the consensus of Muslim community could choose a man of piety as the legitimate leader. Other factions arose in profusion until anarchy became the vogue in many circles. The results produced usurpation of authority resting upon armed force. Islam gives the faithful the right to remove its leaders by violence if need be. Armed struggle over succession to authority, as in the case of the conflict in 744 that gave rise to the Abbasids who overthrew the Ummayads, which substantially removed the distinction between Arab and non-Arab Moslems. The Abassid Caliphs received their support largely from Persia, while the Ummayads gained their support largely from Arabia, Iraq and Syria.

The two major branches of Islam still remain, the Sunnah and the Shiah. The Shiah believe that the community of the faithful on earth are ruled by a semi-divine leader, the imam acts as the mediator between the faithful and the divine. Even though this division had its birth early in the history of Islam, it would not be until 1502 that Shaism became a separate religion-political entity. At that time, it became the official religion of Persia as set forth by Ismail. The Shaih also has a different Hadith from the Sunnah.

Shiah adheres to the concept that only by consensus can the community of the faithful be ruled or guided. Not only the conflict with Christianity would be enlarged by this split, it would augment the discord within Islam itself. As each major division of Christianity claims a monopoly of truth, Roman Catholic, Orthodox Christian, and Protestants, so do the divisions within Islam. This is especially true with regard to the Sunnah and Shaih. To compound the problem, each of the respective branches of Islam claims the monopoly on "truth." Each believes the others must be shown the error of their way.

By the end of the eleventh century, the Crusades brought Christians and Muslims into war against each other. Each openly proclaimed its wars to be "just" and "holy." Consequently, the Crusades left a permanent scar on each that now lies behind the conflict in the Near East at the present day. Today, as in the past, each claim God as their leader, giving divine legitimacy to both.

The great geographic expanse of Islam as outlined previously would crowd Western Christian Society into a relatively small area. Islam took the Christian area of North Africa and by 732 incorporated Iberia and Southern France as far north as the City of Tours. Subsequently, the Crusades by the Western Christians began in Iberia and later into the Near East to recapture the Holy Lands from Islam. These efforts, though successful in Iberia by 1492, were not in the Near East even though an enclave was established, which still holds in modern day Lebanon. These were among the earliest reverses of Islam by its enemies. Islam would overtake Kievan Rus in the 13th century and control the area for some 250 years. By the end of the 15th century, it could lose political control of Kievan Rus. In Iberia the re-conquest by the Christian forces would result in the wholesale slaughter not only of Muslims, but also Jews. In India, where Islam moved in its early expansion, virtually all control would be gained before it would encounter the West.

The expansion of Europe would coincide with the rapid change in Western Europe from an age of agriculture to one shifting to commerce and the development of science and technology as applied to agriculture, medicine and warfare. These developments would coincide with the emergence of the nation-state system. At the same time, the greatest reverses to Islam would take place with the re-conquest of Iberia, as well as other areas in the Mediterranean, the Atlantic and the Indian Ocean from Islamic control. Meanwhile, forces in Muscovy were asserting themselves against the Muslim administration and military power, causing their loss of the area. Finally, the split of Sunnah against Shiah with the assent of Shah Ismail Safavi, would comprise a combination from which there were no Islamic adjustments. Aside from the last matter of Shah Ismail Safavi, these reverses and the loss of India to French and British forces, would be due to superior technology of war used by the commercial and mercantile nation-state system of the West and its consequent expansion of Europe.

There arose far deeper spiritual questions as these reverses were carried out. How does one explain the losses sustained in an Islamic context? Among the faithful many thought:

1. Allah has forsaken us.

2. We, the faithful have forsaken Allah.

3. One cannot question the inscrutable wisdom of Allah.

4. Allah is balancing losses with gains.

5. Let us promote an Islamic renaissance that will support the knowledge and skills for metals and techniques of warfare which sustained us in the past.

6. Allah gave us these skills, but took them from us. We cannot revive what Allah has taken from us without violating Islamic law of the Koran.

7. Let us borrow from the West all its techniques for use against them.

8. This cannot be done, for the faithful would be borrowing what was taken from us by Allah, and that from our enemy, the heretical Christian.

9. We are not following the correct ancestral practice of the past.

10. What is the correct practice of the past? [1]

It would be the corresponding relationship between suffering defeats from the West with growing disquiet between the Sunnah and the Shaih that would erupt with the great leader Shah Ismail Safavi.

It was the violent split between Sunnah and Shiah that was Islam's greatest reverse in many respects. A fanatical Shaih sect arose at the southern end of the Caspian Sea around 1499. The leader, as mentioned above, built a formidable army by 1500 and proclaimed himself as Shah. By 1506, the entire Iranian plateau was his. Still later (1508-1510) he gained Baghdad, most of Iraq and the major portion of the eastern end of his empire.

Ismail Safavi, a fanatical believer in Islam, and an effective administrator and master of military affairs, proclaimed himself as having knowledge of the correct ancestral practice of the past. In time, however, he would turn Islam against itself. He persecuted all Sunnah under his control and then came in conflict with those in the Ottoman Empire who were Sunnah. Ismail Safavi ultimately claimed to be no less than Allah incarnate. This proclamation would turn Sunnah against the heresy of the Shiah beliefs of Safavi. Warfare broke out between one sect against the other. This kind of mutual suppression paralleled the wars of Lutherans against Roman Catholics and the warfare in Switzerland.

From another viewpoint, as Islamic expansion came to an end, the cohesion that existed within it, since the time of Mohammed fell apart. Fractional rivalry, regional conflicts along with doctrinal and sectarian disputes broke out with a vengeance. The results would produce some seventy-two sects divided into two main groups, Sunnah and Shiah. When the expansion of Islam came to an end, it began to break apart. It would be late in the 17th century before the end of expansion would be noticeable. Among the many reasons for the check on Islamic expansion, aside from internal warfare of Islam against Islam and over expansion, the lack of adaptation to the technology of war as was transpiring in the West, was clearly a major factor. The static nature

---

[1] *"The Rise of The West"*, William H. Mc Neill, *The University of Chicago Press, 1963.*

of Islamic law and the belief of the faithful in that law was the predominate failure in making the needed adaptation.

Looking for the correct Islamic practice of the past did not allow Islam to keep up with the rapid scientific advancement of the West. By the 17th century, the backward looking ethos of Islam created rigidity. In the Ottoman Empire it would be Salim the Great, the lawgiver, who would strive to keep out and suppress all dangerous thoughts from his realm. In India, Aurangzeb would do the same. In both instances these events were effects of previous causes, the major split in Islam and the consequent fratricidal wars of the Islamic people. [1]

Early Christians were not unified concerning the teachings of Christ. Neither were the forces of Islam. Many movements arose within Islam in the early centuries after Mohammed had worked to restore what they believed to be true Islam. Much of the various teachings were absorbed into Sunnah teaching.

As early as 644, Islam was divided on its teachings and the third Caliph, Uthman, in that year sought to impose religious uniformity upon the faithful. When Uthman was killed in 656, Ali was proclaimed Caliph. Because he failed to take action against soldiers who killed Uthman, some of his soldiers killed him in a civil war, constituting the first such war among Islamic people.

Those withdrawing from Ali, the Kharijites, as the group was known, believed themselves the possessors of the true teaching. They declared those who did not follow their way as outlaws and unbelievers, proclaiming a "holy war" against the rest of the community, especially its leaders. Warfare and assassination became a common means to an end. Ali was killed in 661 A.D. According to the Kharijite version of the Holy Koran, they were given the right to overthrow Caliphs perceived to be unjust. Although this movement was crushed, it set the prototype for the fundamentalists of today.

Because of the personal qualities of Ali, and since he was a member of Mohammed's family, a movement arose around him. It was hoped that the social disorder of the time could be ended by this leadership. The Shiah,

---

[1] *"Man's Religions"*, John B. Noss, MacMillan, 1963. *"The Religions of Man"*, Huston Smith, Perennial Library. *"Islam In Focus"*, Islamic Teaching Center, Chicago, IL. *"Hamonudah Abdiati"*, American Trust Publications, Indianapolis, IN, 1975. *"Faith and Power, The Politics of Islam"*, Edward Mortimer, Random House, 1982.

centering around Ali, could oppose the Sunnah. The Shiah believed Mohammed had predicted a future prophet or leader who was to appear among them before the end of time, and the Mahdi would be one directly chosen by Allah. This would set the Shaih apart from the Sunnah. The former believe Ali was the first in a succession of imams (learned men). These personages are believed to give the correct interpretations of the Koran. Although not equal to Mohammed, these divinely inspired leaders would oppose any state, if need be, whereas the Sunnah would not separate church and state.

Believing the 12th imam was hidden among the faithful, the Shaih believe in time this one will appear as Mahdi to purify the world. The Shaih became the official religion of Persia, now Iran, at the outset of the 16th century.

For several centuries this minority existed under the Sunnah. Giving spiritual authority and guidance, and not taking physical control of the state was their fashion. The hidden imam would correct the world when the time evolves in an undisclosed future.

Among other segments of Shiah believers, the imam is held to have authority to overthrow corrupt regimes when possible. Following Ismail, other Shaih think the Koran has an inner meaning secretly carried from Ali through the successive imams. Not only are these teachings gained by intensive training, but the teachings are also guarded. In time, the Shaih took to violence and terrorism -- becoming feared by all other segments of Islam as well as Christians, Jews, Zorastrians and those not of The Book.

Before Ismail, arising in the 11th century, there was one Hasan Ibn al-Sabbah, who became known as "the Old Man of the Mountain." The leader of this group in Persia led armies and guerrilla warfare, sending missions into camps of opposing groups to safeguard their own strongholds. The name "Assassins" became attached to them.

Another segment of Islam that is disclaimed in some measure by Sunnis as being true Muslims is the Alawis. Contrary to Islamic teaching, Alawis hold Ali to have been divine. This group is in Syria today.

One of the Fatimid, Caliphi Hakim 966-1002, proclaimed himself as God manifest. From the teachings of Darasi, who made this proclamation, arose the Druses' movement, who believe that Hakim will reappear in the future. Furthermore, the teachings are secret and revealed only to the faithful upon attaining the fortieth year of life. Furthermore, one cannot be converted to the faith. One becomes a member only by birth into a family of the faithful.

Another group founded by Muslims, but by those who broke from the faith in the 19th century, was a Messianic movement sweeping through Iran known as "Babism." Proclaiming himself to be the gate to the 12th imam, Ali Mohammed Shiraz, set forth a new order —superseding the Koran in the mid-nineteenth century. From this arose the Bah'i religion. Not being Muslim, but founded by Muslims and claiming to supersede the Koran by its teachings, this faith has been the target of intense persecution since its origin because to break from Islam in such a fashion is a capital offense under Islamic law.

It appears as though much of the Islamic world is undergoing similar changes due to the thrust of industrialization of the Western world, the establishment of Israel, and the acceleration of industrial power by the former U.S.S.R. In the 19th century, the United States faced the problem of a changing order from agriculture to industrialization with its consequent changes from slave labor to non-slave labor. The southern states had institutions and ideology, philosophy and religion to support an order threatened by the change coming from England and Europe and then from the New England states. Failure to adjust to these changes peaceably, produced the Civil War. The same change in the Germanies prior to and after German unification (1871) would play a dominant role in the rise of Nazism and Fascism in the 20th century.

Currently, the Western powers, the former U.S.S.R. states and Japan have an industrial order built upon petroleum. Much of this strategic material is in the Islamic world, a zone conflict of culture and power in the Near East. The conflicting ideas are Zionism, Christianity, Islam and Bah'i, and the nationalistic movements in the former Soviet Union.

Small wonder that in the Near East a crisis remains. From the origin of Christianity there has arisen an area of violence, accentuated by Christian heresy. Prevailing in Lebanon are at least ten different versions of historic Christianity at bitter odds with themselves. These divisions also exist in the same area within Islam and Judaism. Among the Christians, there are Maronite, Syrian Orthodox and Roman Catholic, Greek Orthodox and Catholic, Armenian Orthodox, Catholic, Chaldean and Assyrian Nestorians, and Roman Catholics. These various religious factions increase the role of violence and terror, and act as a catalyst to the fragmentation of the human spirit.

In the movement of Islam into the area, religious persecution arose. By 632 A.D., at the time of the death of Mohammed, Islam was at war with its Roman and Persian neighbors. The faithful believed that by order of God, Islam had to be made known to the outside world. To do so, important borders had to be crossed. Requiring large military force, expansion into non-Arabic land came by force of arms. Some Persians and Romans openly received them, and though Christians or Jews, became converts. Those that did not, and held on to their faith, paid tribute (Zakah).

Christians and Jews remaining faithful to their respective creeds were guaranteed protection, security and freedom. Furthermore, any danger to the tax paying Jews or Christians was considered a danger to Islam. These abiding subjects were required not to be of any trouble to their religious counterparts in the Muslim community. Refusing to accept Islam and resistance to it was considered treacherous. These acts needed to be suppressed in order to protect the state. Force was used when needed to bring the non-Muslims to their senses, to show they must share responsibility for social order.

The Koran clearly states that war is a necessity so long as injustice and ambition exists. War is a fact of life which cannot be overlooked as a matter of human conduct. Accordingly, The Koran says:

> Fighting is prescribed for you, and ye dislike it. But it is possible that ye dislike a thing which is good for you, and that ye love a thing which is bad for you. But God knoweth and ye know not.

Sura II, 216. All quotations are from The Holy Qur'an, A. Yusuf Ali, The Islamic Center, Washington, D.C., 1978.

From the commentary, The Koran, page 84, is found the following:

> To fight in the cause of truth is one of the highest forms of charity. What can you offer that is more precious than your own life. But here again the limitations come in. If you are a mere brawler, or a selfish aggressive person, or a vain-glorious bully, you deserve the highest censure. If you offer our life to the righteous imam, who is only guided by God, you are an unselfish hero. God knows the value of things better than you do.

To the faithful, war is a matter of last resort. War is to be engaged in only when there is an aggressor. The Muslim is commanded not to begin aggressive warfare.

For the non-Muslim Sura VII, p. 97, the following speaks of those who defy God's law:

> Did the people of the towns feel secure against the coming of our wrath by night while they were asleep?

Did they feel secure against the plans of God? But no one can feel secure from the plan of God, except those (doomed) to ruin.

In the commentary on the second verse, page 370, is the following:

". . . the nations which as a body could not be won over to God's law perished."

This refers to the story of Moses and the bondage to Egypt --the rescue of the Israelites and their wanderings, and their proving themselves unworthy and being left to wander in a new sense when they rejected the new Prophet (Mohammed) who came to renew God's message.

In reference to Jews rejecting Mohammed, Footnote 1141 on page 392, the following is stated:

The dispersal of the Jews is a great fact in the world's history. Nor has their persecution ended yet, nor is it likely to end as far as we can foresee.

For further reference to those nations as a body that could not be won over to God's law, in the commentary to Sura VII, page 167, a cross reference to Deut. 11:20 is ginen: "A curse if ye will not obey the commandments of the Lord your God." Also see Deut. 27:49, . . . "the Lord shall bring a nation against thee from afar, and from the end of the earth, as swift as the eagle flies."

For those who disobey God's will, Sura XXII, pages 1-21 deals with those to whom God has been made known and yet reject Him. They will become outlaws in His Kingdom, making friends with Evil —which is to be a rebel in God's Kingdom.

Defiance of God's law is described as follows:

"Over their heads will be poured out boiling water. With it will be scalded what is without their broken bodies as well as (their skins)."

The commentary on page 855 states that in physical terms the punishment shall be all-prevailing, not superficial, and none shall escape the final punishment when the time of repentance has passed. The unbelievers will wish they had believed and will be covered with shame.

Special consideration is given those who suffer evil in the cause of God.

They shall have the highest rank in the sight of God (Sura IX, 20). In the commentary on this, the following is a paraphrase: The Jihad (Muslim Holy War), may require fighting in God's cause as a form of self-sacrifice. The essence required is a true and sincere faith, and an earnest and sworn faith involving the sacrifice (if need be) of life, person or property in the service of God. Brutal fighting opposes the spirit of Jihad, and the scholar's pen and the money of the wealthy may be a valuable form of Jihad. Those fighting are promised a mercy specially from Himself; His own good pleasure, gardens of perpetual delight, the supreme reward, God's own Presence or nearness.

From a commentary of the Koran, page 76, is the following comment in paraphrase on the issue of fighting in the cause of God. In general, Islam is a religion of peace and good faith. Its men will not acquiesce in wrong-doing. Holding life is cheap, they will sacrifice their lives to uphold their religion. They believe in constant striving by all means of their power for the establishment of truth and righteousness. They know war to be an evil, but will not flinch from it where honor demands it, and a righteous imam commands it. Then, they are not serving carnal ends. This philosophy supports the intensity of violence and cheapens life for all involved.

War is permissible in self-defense and under defined conditions. When these conditions are present, then war must be pushed with vigor to restore peace and freedom and the worship of God.

Sura IV, 84 states the following:

> Then fight in God's cause, thou art held responsible only for thyself —and rouse the believers. It may be that God will restrain the fury of the unbelievers, for God is the strongest in might and in punishment.

In the commentary on this point, page 206 observes the following:

Muhammad, as an example, inspired his men. Where he saw himself as carrying out God's plan, nothing can resist it. If the enemy happens to have strength, power or resources, God's strength, power and resources are infinitely greater. If the enemy is meditating punishment on the righteous for their righteousness, God's punishment for such wickedness will be infinitely greater and more effective.

For those who fight in the cause of God and are slain, the reward is great. See the following: Sura VIII, 9; IX, 29, 133; XXII, 39-41; ILVII, 4, 20; and XIVIII, 17.

A final note on apostates is required. Sura XLVII, 25 states:

> Those who turn back as apostates after guidance was clearly shown to be the Evil One has instigated these and busied them up with false hopes.

The commentary on page 1385 states:

"Such men are entirely in the hands of Evil. They follow its suggestions, and their hopes are built upon deceptions."

From a speech given by the Ayatollah Ruhollo Khomeini on December 12, 1984, the birth date of Muhammad, this excerpt appeared in the January 11, 1985 issue of *Le Nouvel Observateur:*

> If one permits an infidel to continue in his role as a corrupter of the earth, his moral suffering will be all the worse. If one kills the infidel, and thus stops him from perpetrating his misdeeds, his death will be a blessing to him. For if he remains alive, he will become more and more corrupt. This is a surgical operation commanded by God the all-powerful.

> Those who imagine that our time on earth is a divine gift, those who believe that eating and sleeping like animals are gifts from God, say that Islam should not inflict punishments. But those who follow the teachings of the Koran know that Islam must apply the lex tailionis, and thus they must kill. Those who have knowledge of the suffering in the life to come realize that cutting off the hand of someone for a crime he has committed is of benefit to him. In the beyond he will thank those who, on earth, executed the will of God. War is a blessing for the world and for all nations. It is God who incites men to fight and kill. The Koran says: 'Fight until all corruption and all rebellion have ceased.' The wars the Prophet led against the infidels were a blessing for all humanity. Imagine that we soon win the war (against Iraq). That will not be enough, for corruption and resistance to Islam will still exist. The Koran says: 'War, war until victory.' A religion without war is an incomplete religion. If His Holiness Jesus —blessings upon Him— had been given more time to live, he would have acted as Moses did, and wielded the sword. Those who believe that Jesus did not have 'a head for such things,' that He was not interested in war, see in Him nothing more than a simple preacher, and not a prophet. A

prophet is all —powerful. Through war he purifies the earth. The mullahs with corrupt hearts who say that all this is contrary to the teachings of the Koran are unworthy to Islam. Thanks to God, our young people are now, to the limits of their means, putting God's commandments into action. They know that to kill the unbelievers is one of Man's greatest missions.

An article in Harpers [1] states that with the justification for the use of violence against the non-believer, and the drive within Islam itself to find the correct ancestral practice of the past, the conflicts within the faith gave rise to violence.

Internal conflict has made it easier for Western Christian powers and Czarist Orthodox Christianity as well to progress toward their acclaimed goals. With the aftermath of the First and Second World Wars, there has been a drastic acceleration of the internal conflicts of Islam as well as with Israel and the West.

The people of the Near East led a life which remained virtually unchanged for centuries. However, unlike the Near East, the Western Christian Society championed the advent of the renaissance. The agrarian social base of Western Christian Society changed drastically as the result of the commercial, mercantile and industrial revolutions. Consequently, these forces were extremely fundamental in helping to bring about the final collapse of the universal structure of the Church of Rome.

Within the Twentieth Century, Islam has been threatened by similar forces within its area by industrialization from the West and its consequent disruptions of Islamic mores. In conjunction with this, is the demand for Near Eastern oil and the clash of interest fostered by the super power of the former Soviet Union and the United States.

The demand for oil has brought about some changes within Saudi Arabia, (see The Kingdom, Robert Lucy) and the same is true of Kuwait, and the Abu Dhabi Sheikdoms, Iraq, Iran, and to a lesser degree, Egypt.

The establishment of Israel in the same area with the displacement of Palestinians has augmented the problem. Many Palestinians are as determined to regain their homeland as were the Jews in exile. The paradox lies in that each claims the same land. Israel has its divisions of Jews within Israel as much

---

[1]*Harpers, 1985.*

as the divided Muslims.

In the three Arab-Israeli wars fought before Israeli invasion of Southern Lebanon (in 1982), Israel had been successful. Now with the invasion and partial withdrawal from Lebanon, Israel is still faced with an opponent which will not sue for peace. Israel has won battles to regain their "promised land," but they have yet to attain peace. This cannot be done until Israel can convince the Arab world to accept its existence by their own Arab convictions. Israel cannot disengage itself from Arabic contact. There is no place to strike and deal a fatal blow to Arab authority. From a focal point, Israel is faced by the Arab world beyond the river Jordan to the Zagros Mountains and the Persian Gulf when looking eastward. To the west, it stretches to the Atlantic; to the south, to Aden and the Sudan; and to the north, there is Syria.

In addition, there are many Muslims within Israel itself. In fact, their population seems to be growing more in Israel and occupied territory at a greater pace than the Israeli population, including immigrants to Israel. Consequently, Israel and the Arab-Muslim-Christian world is inter-locked geographically and spiritually. Their respective claims to theological uniqueness has bred and doubtless lead to more violence.

As Israel is surrounded by hostile theological forces, the same is true for Islam. Israel is a house divided, but it also confronts the present day commonwealth of the former Soviet Union with hostile philosophical-opposition to Judaism. Therefore, the Russian Orthodox centuries-old fear of Islam cannot but have an influence in the process of the new Republic's thinking. A large portion of the people of the New Republics are Muslim, and their roots have been there for centuries. The people of the commonwealth, and Iran as well, are concerned about the Russian Orthodoxy. The Islamic world fears the forces of Western Europe because of their Christian ideas and support of Israel; notwithstanding the power of the United States. Islam has a legacy of the violence which it brought into India centuries ago, not to mention the violence that erupted between Hindu and Islam when the British were forced to retreat after the Second World War. There remains the possible Islamic-Sikh connection in the turbulence of 1984, which shook the foundation of Indian stability, to be followed by the assassination of Prime Minister Gandhi. And still open to questions are: just what connections there may be between the events in India and the forces within the Islamic world. Nonetheless, neither Pakistan nor India is safe at their contiguous border.

The Islamic view of God is alien to Hinduism. The Muslims believe that they hold the only correct approach to the unknown, which is Allah. The Hindu, however, takes this as only one view of many approaches. The two declared opposites and much bloodshed has come about as the result of these divergent points of view. Hinduism, as discussed by world historian, Arnold Toynbee, has a scope of passageways to the unknown which are as broad and varied as a spectrum. The antecedents of Hinduism reach into the past some 5,000 years. Hindu scholars have studied virtually every religious thought known to humankind and many have become renown scholars in the various beliefs that have emerged within India as well as those introduced from outside India.

This factor became a point of great conflict when the adherents of Islam came face-to-face with scholars who were thorough in their knowledge of the faith, and could speak, read and write the language of the Holy Koran, but would not reject their own faith and become believers of Islam.

When a great number of *Untouchables* became converts to Islam, it created a serious conflict within the heart of India, especially since the Hindu refused to accept the Islamic faith.

In several Islamic states, there are many versions of Christianity. In Saudi Arabia, Christian services are not permitted as a matter of law.

Consequently, Islam has internal and external religious fears as well, as it did from the outset in many respects. All portend to violence.

Saudi Arabia's opposition to Christianity and the West is, in part, indicated by its apprehension to adjust to the influx of Western laborers working alongside Saudi Arabian laborers in Western technology, relative to the oil industry. Great pains are taken to assure the Wahhabi (preferentially known as unitarians) interpretation of the Holy Koran to the faithful in order to avoid disruption within the country as industrialization and Western thought come into the country. There is also in Saudi Arabia a feeling of apprehension for the presence of a high number of foreign Muslims, the Shaih, and for the non-Muslim Western people as well. The problem is how to maintain Wahhabi Islamic law without contamination. The tranquility of the Kingdom of Saud was shattered on November 20, 1979, when a fanatical person claiming to be the Mahdi (he who is right-guided) with a group of armed associates attempted to take over the Grand Mosque in Mecca.

Iran illustrates the external as well as the internal problems of Islam. After the Second World War, the United States proposed to build a bastion of power in Iran as a safe guard against the Soviet expansion to the Indian Ocean, the Persian Gulf, and to India, as well. The Shah, with great oil resources in the area, encouraged rapid oil development with all the related factors that came with it. With heavy militarization promoted as a necessary adjunct of the Shah's aspirations, the forces produced a deep alienation of the religious scholars because of their fear of Western influence, not only upon the Shah, but among the majority of the Shaih people of Iran. The introduction of alien values considered as evil created an acute breach between the followers of Ayatollah Khomeini and the Shah, himself. Attacks upon Western industrialization and all related matters in Iran were inspired by the Iranian Mullah, who denounced big business and the advantage it gave to infidels to alter the traditional life of the people of Iran.

When the fundamentalist, Juhayman, arose in Saudi Arabia, in November, 1979, and proclaimed himself brother of the Mahdi, he denounced the Kingdom of Saud in the same manner as Khomeini had denounced the government of the Shah. There, Khomeini had demonstrated an ability to bring down the mighty Shah through the teachings of the Word of Allah by Shaih teachings. These illustrations, coupled with the assassination of Anwar al Sadat of Egypt by Islamic fundamentalists, show how hostile and violent the adjustments can be. This violence is all the more perilous because it is an "holy war."

The industrial revolution is now just two hundred years old. Whenever it has reached out, almost without exception, it has disrupted institutions, social structures and their accompanying ideology. Violence has been the handmaiden of change. Industrial growth, so often associated with progress, is actually applied to agriculture, medicine and military affairs of state. Within the last two hundred years, it has turned culture against culture, and religion against religion among the various societies of the world.

Perhaps it would be better if the Islamic world began an adjustment to industrialization as peacefully as possible. Arnold J. Toynbee, in his *A Study of History,* has detailed the problems involved in peaceful transition. For any social order to choose some of the aspects of another culture without bringing the undesired aspects into its own framework may be impossible. Many other elements enter into it, like barnacles that cling to a ship when coming into port after long at sea. So the Islamic world is caught in a dilemma: It is bound by tradition to resist change yet, at the same time, in need of industrialization to defend itself. If gradual adjustment fails because of the acceleration of technology, then Iran's experience will be repeated. Much fear exists that The Kingdom of Saud may fail in its attempt at gradual change, because it is the center of the Islamic world in which the faith is deeply rooted. Finally, what will happen when its great oil resources are depleted? Will some undisclosed Mahdi arise and proclaim events to be from Allah and assail the leaders of state for the misfortune?

The United States failed to adjust to industrialization in the Nineteenth Century. And so did Germany, Italy, Spain, Czarist Russia, the Ottoman Empire, Imperial China, and Latin America in the Nineteenth and Twentieth centuries. In all these instances, the social/religious philosophical orders failed to make peaceful psycho-spiritual adjustments. Charismatic leaders arose in many instances in the midst of these changes. John Brown, Porfirio Diaz, Juan Peron, Lenin, Mussolini, Franco, Hitler, Hirohito, Mao Tse Tung, Khomeini, to name a few of the more prominent ones, all rode the tide of violence at full tilt.

Currently, and on into the unforeseeable future, the non-Islamic world would be advised to approach the Islamic world, and all other developing nations and societies, as well, with a keen awareness of their own defects, including their self-assumed elitist mentality and spirituality. Each would be better advised to lay aside their own assumed uniqueness of spiritual quest. The problems of a spiritual nature that all nations face are multi-faceted. A genuine respect should be expressed toward the cultural aspects among all nations.

Upon examination, there are points upon which most nations can agree as to some concept of peace, justice and compassion, for their respective peoples. However, as nations demand preeminence over other nations, whatever affirmative aspects available may diminish. Currently, nation-states and societies amplify the role of violence which all are engaged in —the legal, moral, and covert guerrilla warfare. It is feared that as religious theories are used increasingly to justify the use of violence, or the threat of its use, these violent aspects of religion will supersede all other motives. Their demands for self-admitted uniqueness has often led to violence. What will happen to the affirmative aspects, if this religious demand continues? The far-reaching results may be that the youth reared in such an atmosphere may come to disregard the line between the *moral-immoral and the legal-illegal* use of violence. There also is the possibility that they may perceive their leaders of state and religious institutions as justifying violence. Violence could therefore become the prevailing knowledge of the day and even worse; it could destroy any faith in a just and compassionate society. Should this come to pass, violence would decimate affirmative relations within and among nations, and also destroy any chance for a standard of conduct which protects the many against the few. If this comes to pass, Thomas Hobbes and Niccoli Machiavelli will be proven correct.

Islam, Christianity, and Judaism believe in absolutes. Metaphysics, theological and natural theology, and objective revelation, are beginning to collapse in the Christian world; and they are under attack in the Islamic world as well. The West faces problems of living without convincing absolutes, without dogmas. Moreover, there are concerns within Islam about a threat to the same absolutes. [1]

[1] *"Arab and Jew, Wounded Spirits In a Promised Land"*, David K. Shipler, Times Book, 1986. *"The Arab World Today"*, Morroe Burger, Double Day, 1962. *"The Highwalls of Jerusalem"*, Ronald Sanders, Holt Rinehart, 1963. *"Blood Brothers"*, Elias Chacour, Chosen Books, 1984. *"Shedding Light On Lebanon"*, John Keegan, The Atlantic Monthly.

CHAPTER FOUR

A BRIEF HISTORY OF CHINA AND JAPAN

Violence, with its devastating effect on society is fast becoming so universal that concerned citizens should cast off their provincial prejudices and fragmented thinking and realize that it has motivated and inspired countless world leaders down through the ages —including those of China and Japan.

Confucianism and Shinto do not appear to be related to Christianity and Islam. Christianity and Islam are monothestic in nature while Confucianism and Shinto are not. Chrisitianity and Islam proclaim to be universal religions while Shinto is confined almost entirely to Japan and does not claim universality. Shinto, in many respects may be considered a national religion. However, Confucianism —whether it is in fact deemed a religion or not— seems to have a universal appeal.

The distinctive character of Confucianism and Shinto arises from the origins of China and Japan, a remote region of the world, the center point from which Judao-Christian-Islamic people arose. It appears that the Chinese and the Japanese ascended from China, Korea and, perhaps Southeast Asia.

Sumer and Egypt, though separated by great geographical distances, including huge mountain ranges, had a highly developed society long before the Chinese society, and long before the emergence of the West with Christian-Islamic religions.

The ancient people of China knew nothing of India, Mesopotamia or Egypt at the beginning of their writing around 1800 B.C. Consequently, the Chinese culture would be dissimilarly fashioned yet highly developed long before the forces of Christianity and Islam appeared on the scene.

China's cultural diffenences, inherent in the background and psycho-dynamics of these divergent people, and the language barrier as well, played a great role in our perception of them. The philosophy of Confucianism and the religion of Shinto are presented together here in order to explain how ancient China influenced Japan. The Japanese borrowed extensively in various ways from the Chinese and made changes in compliance with their own objectives.

Conflicting opinions abound regarding Confucianism and Shinto as substantive religions, the validity of which goes beyond the scope of this study. Each has had, and remains to have, a profound influence on millions of Chinese and Japanese people, and the rest of the world as well.

Shinto is a word which means: the "Way of the Gods." Early Shinto represented the worship of nature in all its manifestations, including mountains, rocks, trees, plants, waterfalls, and numerous forms of fertility symbols. It is believed that all objects possess *kami* (defined as the essence of all objects). Humans are deemed to also have kami, referring to the special characteristics which one possesses. There is nothing superhuman nor moral about it for the Spirit world of kami is believed to be an exact shadow of the real world. Early Shinto-associated with beauty and joy- was a nameless faith having respect for all nature. Shinto grew out of polytheism and without doubt merged with mythology to embrace a Sun Goddess. From many Japanese records we find that those who designed and enforced the merger did so to purposely depict Shinto as being superior to other faiths.

Japan's ancestors are thought to have migrated from Korea, China, and perhaps from Southeast Asia. They had a highly developed civilization, long before they began to migrate to Japan, at the beginning of the Christian era. The Japanese drew heavily from the ancient people of China who were advanced in domestic agriculture, urban life, the division of labor, universal religion, philosophy, and writing. [1] Midway through the 18th century B.C., the chinese had all the elements of a higher civilization, their dynastic system having existed for centuries. The study of Confucianism and Taoism, along with the great Chinese classics, had begun in China prior to the Christian era. The study and pratice of Buddhism also was in China even before the Japanese developed writing in the 7th century A.D.

The major purpose of Shinto throughout Japanese history was to establish an antiquity and if possible a national dignity which would surpass those of their mainland neighbors, China and Korea. [2] According to legend, Jimmu, the first Japanese emperor, lived around 660 B.C. Japanese scholars selected this date around 601 A.D. —some eight hundred years later. The validity of Japan's history cannot be sequentially established prior to 400 A.D.

---

[1] *The works of Arnold Toynbee, "The Study of History", were previously referred to in this book. The volums referring to China and Japan are too numerous to list.*

[2] *"The National Faith of Japan, A Study of Modern Shinto", p.19, D.C. Holton. "Japan, A Short Cultural History", G.B. Sansone, Appleton Century Crofts, New York, 1962. This is an excellent source of information.*

The Japanese adopted from China the system of recording important events in their history in 712 and 720 A.D. These records, drawn from oral history, are the Jojiki and Nihon Shoki. A study of genealogical records shows that all the famous Japanese families were united in some way with the birth of Ama-n-hohi, the Heavenly Burning Sun. This data was apparently selected to support the claims of certain clans over others, hence their assertion to dignity and early antiquity. Records of the Yamato emperors are in Kohiti and Nihon Shoki and today their descendants, the longest ruling line in history, are still in control of Japan. Coming from the Sun Goddess, as referred to previously, this line of emperors combined tradition with mythology and religion, which then emerged into Shinto. The legend of the sacred sword, the spear, the jewels and the mirror all have a Korean background.

The lineage of Japan seems to have originated from the Sun Line founded by Ninigi, grandson of the Sun Goddess. Early myths emanated from northern Japan in Kyushri, an area facing eastward from Hyuga, meaning "Facing the Sun." It is thought to have been a place for sun-worshippers. Legend is that Ninigi brought with him three Imperial Regalia: a bronze mirror representing the Sun Goddess, a Susa-no-o's iron sword and a carved jewel, all of which were symbols of Japan authority. The title of their legendary emperor, Jimmu, which means "Divine Warrior," who founded the Japanese state around 660 B.C, was the great grandson of Ninigi." [1]

Shinto, in the initial, era was established upon vague ideas of a universe with many sentient parts, based on kindly, gracious aspects which today in Japan is still evident. Divinity was assigned to the sun and the moon and all other manifestations of beauty. Despite the violent storms, floods, and earthquakes that Japan experienced, its people spoke of their land as the Land of Luxuriant Reed Plains, the Land of Fresh Rice Ears of a Thousand Autumns.

In Shinto, while growth and beauty were desireable, death was not and, consequently, numerous rituals sprang up around it which had a profound influence in later Jananese history. There is little evidence of spirituality in Japanese mythology and oral tradition. There is no distinct theory of life and

---

[1]*"East Asia, The Great Tradition,"* Edwin O. Reischauer, and John K. Fairbank, *Harvard University, Houghton Mifflin Company, Boston, 1960, p. 465-66. Extensive use of this volume was made as well as, "East Asia, The Modern Transformation", Vol. 2, Edwin O. Reichauer, and John K. Fairbank, Houghton Mifflin, 1965.*

death, nor of body and spirit, and if such theories did, in fact, occur, they were influenced by China. The early tribes of Japan had separate gods and over the process of time, as various tribes came together under one leader, Shinto emerged as the dominate faith. Various clans who were religious became so closely coordinated that the words which were interpreted as: "religious observance" was the earliest known Japanese definition for government and were organized and carried out by the minister of the sovereigns.

Early records reveal that the Japanese emperors served in a dual capacity: one as high priest and one as a secular ruler. Reischauer states that the word government, matsurigoto, literally means "worship;" and miya means "palace" and "shrine." [1] He further contends that in comparison with other Asian and European faiths, Shinto is primitive in comparison and elements of it were secure by the fifth and sixth centuries which have survived to the present. [2]

Although these early records have been given careful scrutiny, they do not suggest at which point these religious/political forces evolved as one in the pantheons of Yamato and Idzumo. Early records, however, do indicate Shinto to be a religion of ritual purity. Since death was looked upon as an impure act, and because of the stigma attached to it, consequently, at the death of an emperor, the capital would be changed to another city. Death was associated with uncleaniiness, therefore, the place where a previous ruler resided was also perceived to be unclean. In the performance of the great Purification Ritual, subsequent to the death of an emperor, those executing the ceremony must be free of all moral guilt. This process continued for a long period in early Japanese history. A religion that in principle was aligned with the worship of nature (animistic, magic) in time merged with the dominate political system of Japan.

In Japan, an important progression emerged from the scheme of borrowing and adopting Chinese customs. Confucius (551-479 B.C.), chose a revolutionary position in his day of social turmoil among the feudal states. He maintained that virtue comes not from the intrinsic quality of a person, nor from their nobility of birth, but as the result of personal effort. Confucius placed great emphasis on ritual behavior, on observance of the rules of society, on respect for the self, and on respect for others. Perhaps the climax is a mutual sense of respect and reciprocity. This complex system of relationships and mutual respect functioned within the family, within the village, within the province, and

---

[1]*Reichauer, Fairbank, op. cit., Vol. 1, p. 471.*

[2]*Ibid. r pp.*

finally, within the empire. It was proclaimed as an edict to be obeyed within each area and in the respective spheres of social order, and that which must give respect and reciprocity on each level to all those over whom authority was given. This applied to all, from the emperor, to the ruler, down to the parents presiding over families in the society.

One of the principal features in Chinese classic thought is filial piety. Confucius believed that sacrifices should be made to one's ancestors in the same spirit as one who shows courteous treatment to a friend. Long before Confucius, there was a book of poetry with the phrase, "No one is to be looked up to like a father.   No one is to be depended upon like a mother." This became not only a moral obligation, but a legal one as well. One's obligation to show reverence to one's parents, to ones grandparents, to one's emperor, and to one's former emperor, also functioned reciprocally from the top down.

With the exception of obligation from emperor to common man, much of Japan's principles of devotion was borrowed from China. Only the State in Japan can grant loyalty to the family. Subsequently, nature worship became an organized cult in Japan, bound to the political system by the process of dedication to ancestors, past and present. There was, however, in Japan, an implication toward divinity in the worship of deceased emperors. Again, Japan borrowed a theory from China and implemented it within their own territory, thus declaring the emperor head of a centralized state.

The imperial interests of Japan were obviously fashioned after the disciplinarian order of the Han Dynasty (221 B.C. - 222 A.D.), which, at best, were not ideas of Confucius or Mencius, but ideas of the Legalist, a strong and highly stratified centralized state, established during the Han Dynasty. In many respects, the Legalist borrowed from the Chin Dynasty (221 B.C. - 200 B.C., whose intensely authoritarian rulers endeavored to destroy all the records of Confucius and Mencius, as well. There were, in fact, a number of Han rulers who believed that human nature was wicked. Although the people had the predilection toward being good, the rulers theorized that, without the aid of a king, this was not possible. Although, Mencius believed human nature was good, Confucius, however, gave no opinion on the issue, being perceivably judicious and, perhaps, much too wise.

The Chinese Civil Service System, initiated during the Han Dynasty, corresponded with the thinking of the major population of China. Not to be ignored by any successful ruler were the teachings of Confucius which had been deeply rooted in the minds of the people. Therefore, the Han Dynasty, a combination of authoritarian rule, and Confucian thought came to be known as the teachings of Confucius and Mencius. Although, Emperor Wu (141 - 81 B.C., the greatest ruler of the Han, attempted to twist Confucian thought from its original premise, [1] and adjust it to support a monarchial position, he was however, not completely successful.

It shall be explained in subsequent how Japanese government officials took Chinese ideas and molded them into their situation and aspirations.

In Japan, the imperial clan was first in rank for they were descendants from the Sun Goddess, who was related to Jimmu, reputed to be JaDan's first Emperor, who was also bound to Shinto. Shinto, founded as the state religion of Japan by the 6th century A.D., was as political as it was religious. There is much evidence to support the fact that the early rulers of Japan preferred their people worship the "founders of the land," and to disregard the religions of foreign people, including Taoism, Confucianism and Buddhism. This petition to a national god, to the exclusion of a universal appeal, would cut away a fundamental characteristic of a higher religion which, by definition, is neither confined to one geographic area nor to any one society.

When we examine the Chinese belief system further, we begin to see how these ideas were used in Japan. For example, according to Reichauer and Fairbanks *History of East Asia,* Volume One, p. 50, the Chinese word T'ien is translated to mean "Heaven." They state their belief that the word T'ien, is anthropomorphic in origin. Their idea, however, is countered by H.G. Creei's *Chinese Thought from Confucius to Mao-Tse-tung,* [2] who does not believe the word, Heaven, is anthropomorphic. He states that the word was seldom conceived as such in Confucius' time when it represented some vaguely conceived moral force in the universe. It was felt that somewhere there was a power that stood on the side of the lonely man who struggles for the right.

Confucius made no reference to a king as the Son of Heaven who ruled with the support of his ancestors living in heaven who supervised the lives of people. The Japanese affirm that their Emperors all come from the Sun Goddess. The Chinese believe that a monarch is virtuous and that he works for

---

[1] *Perhaps the greatest classic on war was written some 2,300 years ago by Sun Tzu, "The Art of War", translated by Samuel B. Griffith, Oxford University Press, 1963. In many ways this work surpasses the 19th Century work of Clausewitz's "On War." Sun Tzu states that the purpose of war is not annihilation of the enemy but victory over them.*

[2] *Chinese Thought From Confucius to Mao-Tse-tung, H.G. Creel, A Mentor Book, 1953.*

the benefit of his people. Desiring success for the self, the ideal Chinese monarch strives for the success of others. This can only be achieved by universal education of the people as the foundation of the state to bring welfare to all. Capable men as administrators were clearly a *sine qua non*.

Mencius supported Confucius on the point that if the ruler failed to promote the welfare of the people, he should be removed. "Heaven sees and hears as my people see and hear." To Mencius, even a hereditary monarch received his throne as a gift from his people. The concept of the middle way is one of the compromises and Confucius and Mencius denied unlimited authority to the state.

In China, the Mandate of an emperor depended on the virtue of the one holding office. The occupant served as a model for all people of the land. It was therefore not a question of patrimonial power with a religious base that gave the emperor status, as it was in Japan. Status was gained by one's concern with simple generosity, coupled with concern with each individuals well being. Men possessed the quality to make themselves good, to have humanity, a sense of duty, politeness and knowledge, qualities which could be either developed or stifled.

Shinto would take over ancestral piety, as man was a part of nature, one's ancestors became the intermediary between man and nature. All ancestors of the original Clan made Japan a divine nation, believing as they did that the emperors emerged from the Sun Goddess. Consequently, Shinto presented two faces, one to reconcile man to nature, and the other to make Japan exclusive and isolated.

In the pre-Christian Greek and Roman world, the religion of the people consecrated the forces of nature. Inasmuch as man is a part of nature, he organizes into social groups, making the collective power overshadow other natural forces, and the gods which symbolize human institutions; the ultimate being the nation. [1] This is comparable to the Greek city-state and its pantheons.

As early as the seventh century, a practice evolved in Japan which continued for a thousand years. The emperor or empress had advisors who took the initiative on matters of policy, having a semblance of authority which covered the actual government in such a way as to take responsibility for

---

[1]*"Choose Life"*, Arnold Toynbee, *Oxford University Press, 1976.*

matters of state and, thereby protecting the ruler when policy failed. The government would operate from behind the scenes. At the beginning of the 7th century, the Fujiwara Clan, one of the most remarkable clans in history and clearly the most prominent in Japan, would surround and control the throne until 1945. Japan's government, fashioned from the Chinese model, became centralized, minus responsibility from the top down. Contrary to the Chinese, who promoted education among its people, Japan restricted it to the elite class, another instance in which the Chinese features of government were adopted only as they served Japan's purpose.

The Emperor had become the link between the people and their ancestors by the 8th century. This gave a new approach to Shinto which would gradually separate from the nature worship of the people. Confucianism and Buddhism also would be severed from Shinto. Confucianism would be separated for apparent reasons. Buddhism would be excluded from the plans of state since its teaching emphasizes "cherishing all life." The universal teachings incorporated in the Dharma or doctrines of Buddhism would be another point of conflict. Dharma, in the broadest sense, intimates all phenomena are subject to the law of causation, a fundamental truth which comprises the very core of the Buddha's teaching.

The Kamakura period (1185 - 1333) was a time of feudalism when economic and social organization was based on the holding land from a lord to his vassal -one to whom land rights were granted by the lord of the land. Also, at this time, there was religious fervor and constant warfare when numerous warriors became Buddhists, often taking religious orders after completing their military obligation. Buddhism had a powerfully positive influence on these warriors who failed to identify with their faith of feudal ethics. This period of liberation had also had a profound effect on people in the lower level of society. As Buddhism spread among the people, the effect of its teachings seemed to elevate them, creating a spirit of equality among men and women.

The Nichiren would be the only sect to stir up great problems. Nichiren (1222 - 1282) made Buddhism in conformity with his beliefs, promoting his interpretation of it as the only correct one. Thinking that his teachings would protect Japan, it became known as Japanese Buddhism, at best, an oxymoron. During his time Japan would suffer fire, floods, famine and earthquakes. Nichiren maintained that these disasters occurred because the false teachings prompted The Buddha to withdraw his protection from Japan. Nichiren followers were fanatical nationalists who considered Japan the spiritual center of the world and were intolerant of all other sects. This fanatical sect, dissimilar to any other Buddhist society, would rise up in support of Hirohito in the 20th century. Nichiren proposes nationalism, as opposed to any other group, violence against peace, and the one way as opposed to many paths.

Japan had not been ruled by a unified command for some two hundred and fifty years until it was brought about by Hideyoshi (1536 - 1598), in the year 1590. The result was the establishment of the Tokugawa period of Japan, (1603 - 1861). Although the emperor had little power during this period, the shogunate rulers (military governors) derived their authority, in theory, from the emperor, and this was the position of Tokugawa (1542 - 1616). During the previous period of feudal disorder and lack of central government, many monasteries became military strong holds. The strongest was Enryakuji on Mount Hiei where it was dominated by warring monks. But their power was broken by Oda Nobunaga (1534 - 82), a great unifier. Another unifier was Hideyoshi (1536 - 98), and then Tokugawa Ieyasu (1542 - 1616). These men were able to consolidate and steer the course of Japan until the Meiji Restoration in 1867. This period is called Tokugawa Shogunate. The rulers turned to Confucianism in order to gain a stable government with an ethical code of conduct. Great emphasis was placed upon order, loyalty and civil service bureaucratic rule. This was a distorted version of Confucianism by the Han Dynasty, as explained previously. The position of emperor from Nobunaga, Hideyhoshi, and Ieyasu, took on a divine status during this period.

The First Class Government Shrines of Special Rank, dedicated to the men mentioned above, who were listed as deities, were the foundation of Japan's Shogunate rule. The moral basis of the system placed on the hierarchy of the family operated throughout the social order of Janan. The one great difference from Confucianism was: the loyalty to one's lord took precedence over the loyalty to one's family. Consideration of debt to which one owed their superiors did not require the element of reciprocity, as did that of China. Japan's citizens were incited to do more than that which was socially expected. Unlike the egalitarian system of China, Japan's conscientious drive was charged with anxiety and in time led to a rigid formalism.

Nationalism escalated during the Tokugawa period, along with an acute awareness that imperious European powers were expanding into the Western Hemisphere, Africa, India, the Near East, and into Southeast Asia. Japan's observation of Europe's overall assault caused great consternation among its rulers for their concern was that Japan, and China as well, might be the next target of aggression. Japan therefore, entered into self-imposed isolation from the rest of the orient and from the occident (countries west of Asia), while building the Imperial House into Shinto idealization and deification, which established the basis for the Restoration. Although Japanese authorities were aware of Western developments by the Dutch, on an artificial island near

Nagasaki, they were nonetheless permitted to act as liaison to Japan. The extensive data furnished to Japan by the Dutch became known as "Dutch Learning," for the way in which the scientific development of the language was used for information. There appeared as early as 1745 a Dutch-Japanese dictionary. Scientific developments spread throughout Japan and by 1770 a medical university was established which included the study of agricultural plants, medicinal herbs, botany, electricity, and asbestos, to name a few.

As the West increased in growth of military power and nationalism, the Japanese began to criticize the administrative and military strength of the Tokugawa System. Some Japanese administrators advocated ending the self-imposed isolation and the Tokugawa System which proposed that Japan become the "England of the East," with its Imperial expansion on the mainland to the north, to make it a world power.

There came from the West a powerful shock wave to break the weakened wall of Japan's exterior which was the intervention of Commodore Perry from the United States in 1850-53. The Japanese had held a proud and disdainful posture of isolation which was fast coming to an end. Having observed Western imperial colonization, the Japanese were thrashing about for a means to meet the forthcoming thrust from the outside. The United States, to no avail, had tried to break Japan's barriers. But for myriad reasons Commodore Perry would succeed. The Japanese, conscious of Western aggression in China in the recent Opium War, (1839-42), was also aware that the Shogunate, who had been powerful in previous years, was now weak. There was now great policy divisions and no coordinated power behind one leader. Consequently, in the face of superior armed forces, the Shogun could not deal effectively with the problems presented by Perry to open trade with the West.

A search was begun to find a means by which Japan could change its course. The dynastic system of China became a model for Japan. Their leader built upon their own imperial line and Shinto was the vehicle. Prior to the restoration in the 18th and 19th century, Japan was consolidating itself as China was beginning to fall into early stages of decline under the Manchu Dynasty. Japan's superiority was attributed by its rulers to their own divinely appointed line of emperors. During the Shogunate, Japanese scholars collected aspects of China's history and thought, excluding the fundamental differences, and molded them as a means to serve their own purpose.

The Shogunate, because of mounting internal governmental weaknesses and failing to handle the threat from the outside, was overthrown and by 1868 the revolutionaries had a new emperor. For centuries the emperor had been subservient to the Shogun. The restoration of the emperor from the subordinate role marked the beginning of modern day Japan. Central authority would focus around the emperor. For centuries Japan had been ruled from behind a veil. The Japanese did not expect personal rule by its restored emperor, since it had not been done for over one thousand years. The new Emperor Mutsuhito took over in 1868 and ruled until 1912. Responsibility for failed or unpopular programs was readily accepted by Mutsuhito's agents. Japan championed an imperial government and whose success was attributed to divided opposition and promoting popular measures for the people of Japan.

The new leaders found Confucianism to be unsuitable for Japan; their purpose was to industrialize, to rearrange the finances, and construct an army round a restored emperor in a unified state. A constitution was adopted which was industrial in structure, however, its religion and ancient ideas were preserved. This was the technique by which the West, China, Czarist Russia, and later, South East Asia and the Soviet Union would have to confront.

The year 1868 is referred to as Meiji "Enlightened Rule." After his death, in 1912, the emperor Mutsuhito, known as Meiji Emperor, became the symbol of Japan's modernization. Thus, the Fujiwara aristocracy would continue to control governmental affairs through 1945 until today.

The purpose of the Japanese government after the restoration of 1868 and the constitution of 1889 was to prepare for military confrontation with the western imperial states. Japan had aspirations of becoming the England of the Far East. To succeed in this endeavor it would have to unite its social institutions of banking, finance, labor, management and social loyalties and still preserve its ancient rituals. The most influential institution to be preserved was Shinto, from which a revived interest had been evolving. Under this constitution, the Meiji Emperor would be semi-theocratic, built upon the premise of the great antiquity of Japan reaching back to some 660 B.C. Shinto was the "True Way" to its proponents, transmitted to Japan by a divinely descended imperial line. The Fujiwara family had advised the imperial family for centuries in order to protect them from the responsibility of failure. The Emperor was known as "The Great Way," "The Dawn in The Palace," and "The Steps to Heaven." State Shinto revered the Japanese people, and its leader, the divine offspring of the Sun Goddess, offered collective divinity to them for the honor to worship a god who was perpetually embodied in the Emperor.

The Japanese people must perform civic ceremonies, not by personal choice, however, but prompted by duty and honor with gratitude to the Emperor's ancestors; and a failure to do so was evidence of disloyalty. Japan's scholars had stressed the divinity and uniqueness of ancient spirit worship to such an extent that by the beginning of the 18th century, Shinto came to be known as the way of the ghosts. The ghosts, previous emperors, to whose worship had come to be that of the dead.

To obtain these ends, a constitution was drafted in 1883 that was put into force in 1889. The basic structure of this constitution was drawn from that of The Second German Reich, set forth by Chancellor Prince Otto Von Bismarck, the Iron Chancellor of Germany. This was also a period in which Western scholars were easily seduced by anything proposing to be a constitution. It would be assumed to be in some fashion from the British combination of a constitution, written and unwritten, or from the United States Constitution. Careful examination would reveal the Japanese constitution to contain none of the features of either the British or United States Constitution. It was in form and content clearly Prussian, or Second Reich.

The Meiji constitution was deemed a gift from the Emperor, his person being sacred and endowed with executive power, although his legislative authority was limited by the consent of the Imperial Diet. This, however, formed no barrier, for in reality the Emperor could dismiss the Diet and the House of Representatives at his pleasure. As for the judicial system, it was nothing more than an extension of his own authority. The rights of free speech and press could go no further than "limits not prejudicial to peace and order" which were determined by the Emperor. The Emperor was the supreme commander of the armed forces and all cabinet members were directly responsible to him. From these powers the Emperor formulated all imperial policy for warfare without fear of losing control of the Japanese Diet or House of Representatives. So great was his authority that it was believed to give clear moral leadership over any member of the government and over the elected Diet. Carrying the point to its ultimate end, the general staff of the army and navy had the authority to say they were the rightful interpreters of the "imperial will."

Japanese elite scholars in the 19th and 20th centuries believed Japan to be superior to all nations. Their national policy, they said, contained what other nations lacked —a people's moral character bound to a "sacred and inviolable" emperor and his ancestors by "Filial Deity." Japan was, to the elite, an organic state headed by an emperor in the same fashion as the human head rules the affairs of one's body. Some Japanese elite even believed Japan's national policy was eternal and that the Imperial Household was "coequal with heaven and earth." Consequently, they held that their Emperor is the embodiment of moral order manifesting ultimate value. Furthermore, the Emperor is viewed as "the eternal culmination of the True, the Good, and the Beautiful throughout all ages and in all places."

Japan is perceived as the "family state" and the family as a continual religious service for ancestors. The social order looks at loyalty to the state and filial piety as one and the same. Ultimately, the Emperor is viewed as the mystic body of the state. To support this mystic structure, Japanese youth are brought up to believe that survival of the family is the primary factor. Until a man reaches the age of forty-one, he is considered a debtor to society. Should he happen to die of natural causes prior to that age, his spirit will attain very little because of the lack of accomplishment during his lifetime. If, however, a man dies in battle, much is accomplished and he is promoted in rank and placed in the heavenly abode of warrior ghosts, which is the Yasukini Shrine in Tokyo.

Hirohito, prior to becoming Emperor in 1926, was taught that the strong nations of the world were England and Russia (prior to World War l), with the United States a close third. China was seen as degenerate and could not be a partner with Japan against the West. Consequently, Japan must match the power of the Aryan Clans of the West alone.

When Hirohito became of age in 1915, he presented himself at the palace shrine with two swords of the Samurai, to be anointed as a warrior. Around 1920, he was taught that his role was to liberate the world. To free the universe would be the work of spirits. When Hirohito became Emperor in 1926, at the death of Emperor Taisho, he was taken to the Imperial Family Shrine in the palace forest. Entering the holy of 'Holies,' in private ceremony, he stood before the spirits and the imperial regalia, and as he touched the fragile brocade bag supposedly containing the sacred green jewels, he declared himself the new Emperor of Japan. He then lifted the replica of the sacred sword of power taken from the tail of a dragon by the son of a sun goddess.

Holding the replica of a bronze mirror and gazing into it, only he could see the sun goddess and commune with her. He took the name "Peace Manifest." for the name of his reign. Among his people, Emperor Hirohito encouraged the idea that he was the Zeus in the Shinto of great spirits. Some of his supporters urged people to believe that he was a living god and the high priest of the dead. He was so impressed with his status by 1936 that he changed the signature he used on state documents from "Supreme of the Great Land of Japan" to "Heavenly Emperor of the Great Land of Japan."

Japan's Imperial Conspiracy [1] by David Bergamini, thought to be the most definitive account of Japanese Imperial policy, was drawn from Japanese government documents and extensive interviews with high Japanese governmental officials. It makes clear that Japan's attempt to overthrow of China, Manchuria, South East Asia, the Philippines, India, and the United States, was planned in detail by Emperor Hirohito; he was seen to do this in his role as the spiritual embodiment of the nation. As a matter of faith, as late as 1945, the majority of the Japanese believed the Emperor and Japan were one and the same and that their fates were intertwined.

Hirohito planned to enforce the family rule over the nation and to expel the barbarians from Japan. More people were slaughtered in the 1937 rape of Nanking than in Hiroshima and Nagasaki combined. The invasion of Pearl Harbor in 1941, and Hiroshima were seen as the result of a burden placed on the Emperor by imperial ancestors; it was a holy mission. Evidence is clear that he furthermore planned Asia for Asians, of course, meaning Japan, in the same manner as that of the Nazi German Nordic theory. Finally, he had planned to war against Nazi Germany. There could clearly be only one superior people in the world and that must be imperial Japan.

Twenty one months prior to Pearl Harbor, on February 11, 1940, when Hirohito was faced with the forthcoming war with the United Sates, he went to the town of his ancestors at Yamato. He prayed at the shrine of the Sun Goddess, the Holy of Holies housing the ancient imperial symbols.

The point of extreme deification is pointed out by Bergamini who writes that when Hirohito spoke in the Phoenix Hall of the Imperial Palace, he was considered a god king who could make no mistakes. On these occasions he spoke with a high pitched voice and was considered the national Shinto high priest. When speaking outside of this room he was acknowledged to be human and fallible.

Educated Japanese, including Hirohito himself, never considered the Emperor a god in the omnipotent/omnipresent Western sense. Rather, he was a Kami, or immortal spirit in all things Japanese, even the rocks and trees and women were thought to possess a share of it. The Emperor had the largest and most potent share. To the Japanese mind there was nothing superhuman or moral about Kami; it was the distilled essence of a man, his special charm and efficacy. The spirit world to which Kami belonged was an exact shadow of the

---

[1]*"Japan's Imperial Conspiracy", David Bergamini, William Morrow, New York, 1971. This, in my opinion, is the most graphic account of the subject, available.*

real world. Subject to the Potsdam Declaration, the Emperor was required to surrender or be destroyed. Among the conditions for surrender was a disavowal of his divinity. Bergamini informs us that the Emperor and General MacArthur agreed on a statement to be delivered to the Japanese people on New Year's Day, January, 1, 1946.

The Emperor simply reiterated what his grandfather, Emperor Meiji had stated in 1868, implying that he would occupy an humble position and govern in accordance with the customs of the land. The essence of his agreement is defined in Bergamini's statement wherein he quotes the Emperor:

> The ties between Us and Our people have always stood on mutual trust and affection. They do not depend upon mere legends and myths. They are not predicated upon the false concept that the Emperor is divine and that the Japanese people are superior to other races and fated to rule the world.

Hirohito published his annual thirty-one-syllable tanka for the New Year's poetry contest, suggesting that his subjects must not be confused by the frosting of dissimulation forced upon them by circumstances:

> 'Courageous the pine
> that does not change its color
> under winter snow.
> Truly the men of Japan
> should be a forest of pines.'

To further paraphrase Bergamini, the educated Japanese and the Emperor knew that nothing was given up when the terms of peace were presented to the Emperor for signature. This was a clear case where Western leaders were unaware of the basic premise of Japanese thought. The Emperor was aware of that fact and signed the peace terms and gave up nothing pertaining to Japanese ideas about the Emperor and his place in Japanese thought. Nothing has changed in that position from 1945 to the present.

Shinto, which has endured for centuries still exists today. It is, in many respects, a national ideology or religion in the same way that the Greek city-states confined their religion to their one locality. Bergamini states that as of 1971 the operation of the Emperor continues behind a veil in the same fashion in affairs of the state as it has for centuries. It has been behind this veil that Japan prepared to subjugate the Korean, the Chinese, and all other Asian people. The China-Japanese War of 1894-95; the Russo-Japanese War of 1904-05, the Japanese in World War One, the Japanese invasion of Manchuria and its "New order in Asia," 1938, the "Greater East Asia Co-Prosperity Sphere," and its role in the Second World War, including the Rape of Nanking, and Pearl Harbor, was done under the direction of Japan's emperors in the name of Shinto. [1]

China, under the ethos of the "Mandate of Heaven" from the time of the Duke of Chou 1122 B.C., removed the dynastic rulers through the ages, until the end of the dynastic system in 1911. The same mandate also played a role in the overthrow of Chiang Kai-shek and the victory of The People's Republic of China. [2]

Sir William Flood Webb of Brisbane, Australia, wrote the introduction to Japan's Imperial Conspiracy. He was Chief Justice of the Australian State of Queensland, and later became a Justice of the High Court of Australia, and finally, headed the bench of eleven judges from eleven nations known as the International Military Tribunal for the Far East, which sat In Tokyo from May, 1946 to November, 1948. He states that more than half the material is new to English speaking people and some is controversial. "I would judge, however, that the book has the highest importance and will cause a major readjustment in western views or oriental history." He states the data is more convincing than that brought out by the prosecution because a major portion of the material was not available until after 1960.

As for Bergamini, who learned again to speak and write Japanese, he recruited an army of research assistants who read the entire Japanese Volume in war literature. Collateral data was also obtained in English, French and German and additionally, 50,000 pages of war trial material and 30,000 pages of captured Japanese documents and 212 reference books. In addition to this,

---

[1]*Ibid., pp.*

[2]*"The Great Chinese Revolution, 1800 - 1985", John K. Fairbank, Harper and Row, 1986. This covers the collapse of the last dynasty and the struggle of the Chinese present government. Other works consulted on China are: "Buddhism in Chinese History", Arthur Wright, Stanford University Press, 1959. "Buddhism, The Light of Asia", Kenneth K. S. Chen, Barron's Education Series. "Buddhism in China", An Historical Survey, Kenneth K. S. Chen, Princeton University Press, 1964.*
    My many years of close friendship with Dr. C.C. Shih, retired professor of Chinese History in the East Asian Department at the University of Toronto, has proven a great enlightenment to me.

Bergamini conducted interviews with a host of Japanese military men, most of whom were generals and lieutenants.

CHAPTER FIVE

THE FUTURE OF CHINA AND JAPAN

Centuries ago, The Buddha stated: "If you want to know the past, cause, look at your present life, effect. If you want to know the future, effect, look at your present, cause." This statement promises a deleterious future unless drastic changes occur relating to the ethical support of violence.

Customs, when institutionalized in an organized state have a profound influence on those subject to them, despite the changes which come about as they pass on from generation to generation. The sanction of violence has been entrenched in social and ideological thought from the emergence of the first temple communities and until the world community commits to an enormous effort to change the collective pattern of theological and ethical thought, there is little hope to ameliorate the world for future generations.

There is the perception that all present cultural conflicts which create violence are the effects of previous causes in which all societies have participated. The future depends on the way societies deal with situations arising from present actions or reactions. Without fear of exaggeration, the violence of today which flows from a limitless past into an unending future is the result of the causes of yesterday. Previous thoughts primarily centralized upon violence while excluding the causes, and not being peacefully resolved, ripened into the violence of today. Consequently, violence and its cause becomes self perpetuating. As the knowledge of science and technology expands, in relation to medicine and agriculture, the conflicts are greater in that they become meshed with the ideological conflicts of our time. The formation of politics and its continuation was maintained almost entirely by oral tradition through *customs* of the time from the beginning of urban life, 7250 - 6750 B.C., [1] until the beginning of writing about 4000 B.C.

The purpose of urban politics was to prevent anarchy in the social life of our first temple communities. In order to achieve this, there had to be a

---

[1] *The University of Chicago Magazine, Fall, 1985, "The Worlds First Architecture", Brigitta Carlson: The mount in front of the stream of the first site of settlement of man in the area of the Tigris River.*

balancing of the elements of force and consent.   The two counter-posed
elements developed both customs and traditions.   Rules and regulations
emerged to determine how and when officers should act in defence of the
temple community. To gain social credence for the threat and use of violence,
moral and spiritual concepts were initiated and combined with the rules,
regulations and customs. Humanity has collectively worshipped this form of
human power, in one fashion or another, for thousands of years. The collective
support of violence has moved from the historically Sumerian temple
communities on up through the present day nation-state system of the twentieth
century. And if the future is to be saved from total destruction, it would be
wise to re-evaluate the reasons for sanctioning violence.

Prehistory cults, or man worship, reappears when higher religions lose
their appeal.   This revitalization occurs when leaders of a state or society
identify their religion with the security, the justice and the military forces of
government. When the ruling elite of a society faces an internal or external
crises, and that social order is overthrown, as happened in Czarist Russia and
in the Christian West at the time of the Reformation, their religion is tossed
out upon the garbage heap along with the failed institution.

The supremacy of Russian Orthodoxy prevailed for centuries until the
crisis of the late nineteenth and early twentieth century. [1] But when the Czar
was overthrown, Russian Orthodoxy was tossed out along with him. Total state
control of human life, internal brutal oppression, criticisms from within and
without, and external aggression, were all hallmarks of Russia Czarist
Orthodoxy, carried over into the state theory and practice of the former Soviet
Union. Intensive internal control over human ideas and activity, with increased
technology, built a monolithic state elaborately modeled after the Russian
Orthodox regime. Lenin simply became the new Czar. The ideology of Marx,
built upon the ideas of the Old and New Testament, was carried through from
Christendom, Orthodox style, into Soviet Communism.

Despite the onslaught of the Nazi invasions and the loss of millions of
human lives, Soviet Communism appeared to be firmly fastened over its land
and people.   This clearly shows, however, that despite disruptions,
institutionalized ideas have a long history, with roots going all the way back to

---

[1] *This refers not only to the violent protests by the Russian people in the 19th
century, the abortive revolts of the early 20th century (including the Communist
uprising of 1917 - 1918), but also the Russo-Japanese War, the First World War,
but also the European and United States invasion of Soviet Russia at the end of
the First World War.*

the Caesar, to Emperor Constantine, and to the Grand Prince of Kiev. Consequently, it looks as though external aggression and internal oppression will continue, given its philosophy in world cultural tensions and conflicts.

Japan's experience with Shinto is one such example of ideological belief which supports a state structure, despite the violent intrusion by an alien people motivated by a different ethic. The violent intruder was the United States. The ideology behind the United States invasion was to remove the idea of the Emperor as a god-king, omnipotent and omnipresent, and bring about the separation of church and state. This ideology was ill conceived in the sense of our not knowing the true nature of the Emperor in relation to Shinto. The educated Japanese, including Hirohito himself, never considered the Emperor in the Western sense. Consequently, nothing was given up by signing the treaty of peace.

Buddhism was rejected centuries ago by the Japanese emperors who considered it a foreign religion and disavowed its principle "To Cherish All Life." Buddhism is not confined to any one geographical territory or society. Unlike Buddhism; however, Shinto is a Japanese religion where by the emperor is the embodiment of state and religion, and to whom most Japanese pay supreme loyalty. Combined with their Shinto faith was the aspiration to make Japan the spiritual center of the world: The Japanese of the East would be likened to the Aryans of the West. Inasmuch as there could be only one superior people, Emperor Hirohito had planned to eventually wage war against Nazi Germany to disprove their claim to superiority. [1]

The inseparable presence of the Emperor with Shinto is deeply lodged in Japanese thought and conviction. This presence plays a determinate role for the Fujiwara Clan who acts as a shield for the Emperor and the Royal Family, for Shinto, and for the elite class as well. The Clan's basic policy, going back as far as the 7th century, has been to have the Emperor rule from behind an illusionary *veil*, which illustrates that since the Emperor and Shinto are combined, should any state policy fail, no blame is cast upon the emperor. This was the ultimate reason that the Emperor was not faulted for Japan's catastrophic defeat during the Potsdam Declaration, at the end of World War Two. The Japanese accepted as a matter of faith that "Japan lived or died with the Emperor." Thus, the purpose of having all war campaigns executed from behind a veil gave protection to their Emperor. Should a program fail, the

---

[1]*This lack of historical incidents include Pearl Harbor and the atomic bomb. The Japanese have virtually no knowledge of how Japan became involved in World War Two.*

fault falls, not upon the Emperor, but the ministers. This is an age old practice of Emperor/Shinto worship which has existed for centuries and is today still very much in vogue.

Japan has a deep fear and hostility toward the West, as did Orthodox Czarist Russia and, until recently, the former Soviet Union, each making judgements from their own particular stance. They were invaded by the West and each fought against it as it evolved, seeking isolation in a world in which such policy was becoming increasingly impossible. Orthodox Russia believed in its superiority over all other religious manifestations, and any internal opposition to it was immediately crushed.

Japan has successfully protected its emperors from responsibility of the wars in China, Korea, South East Asia, Czarist Russia and the Soviet Union. The fault was and is placed upon the outside world, and the subordinates of the emperors. The same was true in Czarist Russia when the Czar or Czarina was considered the agent of God on earth and only during the last days of the Czarist rule in 1917-18 did any appreciable number of Russian people place any fault upon the House of Romanov. In the last days of Czarist Russia, great numbers of Russian subjects refused to fault the Czar.

Most Japanese do not fault Emperor Hirohito for Japan's hideous record in Korea, China, and South East Asia. The fault was placed upon the failure of the Emperor's agents, and the United States. The Japanese ruling elite survived Western attacks, whereas the Czarist leaders did not, even though the authoritarian substance remained secure in the former Soviet State theory and practice. August 15, 1985 marked the fortieth anniversary of Japan's defeat in the Second World War. Ceremonies held at Yasukuni Shrine bring into question fundamental points in the Japanese constitution where, at the conclusion of World War Two, State Shinto was abolished, along with war as an instrument of national policy. The constitution also calls for separation of Church and State.

The current Japanese constitution, in a few words, attempts to cut asunder more than a thousand years of religious and ideological practice. Historically, State Shinto verifies nature spirits and encompasses a profoundly deep adoration for the Emperor and the uniqueness of the ways of the Japanese.

Governmental officials did not visit the Yasukuni Shrine for some years after the war because of its connection with war. But on August 15, 1975, senior governmental officials bridged the gap by again going to the Shrine, thereby asserting their belief before the symbol of patriotism. Prime Minister

Nakosone, on August 15, 1985, along with his leading cabinet members, dressed in cutaway coats, visited the Yasukuni Shrine in their official capacities.
This visit marked the twenty third anniversary of the day the Emperor had made the observation to the Shrine. And there on the same grounds as the Shrine is a museum for Japanese war dead with some 2.5 million names inscribed upon small tablets. It is here that the these men, including World War Two war criminals and members of the dreaded secret police, are honored war spirits.

Bitter reaction has come from some Japanese citizens who clearly understood the visit to the Shrine by the Prime Minister and senior cabinet members, as a statement tantamount to Japan's prewar days. The Chinese reaction was in effect the revival of Japanese aggression in China and other Asian countries. It has been asserted that during the course of Japanese aggression some twenty million people were killed in China alone. And throughout the ceremonies not one word of regret or apology was voiced pertaining to the suffering that followed in the wake of Japan's aggression. The Emperor merely bowed.

Japanese opponents of Mr. Nakosone regarded his visit a breach of Japan's constitution which raised the specter of State Shinto, "used by militarist before the war to whip up nationalist fervor." Chinese authorities maintained that the visit was a mockery of Asian sentiments.

James Reston, Jr., of The New York Times, pointed out a thinly veiled arrangement by Japan's elite in attempts to cover up its aggressive past and their designs to revive its military power. Failing to cover up their history, Reston continued, they have attempted to rewrite it. Large numbers of Japanese youth who have grown up since the Second World War have no knowledge of their country's past aggressions. Japan's attacks on China, 1894 and 1931; Japan's militancy over Russia in 1904 and 1905; and Japan's prejudice and atrocities against the Koreans at Hanjing in 1937, are all apparently unknown to the generation of post-war Japan. [1] Japan's scholars do not fault students for their lack of information. Reston explained this as a system of education, the purpose of which was to keep students uninformed, or misinformed, at best.

Prime Minister Nakasone proposed a new educational system and declared "post war Japan is at an end." The education commission of Japan, composed mostly of conservatives, is looking for a means to rebuild traditional

---

[1] *The New York times, January 22, 1989.*

values and morals. His critics say this means scrapping the constitution and teaching patriotism, which undermines the lessons learned from the war.

The Japanese concern for material wealth now seems absolute. The Prime Minister and the Ministry of Education look to the past as a road to the future. Past history is "sanitized" in the approved text books for students. The Japanese invasion of China is called an "advance," the 1937 Nanking massacre is referred to as "mob confusion," with no reference to the 2,300,000 fatalities. The same lighthearted manner is used in reference to Japan's "advance" into Korea, along with prayer to Japanese spirits at Shinto Shrines, forced upon the Koreans and called "encouraged" prayers. Korean girls were forcibly used as "wartime ladies of consolation" for Japanese troops on the front lines. The Chinese and Korean protests over the proposed texts have caused Japan to modify them. But the "ladies of consolation" issue is yet to be resolved.

Collective blame for past wars is now in vogue in Japan. Known as the "confession of a hundred million souls," some say it is an attempt to divert blame from the Emperor. Since he alone had the authority to declare war, he was responsible for everything that was planned and carried out during the war, yet the Japanese are taught that they were the victims. One must ask, what intentions lie behind this revival of post war ethics in Japan?

Some forty five years in the life of Japan is but a span of hours. Shinto, and its ethos have been merged with veneration for the Emperor by the Japanese far beyond a thousand years, and a faction of death enshrouds the interlocking of the two. Japan's drive to formulate their history in such a way as to have it appear to predate that of China —while borrowing extensively from it— therefore exhibiting a greater Japanese culture, discloses a feeling of inferiority in its people.

Previous centuries of bitter feelings toward the West by Japan are now being targeted against the United States. The provisions of the treaty of peace, which called for Japan to remain disarmed —while favored by many— were strongly resented by Japanese conservatives and leaders of the government. The peace treaty put a strict limit on the amount of funds which Japan could spend for weapons. While the old military civilian conservatives have pushed close to that limit, they have not gone beyond it. There are those in the United States who think that the Japanese government should assume a substantial portion of the responsibility in the expense of defending themselves. As Japan grows more disenchanted with its material prosperity, the United States' feeling of resentment mounts because of the overwhelming balance of trade favoring Japan -along with the costs of defending it. Japan's provocation for world recognition and the United States demand that they pay their own way, should generate the precise circumstance for the re-creation of a Japanese military power, one in which Shinto may well take a prominent role.

There are those in Japan who feel the process of reestablishing its prewar status is too slow and those who would also like to see the Western barbarians driven into the sea. This thesis is expressed graphically in an article by Henry Scott Stokes. [1] The following is taken from his essay:

> Yukio Mishima committed suicide on November 25, 1970. This widely acknowledged writer committed an honorable act sanctioned by tradition in Japan. From his writings, he was acclaimed 'the Renaissance man of Japan' by the New York Times Magazine in 1970. [2]

The death of Japan's greatest novelist, Yukio Mishima, caused a great stir among his people. As one who expressed the remilitarization of Japan along with reestablishing its national pride, Donald Keene, Columbia University professor, states that in his view, Mishima will prove to be the most famous Japanese of all time. There are those of course who think otherwise but he has pointed out the existence of a virulent and potentially dangerous group in Japan who are pressing for Japan's remilitarization. Scott Stokes quotes Alvin Toffler as saying the movement also is "ultranationalist and hence-anti-American." Stokes announced that two Japanese prime ministers supported Mishima who organized the Shield Society in 1968, a small private spiritual army. All members are very much to the right. Immediately after the death of Mishima, the two prime ministers, Eisaku Sato, prime minister from 1964 to 1972, and prime minister Yasuhiro Nakasone denounced his actions but never revealed their close association with Mishima's Shield Society.

Stokes asserts that the suicide of Yukio Mishima ranks as the most startling event in Japan since the War. Although it was an anti-American gesture, it was, however a rebuke to the Emperor. He could not openly admonish the Emperor for signing General MacArthur's declaration that he, the Emperor, was not a deity in human form, so chose to silently censure him by the time honored prayerful rite of hara-kiri. Among Mishima's novels were: *Voices of the Dead, The Decay of the Angel, The Temple of the Golden Pavilion,*

---

[1]*Last Samurai, The Withered Soul of Postwar Japan*, Henry Scott Stokes, *Harpers*, October, 1985.

[2]*Yasumari Kawabata, who won the Nobel Prize which Yukio Mishima has so passionately coveted, went so far as to say: "Only one in every three hundred years or so do we find a writer of the quality of Mishima."*

and The Sea of Fertility, in which disdain for postwar Japan is etched in vivid colors.

The rebirth of Japanese Emperor-military-Shinto is not full blown. The drive by Congress and the Pentagon to rid the United States of the cost of Japanese defense, combined with Japanese conservatives efforts to by-pass Article IX of the "peace constitution" of Japan, should nonetheless go far to re-establish post-war Japan. John Foster Dulles, the original cold war warrior, went to Tokyo and asked General MacArthur to find a way to by-pass Article IX, which denied Japan the right to bear arms. The attempt failed, but the United States and Japan have been trying ever since.

Elderly Japanese people remember the events of Manchuria, where military experiments on the Chinese is equivalent to anything done by Dr. Mengele at Auschwitz. Stokes reminds us that such atrocities are not found in text books of the Education Ministry. And he concludes that however much the Japanese people remember the past, they also fear the future.

Given the underlying hatred of the West, the United States in particular, there are those who fear that the Japanese might follow Mishima's statement in his autobiographical essay, "Sun and Steel," in which he says, "peace was the most difficult and abnormal state to live in . . ." Mishima seemed to romanticize world nuclear destruction as the proper aesthetic response to the death of civility, implicit in the idea of a commercialized Japan.

The Japanese elite see their culture as singularly unique, superior to any other social order. Behind their drive of "Asia for the Asians,"there is not only a deep seated hostility toward the Western world, but also the desire to make Japan's history of greater antiquity than that of China. Furthermore, the elite wish to convince themselves of the supremacy of their culture over that of China, whose cultural life style they so eagerly copied. At a profounder level is the desire to make Japan the spiritual center of the world. The deepest layer of motivation is Shinto —the cult of death. The Emperor and the Japanese nation are identified by the elite as one and the same. Together, they stand or fall.

The Emperor is dead. Long live the Emperor. On January 7, 1989, Emperor Hirohito —also known as Emperor Showa— died, and a reign was concluded which had begun some sixty two years ago. Immediately after his death, Akihito, became the new Emperor and received the traditional Shinto symbols of office. Recognizing the challenges facing Japan, the government named his era Heisei, the meaning of which is, "achieving peace." [1]

The demise of Emperor Hirohito opened anew the debate of his role in Japan's wars of aggression. Scholars issued statements calling for an historical study of his war record.

There are some Japanese scholars, critical of his military record, who have received threatening telephone calls. There are those professors who condemned Hirohito's record and hold him responsible for the atrocities Japan's military forces carried out abroad, and also for the suppression of freedom in Japan prior to and during the war. Takako Doi, chairwoman of the Japan Socialist Party, stated that "the Emperor's war responsibility cannot be denied."

Others asserted, as did Prime Minister Noboru Takeshita, that the war "had broken out against his wishes." Such an assertion incited hostile comments from the people of South Korea, who had been under Japanese rule for thirty five years. It also drew strong remarks of disagreement among groups in Britain, New Zealand, Australia and Canada. Bob Tizard, the Minister of Defense in New Zealand, suggested that after the war, the Emperor "should have publicly been shot chopped up." [2]

The BBC-Television program, "Hirohito: Behind the Myth," charged the Emperor with being personally involved in planning the Japanese attack on Pearl Harbor and the deception in which it was cloaked. The program, presented on February 25, 1989, was opposed by Edwin 0. Reichauer, by John Toland, and by Carol Gluck, a professor of history at Columbia University. They had all seen the film prior to public showing. Only Akira Iriye, a professor of history at The University of Chicago, gave a qualified approval of the program.

The program, made possible by Edward Behr, former European Correspondent for Newsweek, stated his views on Hirohito were formulated primarily upon two documents: "the diaries of Marquis Kido," an Imperial Palace official who was in contact with the Emperor before and during the War and "the Sugiyarma Memorandum," published in 1971, by a member of the Imperial Army Staff.

In the case of the Kido diaries, Mr. Behr reports:

---

[1] *The New York Times, January 7, 1989.*

[2] *The New York Times, February 24, 1989.*

We discovered that everything favorable to Hirohito had been extensively quoted by scholars and anything that was not favorable had been ignored. The Sugiyama Memorandum shows some extraordinary frank questioning by Hirohito of his army and navy staffs. For example: in July 1940, eighteen months before Pearl Harbor, Hirohito is asking Sugiyama and Naganol the chief of the Navy General Staff, questions like: 'How many divisions do you intend to send to French Indochina? Is that enough? Shouldn't you have another division in Thailand?' It shows Hirohito in the role of a kind of benevolent instructor questioning bright pupils, picking notes in their plans, not for any moral purpose, but simply to have them behave more efficiently. I can't understand why scholars have overlooked this sort of thing.

The last point ot be raised is to question whether this constituted courtesy or a command. However, in reality, what does it matter? Does it not show that the Emperor was aware of cooperating with and planning the strategy of the war? It is clear that no opposition was shown.

An interesting contrast to the position taken by previously mentioned scholars, is a full page advertisement in The New York Times, February 16, 1989, sponsored by an Ad Hoc Committee on The Case Against Hirohito. It stated that the Emperor assumed direct command of the army headquarters on September, 1941. It further stated that he also appointed many of his own Royal Family as military leaders and advisors under a constitution of which he had supreme command, "the army and navy and the individual ministers are directly responsible to him."

Colonel Tsui Masaobu, the Emperor's brother, presented his plan to the Emperor for the Malay and Philippines campaigns. The day following the capture of Nanking, the Emperor expressed his "supreme satisfaction" to the Chief of Army General Staff and subsequently received Prince Asaka, General Matsui and General Yanagow, the Chief architects of "the Rape of Nanking," whereupon he rewarded each one with a pair of silver vases embossed with the Imperial Chrysanthemum.

It is indeed strange that Japanese and United States scholars who defend Emperor Hirohito never make reference to the International Tribunal for the Far East which took place in Tokyo. From the trial, there is irrefutable evidence which clearly depicts the Emperor's serious involvement in plans for the War which came from the testimony of eye-witnesses, his own generals and relatives, and documents confirming the accounts. The trial, which convened about eight months after the War ended, lasted two and one half years and was conducted in conformity with the process of law in the Anglo-American practice. Not any of the above mentioned scholars refer to David Bergamini's work, "Japan's Imperial Conspiracy." The introduction to this volume was written by Sir William Flood Webb, presiding judge at the International Tribunal for the Far East. He affirms the high degree of the Emperor's implicated involvement in the activity of the war, produced during the trial, points out the vast amount of data which Bergamini made available but was not to be known for years after the trial. This evidence seems conclusive enough to show that the Emperor was no idle puppet awaiting someone to manipulate his arms and legs, let alone his head.

The Emperor was laid to rest in Tokyo on February 24, 1989, in a ritual which reaches far back to the ancient days of yore. In attendance for the occasion were 163 representatives from foreign countries. Some Japanese disapproved of the event, including a small Christian community, a number of constitutional lawyers, and opposing politicians, contending that it glorified the Emperor. Those in opposition also claimed that the reenactment of the Shinto rites, held on the same site as the state sponsored funeral, violated the postwar separation of church and state. This is especially important as Shinto is a indigenous, animistic faith which was used as the religious basis for the ultra-nationalism and military expansion of wartime Japan.

Carried in the funeral ceremony were two sacred sakaki trees, ceremonial boxes of feed, and silk clothes, offered to the spirit of the Emperor, along with other ingredients, evoking a Japan that has all but vanished. A torri gate, a Shinto symbol which marks the entrance to the sacred space, was also carried in the funeral procession.

The Emperor, always operating from behind a veil, as previously explained, was in the rites of death. At the end of the Shinto ceremony, a black partition was drawn, the Shinto symbols were removed, and the ceremonial officials withdrew. The new Emperor, a necessary participant, took part in all the ceremonies. A special place was arranged for special guests who did not wish to witness the Shinto Ceremony.

Has Shinto and the Japanese affairs of state changed? If the past is the doorway to the future, Shinto will not die as the result of a Treaty of Peace. Rituals —long held by tradition— are stronger by far than a peace agreement written and signed on a piece of paper.

The former Soviet Union took over the torch from Czarist Orthodox Russia. The latter professed to have the only true religion as revealed by God and the faithful's assertion that it has the only correct knowledge of the laws of history. Taking over from Czarist Russia in the same pattern, the former Soviet elite believes it must repress all internal dissent, that it has a mandate of history to expand its teachings to an alien, hostile and non-believing world.

Neither pre-war Japan nor Czarist Russia entertained a theory of resistance to state authority by its own people, unless one considers suicide a valid resistance; as might happen in Japan. In short, a theory of revolution as a social movement was not part of either culture's social or religious ideology.

China, with a much longer oral and written tradition, evolved its own sense of uniqueness, in contrast to either Czarist Russia or Japan. In earlier centuries, China's society was locked behind the Himalayas, the highest mountain range in the world, and land locked from India. Protected by vast desert and mountain ranges of the Iranian plateau, it was also insulated from the Tigris and Euphrates, and Egypt, in the valley of the Nile. Chinese isolation from these high cultures left it bordered on the south, north and west by nomadic people. To the east was the sea and the many ancient islands to be known later as Japan. The land bordered people had many contacts with the Chinese from their earliest days. Some traded, some paid tribute, and others waged war.

As the result of the constant pressure on its land frontier, two great factors influenced Chinese history: First would be the concept of The Middle Kingdom. The geographical isolation from other high cultures led Chinese theorists to believed their rulers controlled everything under the heavens. Arising from this concept was the Mandate of Heaven: the concept of reciprocal responsibilities within the family, the village, the province, and the empire evolved in such a manner that the Emperor had to be constantly aware of the Mandate or face revolt. It would not be until midway into the nineteenth century that a Chinese revolution would attempt to overthrow the dynastic system. All previous revolts had been for the purpose of improving the system, however this one wished to destroy it. The second great event to transpire evolved from the first. The Chinese society would move north, west and south. This expansion would push back the frontier and secure it.

The Chinese developed the great Classics, the civil service system, the tax role system, Taoism, Confucianism, and Buddhism. Its painting, architecture, and calligraphy would not be equaled in any other culture.

Coming to China was a line of people and cultures from as far away as the Mediterranean Sea which resulted in a great social order. Gradually, this produced a sense of superiority in the ranks of the Chinese elite. Early in

Chinese society, many tribal people paid tribute to China, and their leaders visited with the heads of state. Today, in line with this ageless tradition and representing the United states was Henry Kissinger, former United States secretary of state, followed by President Richard Nixon, and President George Bush.

It is important to note that the Mandate of Heaven is, in the main, different in its relationship to the state from that of Orthodox-Russian and Western Christian thought. During the primacy of the church and the age of absolute monarchy, it identified with the state order in their religious and philosophical thought.

The Mandate of Heaven was sustained from the Chou dynasty, 1027-256 B.C., through the dynastic system and up until the overthrow of Nationalist China, October 1, 1949. Interwoven with the Chinese Classics, the educational system, and the entire culture, it exists, despite attempts by the Chinese Communist to root it out. A re-examination of Chinese history is underway today by the present day leaders. Just how far it will go remains to be seen. The ancient theory of revolutions is in the psyche of the Chinese people and that cannot be denied. The Chinese leaders are acutely aware that state is responsible for the welfare of the people over whom it has authority. It remains to be seen if Chinese communism can coexist with the Classics and the revolutionary thought of Mencius. A learned Chinese ruler should take into account these serious thoughts.

It is important to note that Moscow looked upon itself as the focal point of World Communism which conflicted with Chinese thought. And now the Chinese leaders are of the opinion that all other governments should come to recognize China as the focal point of World Communism. In agreement with this opinion is Henry Kissinger, former President Richard Nixon, former President Ronald Reagan, and former President George Bush.

CHAPTER SIX

Adolph Hitler was more than just a product of his parents union; he was a product of Western Society. Society collectively fails when it attempts to fault an individual such as Hitler for crimes of violence perpetrated against humanity. When leaders, at times, make serious mistakes in judgement either by an act or by failing to act, they must be held accountable under national and international law.

It is indeed fitting that Western Society examine the historical documents which explain how Fascism spread from Rome -the seat of Roman Catholicism- and how Nazism issued forth from the Reformation, to clearly perceive how Western Christianity spawned the horrible atrocities of German Nazism and Italian and Spanish Fascism.

Data, presented in the first chapter, explained the effects of the Reformation through to Thomas Jefferson. Additional information shall disclose events of the West from the last two centuries (to the time of this writing).

The aftermath of the Protestant Reformation clearly reveals how Western Society became a house divided against itself. There are fundamental factors which support this view: After the collapse of the Church of Rome, a conflict developed among the nation-states in Western Europe. Western Christianity was imposed by imperial military force in the 4th and 5th centuries and merged church and state, expanding into Western Europe, England, Scotland and Ireland, to establish the church as prime agent of spiritual-temporal authority for nearly a thousand years. The church doctrine espoused that mankind must seek redemption from the fall of Adam and Eve, that which could only come about through the church —the mystical body of Christ. Consequently, all authority, temporal and spiritual, came from God, through the church. Thus, the hypothesis that man could not govern himself. The primary purpose of the church was to prepare man for life after death and not for his service on earth.

The Reformation ended the monolithic structure of the church in

Western Society; however, in theory the practice continued in another form. The nation-state system —legalized in 1648 at the end of the Thirty Years War with The Treaty of Westphalia— emerged with the Reformation and the wars of religion. This system began a religious conflict that ended in a power struggle among Christian authorities to fill the vacuum created by the collapse of the Church of Rome.

With the expansion of science and technology, wars became more frequent and more destructive. Attempts to reunify Western Society have failed, although endeavors continue to this hour. Dramatic differences are manifest in attempts at unification, first by the French under Louis XIV, in the latter part of the 17th century and first part of the 18th century, and Napoleon, in the 19th century, and the two subsequent attempts by the Germans in the first half of this century.

Napoleon's ability to wage destructive war far exceeded Louis XIV. Yet, the destruction of Louis XIV far exceeded any previous warrior king. The increase in catastrophic war was evident in Germany's efforts to unify the whole of Europe, and the Soviet Union in World War Two. Henry Stelle Commager, in June, 1985, speaking of the community of culture built over the centuries and how it was largely destroyed by modern nationalism stated the following:

> It, (nationalism) did this by calculated appeals to the worst traits of human nature, and by fostering the pernicious notions that some nations were destined by God and nature and history to rule over others, or even that there was some cosmic law, some 'manifest destiny' that one nation should be more powerful than any others —the psychology that so surely prevails today. It is no wonder that nationalism —in its origin not without logic and usefulness, and in its eighteenth century manifestations not without benevolence —should come to be the most destructive force in history or that it now threatens to put an end to all history. [1]

The second factor in the Western World as a house divided is its refusal to agree on the nature of people and their ability, or lack of ability, to rule themselves. However, these questions remain: Are the people the servants of the state, or is the state the servant of the people? There is much evidence to support the position that the West is lacking in a fundamental philosophy

---

[1]*Academic, November, 1985, The University of Chicago.*

regarding the nature of human beings.

One should further examine these points to discover that the absolute monarchs of Austria, Spain and France were among the first European powers to attempt to reunify Western Society after the collapse of the Church of Rome. Each monarch was Roman Catholic and fought not only other Roman Catholics but Lutherans and the Church of England as well. Although they declared that their authority had come from God, each tried and failed to reestablish Western unity. A number of Roman Catholic Christian monarchs joined forces with Islam against other Roman Catholic nations, and each individual case used religion to gain support for the conflicts. Christianity served to thwart the interest of one nation state against the another. Religion, along with its doctrines, the former primary unifier of a larger society, was now parochial. Science —physical, natural, and medical as well— gradually encountered the same fate and was forced to serve in the interest of national rather than universal goals. Individuals, to whom the church had previously provided spiritual guidance and relative security, was now provided for by the state. Nationalism, with its many differences in Christian appeal, merged with philosophy and science.

The one point upon which all the fragmented society agreed was: that all authority came from God. Mankind, apart from its rulers, was therefore subject to the authority of the state. In other words: man, incapable of ruling himself, was therefore servant of the state. This law prevailed, for the most part, until the latter part of the 18th century. Exceptions, however, were England's example of the Glorious Revolution of 1688-89, the British colonial revolt in North America in 1776 and the French Revolution in 1789. The Glorious Revolution, with the philosophical buttresses of John Locke and the American Revolution with Thomas Jefferson, would set off the philosophical fragmentation of the West. Both Locke and Jefferson would proclaim that man was basically good and therefore capable of governing himself. Consequently, if man be just, the state must be the servant of man and not man the servant of the state.

It should nonetheless be noted that Machiavelli contributed to the philosophical separation of Western Society when he proclaimed that rulers should govern by their increased power of state, both internally and externally, using force when necessary. Although a prince should appear moral at all times; he should never permit that appearance to dictate his rule of action. Leaders of these opposing views continue the debate. Presently, all nations subject to authoritarian rule rests upon the assumption that the masses are incapable of ruling themselves. However, there also are national leaders moving forward with the conviction that people can rule themselves, and are encouraging them to participate in government.

David Hume, in his "Treatise on Human Nature" 1739-40, [1] between the time of John Locke in the 17th century and Thomas Jefferson in the 18th century- would appear to undermine the concept of natural law and the basic ideas of religion. Thus, human conduct would be deprived of direction. Hume lived at the time when royal absolutism was corrupt. Although the English government and its church had serious abuses, compared to other European churches and governments, they were exemplary.

Hume tested the ideas of necessary truths, the unchanging laws of nature, and morality by examining their scientific validity, and contended that the relationships of events and implications drawn from them can only be accepted if acknowledged as facts. He asserted that, at best, one can accept the fact that events do occur in relation to each other. Consequently, he stated that so-called religious truths were therefore no greater than the people's propensity to believe them. Hence, their purpose is of no practical value. These conclusions were devastating to the premise of Hugo Grotius' law of nations -as stated in the Treaty of Westphalia. Any monarch would adhere to the laws of war, of peace, of neutrality, of monarch to monarch, of prisoners of war, of combatants or non-combatants, for as long as they were believed by monarchs; to do so was advantageous.

When philosophical or religious beliefs are challenged, it seems that a strong resistance in the human psyche is aroused. Apparently old metaphysical or religious ideas are resurrected. The effect is not an examination of new ideas, as was the case with Hume, but the reaffirmation of old absolute values.

It may, for example, be that the destruction and defeat of Germany by Napoleon influenced George Frederick Wilhelm Hegel. [2] He argued that sentiment, tradition, custom, and the idealization of history were fundamental to human conduct. Folk poetry, "spirit of the nation" were the roots of national culture. Community religious reverence and loyalty were greater in wisdom than logic. Therein lies the cosmic spirit of nations. Hegel argued that traditional custom and membership within a society produces moral values of the individual, not natural law or reason. Inasmuch as the state is the supreme

---

[1] *"Treatise on Human Nature, 1739-40, David Hume"*, and *"Hume's Philosophy of Human Nature"*, John Laird, London, 1932.

[2] *The Metaphysical Theory of The State*, L.T. Hobhouse, London, 1918. *Reason and Revolution: Hegel and The Rise of Social Theory*, Herbert Maeuse, New York, 1941.

institution of a nation, its role in custom and tradition cannot be understated since each nation has its own unique role in "a divine tactic."

Classifying further, the role of the state, Hegel asserted that The Volkgeist -the spirit of the nation- works through an individual, for the most part, devoid of conscious will. The Hegelian theory, which doubtless influenced German unification, concluded that the nation-state was the essence of political power. This is markedly similar to Machiavelli, inasmuch as Hegel's thesis, and German folklore and tradition, brought about German unification under Bismarck in 1870-71.

The Roman Church gave a sense of spiritual security and identity, postulating that all authority, church and secular, came from God through the church. The dialectic process of Hegel, as applied to history, hypothesizes that he discovered the law of cultural growth, that which separates an advanced population from those less developed. Furthermore, if this be the case, it then establishes veracity in human activity; those things previously done by the church and the laws of God through the church, independent of man, but through man. Since the facts would speak for themselves, this was concluded by not imposing laws on the facts. The vacuum was created by the collapse of the church. Hence, natural law was impregnated by the dialectic process. Hegel, in searching for the absolute in human reason, believed it was found in the state.

Since the collapse of the first German Reich, subsequent to the death of Charlemagne in 814, German territory had been divided into many small states. Military weakness was evident in the Germanies during the Napoleonic wars and, to Hegel, unification was a moral imperative for it would create an institution to which all Germans could be loyal. Hegel believed that the destiny of civilization was bound to German unification and to follow in the footsteps of history, it ultimately could only come about by war.

Hegel believed complete devotion to the state was a cause greater than oneself, since the state was morally superior to civil society, and its leaders, great men of history, were propelled by forces about which they scarcely understood. He believed that leadership came by harmonization with the Spirit world and leaders neither make nor guide this force, for it lies below the surface of past events. The German state, in Hegel's mind, was in the eminent interest of civilization, having an aura of divine essence and moral mysticism deserving of one's deepest loyalty. Rights of the individual are subordinate to the interest of the state.

There appears here to be a resemblance with the structure and thesis of the Roman Church: the hypothesis that the universal church is the essence of morality, superior to secular authority, guided by the popes chosen from above. This (force from above) leads the head of the church.   The church is an institution, greater than oneself, to which total loyalty should be given, as both give to one an identity and ultimate purpose.   The ultimate goal for the German people, as far as Hegel could see, was unification achieved by war. And violence through war is clearly an acceptable means to an end.

Marx [1] would take the Hegelian dialectic process and apply it not to nations, but as a means of interpreting the international scope of the movement of history. As Marx applied the dialectic, it became known as "scientific socialism." The key word is "scientific." Following through on this premise, it would give certainty to human activity and with certainty, it would give security. The dialectic was to replace the divine law of the church and natural law. Man's quest for a goal and certainty would be assured by the operation of opposite forces, thesis and antithesis, which would merge into a future synthesis.   To Marx, this was the pattern of all logical human development, deemed to be without error.

Still, from another view, Hegel, believed the culmination of European society would be the unification of Germany, whereas Marx held to the belief that the end of social history would come with the rise of the proletariat. Both men aimed to accomplish their goals through violence, in the same fashion as in The Book of Revelations. These goals were to be gained by forces outside the scope of human control. Mechanistic in nature, a careful study of John Calvin's predestination reveals a remarkably similar thought. And in all cases, violence is given moral and spiritual approval.

The culmination of long historical forces is seen in Fascism and Nazism. Each terminated in a paramount leader, Il Duce, Mussolini who aspired to restore the ancient glory of the Roman Empire, and Der Fuhrer, Adolph Hitler, who endeavored to build the Third Reich to last a thousand years, founded on an ancient mystic belief of pure Aryans which would dominate all non-Aryan people. Both dictators made a strong appeal to the past; the glorious Roman Empire, and the mythical Aryan purity, while espousing morality.

Both Italy and Germany were late in becoming unified, compared to the other nation-states of Europe (1870-71). For centuries, each was fragmented into city-states or small kingdoms, and there was strong loyalty to the princes

---

[1] *The Communist Manifesto, 1848, Karl Marx and Friedrich Engels. Capital, Karl Marx, Edited by Friedrich Engles, Encyclopedia Britannica, Inc., Chicago.*

or monarchs, as well as to the administrative structure of the state, the schools and the churches.

Mussolini and Hitler were venerated by appealing to past glories of violence, philosophy and mythology, thus were they able to gain ascendancy, evoking both real and mythical figures of the past which bound them to twentieth century nationalism and military power.

The Italian and German precursors of Fascism and Nazism appealed to the anti-intellectual cult. The mystic of the state which was embodied in the ruler, identified with glory and power as an end in itself. This collective identity gave the people a sense of security in an age when fragmented Italy and Germany was surrounded by highly developed industrialization.

For centuries, a strong resentment against Jews was deeply imbedded in Christian thought. It was believed that Jews constituted a culture apart from Christians and was judged not to be in the interest of unified Germany. Consequently, they were deemed enemies of the church. The Reformation and the Lutheran movement did nothing to diminish this resentment. These feelings escalated during the latter part of the nineteenth century.

The nineteenth century Germans thought, for the most part, like Oswald Spengler, [1] who resolved that history was a struggle of cultures: Europe against Asia; white people against colored people, etc. The Lutherans and the Church of Rome also believed its theology superior; not only to other Christian thought, but to all non-Christian theology. This particular concept, extremely dominate in Germanic belief, along with National Socialism, completely permeated Adolph Hitler's viewpoint.

The Fascist and Nazi systems both agreed on different goals: Italy had not been unified for centuries, until 1870-71, and from that period until the end of the first World War, there was little time to bring Italy together, psychologically and spiritually. But Mussolini was prepared to force Italy into a revived Roman Empire. However, this would conflict with Hitler's aspirations to dominate Europe and expand to the East and beyond.

At the end of World War One, the German monarchy was supported by the aristocracy, the army, the navy, the civil servants, the trade unions, the colleges and universities, the Protestant, Lutheran and Catholic clergy, and by the political parties. Having been born and bred into German ethics, now as

---

[1] *"The Decline of The West"*, 2 Volumes, Oswald Spengler, New York, 1926.

the war came to an end, the infrastructure began to crumble. The monarch had abdicated. Kaiser Wilhelm was in exile. Germany then tried democracy; but without success. Nothing seemed to fill the void —psycho spiritual leadership— which had been created by the collapse of the House of Hohenzollern.

The German Republic, under the Weimar Constitution, clearly did not capture the loyalty that its people had given the monarchy. However, this factor did not slip by Hitler —the little corporal with a gargantuan appetite for power. Just as Mussolini —not the House of Savoy— resolved Italy's conflicts after the first World War, so did Hitler fill the "monarch" void in Germany.

The old institutions failed. All major institutions in Germany merged at the peak of the Reich where collective loyalty focused on the monarch. In Italy, the House of Savoy was not in control long enough to create a kind of cohesive patronage to the degree that the House of Hohenzollern had in Germany. In Italy, the monarchy and the Vatican had also been at war with each other for years. Therefore, at the end of the first World War, the church and the monarchy had failed the interests of Italy.

In both Nazism and Fascism the leaders are above the morality of their subjects. Both leaders scorned Christianity. Both remained Roman Catholic and made extensive use of the church, Mussolini by the Concordat and Hitler by receiving the open blessings of The Holy Father. Their interests were the same. Violent opposition to a common enemy bound them together. The enemy was Communism. The sense of a common cause between Adolph Hitler, the leader of the Third Reich, and the Roman Catholic Church was agreed upon in 1933:

> The Concordat —as the Holy See preferred to call the pact— was signed by Pius XII and Hitler in 1933. It ordered the Holy See's clergy to swear oaths of fealty to Hitler and The Third Reich. It further ordered that prayers were to be said publicly for the Fuhrer and Germany by Catholic bishops and priests The Church, in effect, pledged never to oppose Hitler's dictatorship. [1]

From "*La Popessa,*" one finds the following: "Pius XII, in the choice between Nazism and Communism, was solidly behind the June, 1941 invasion of the Soviet Union by Nazi Germany. "Pius XII said novenas for the Nazis and

---

[1] *"La Popessa", p. 198, Paul L. Murphy with R. Rene Arlington, Warren Books, 1983.*

asked God to intercede for their total victory in Russia." [1]

In a similar fashion, Mussolini had made peace with the papacy in the Lateran agreement of 1929. The Vatican was recognized as an independent state. Mussolini gave large sums of money to the Vatican and the Roman Church was recognized as the only state religion. In return, the papacy urged Italians to support Mussolini's government.

It is clear that the papacy favored Nazism in the fight against Communism. The conflict was designated "in defense of Christian culture" similar to Teutonic Knights, a military religious order founded in the 12th century in the Holy Land during Third Crusade. Late in the 11th century they conquered the heathen Prussians and established the order as the government of Prussia. The church in Austria assured Hitler that so long as it had its liberties, Austria's truest sons would support the Reich. The Nazi law for the Protection of German Blood and Honor was supported in Austria.

Hitler, after his rise to power in Germany, was spoken of as a savior "... the only man of the century who possesses strength to take into his hands the thunderbolt of God and fashion it anew for mankind." John Toland in his book *Adolph Hitler* reports that some Catholic clergy spoke of Hitler as a Messiah, or God, [2] the creator of the world, that the church gave special blessings to him and his people. Toland states in relation to the Final Solution of Jews in December 10, 1941, that the killing of the Jews was carried out under the injunction of God to cleanse the world of vermin. Furthermore, Hitler declared that he was a Catholic and would always remain so. [3] He said he was carrying out church teachings that Jews were the killer of God. Even though Hitler remained a Roman Catholic, he and the church used each other to their mutual advantage.

The laws of war, peace, and neutrality had been placed in the Treaty of Westphalia in 1648. This body of law recognized the new order, the nation-state system of today. The subjects of each monarch were to obey the enforced laws of monarchs, deemed to be agents of God on earth. To whom were the monarchs subject? They were subject or answered to God alone for any infraction of His law. What were the restraints upon absolute monarchs from 1648 through the end of the 19th century? Did they not fight each other in Europe, the New World, Africa, the Near East, and Asia? Their restraints

---

[1] *Ibid. p. 19.*
[2] *Ibid. p. 320, 730.*
[3] *Ibid. p. 528.*

were weak when dealing with the French Revolution, the Napoleonic Wars, and
the European revolts of 1848. This system of 1648 was clearly failing in its
quest for internal, and international peace as well.

Both Mussolini and Hitler would go beyond The Prince, as previously
stated, in that the former would appeal to the mystic past and project it to the
future, the rebuilding of the Roman Empire. Hitler would do the same by
appealing to the irrational will, group instinct, and racial instinct inherent in the
blood. Both men emphasized a life of heroism and self-sacrifice, with a twist
on ideas of Charles Darwin, Henry James, and Sigmund Freud. To Hitler this
would mean that life is motivated by dark, unexplained forces in the folk,
people or nation. The result in both cases was the emergence of group worship.
In Italy, it would be El Duce; in Germany, Der Fuhrer. This was twentieth
century tribalism based upon a different hypothesis. Each social order
demanded the same obedience as did the papacy in former days and the
absolute monarchs. The new basis was an appeal to the deepest hatred from
those at the lowest level of society in Italy and Germany against the morality
of those at the top of the systems which each was taking over.

Hitler was a fanatic admirer of the German composer, Richard Wagner.
Deep in the history of Wagnerian thought and an inspiration for his greatest
works, Tristan and Isolde and Parsival, was the famous 12th century poet and
minnesinger, Wolfram Von Eschenbach. Inspired by the combination of Wagner
and Von Eschenbach, Hitler led himself to believe he had found a Western
path to a transcendental state of consciousness.

Hitler is known to have read about Yoga, but is not known to have
practiced it. He also firmly stated that he did not want to find himself in "the
skin of Buddha."

Though Hitler was raised a Roman Catholic— and remained one
throughout his life— he was unstinting in his contempt for Christianity, believing
it led one to weakness and subservience.

In Parsival and Tristan and Isolde, Hitler believed he found that blood
itself should contain the secret of spiritual illumination and into the mysteries
of The Holy Grail, and the story of The Spear of Longinus, which according to
legend, had pierced the side of Christ. Hitler could accept, as well as Wagner,
an identification with Christ, since Wagner believed Christ was pure Aryan and
not a Jew.

In the legend of The Spear of Longinus, [1] also known as *The Spear of Destiny,* the story states that whosoever claims the spear and understands occult powers it serves, holds the destiny of the world in his hands.

The Grail is described by the minnesinger as a *Precious Stone,* and that it was the symbol of the pineal gland located beneath the brain —*The Third Eye.* The whole plot of The Holy Grail was to open and activate The Third Eye, revealing the hidden secret of *Time* and the meaning of human destiny.

Hitler was influenced by Guido Von List, the organizer of the Blood Lodge, which substituted The Swastika for the cross in theitual of black magic, Trevor Ravenscroft [2] asserts that Hitler and the Nazi Party recognized Christ with the same certainty of Francis of Assisi. Hitler had only contempt for Christ and viewed The Spear of Destiny (located in the Treasure House at Hofburg in Vienna) as a symbol of the war of the world —a conflict "between the hierarchies of Light and Darkness."

According to Dr. Walter Johannes Stein —a Vienna born scientist and Doctor of Philosophy who died in 1957— who acted as the confidential adviser to Sir Winston Churchill during World War Two regarding the mind and motivation of Hitler and other leading members of the Nazi party, few people realize the role that the occult played in the Nazi movement, and to what extent. He also states that the Nuremburg Trials failed to grasp the evil work behind National Socialism; however, it would not be until the publication of Aldous Huxley's *The Doors of Perception* in which Dr. Stein decided to make public his intensive findings on the occult.

Dr. Stein wrote a noteworthy work entitled "The Ninth Century", [3] and other stories of the Grail in Britain, France, and in Ireland. Although he did not live to see the psychedelic age come to pass, Dr. Stein forsaw the widespread use of mind expanding drugs throughout Europe and the United States, providing millions of people with a perilous path to transcendent experiences for which they would not be prepared. He believed this would come about because of ". . .the inevitable reaction to the petrified religious

---

[1] *"The Spear of Destiny"*, Trevor Ravenscroft, Bantam Books, Ct. P. Putnam's Sons, 1973, 1974. *This book is vital to Hitler's background, which is not widely published.*

[2] *Ibid. p. 260.*

[3] *The Ninth Century and The Holy Grail, Stein Piv686/GF ST 513, 1988, M.S.U. This book is available only at Michigan State University Library, Lansing, MI or Boston University, Boston, MA.*

dogmatism and materialistic complacency of the established order in the West which even the cataclysmic events of Hitler's war had failed to shift." [1]

Dr. Stein knew Adolph Hitler and studied him carefully for a considerable time in Austria. He met Hitler in late summer 1912, and was in continuous contact with him until the spring of 1913. Stein found that Hitler had attained a higher level of consciousness by means of drugs and had made a penetrating study of medieval occultism and ritual magic from which he formulated the Nazi Weltanschauung. He continued to closely observe Hitler and the founding of the Nazi Party along with Dietrich Eckart, Houston Stewart Chamberlain and Professor Karl Haushofer.

When Reichsführer Heinrich Himmler ordered Stein's arrest in 1933, to press him into the SS Occult Bureau, he escaped to England, bringing the knowledge of occultism of the Nazi Party. Stein was a spy for Britain in World War Two and an advisor to Churchill in relation to the psyche of Hitler.

During his study of Hitler and the Nazi Party, Dr. Stein observed that the occult circle of the Thule Group/Society reached far into every facet of government. It included judges, police chiefs, barristers, lawyers, university professors and lecturers, aristocratic members of former members of royal families, leading industrialists, surgeons, physicians and influential bourgeois . There were officers and ex-officers of the Reichswehr as well as members of the German Workers' Party.

It was none other than Dietrich Eckart who introduced Hitler into the Thule Group, along with Alfred Rosenberg, who presented to Hitler *"The Protocols of the Elders of Zion"*, an appendix to a work called *"The Anti-Christ"*.

Could the Nazi movement, arising as it did in the same area of the Germanies, at the seat of the Reformation of the 16th century and the onslaught of religious wars and revolts that reached far into the 17th century, have a correlation with the rise of Italian fascism in Rome, the center of Roman Catholicism? Previous material has shown how Western Christianity used its own theology in the suppression of Christian theory not adhered to by Rome, and had waged war against Islam and the Eastern Orthodox version of Christianity as well. The Church of Rome used the sword to plant itself astride the religious beliefs of those of the pre-Christians wherever the church expanded in Western Europe, England, Scotland and Ireland. Armed forces with secular and ecclesiastical courts endeavored to uproot all aspects of

---

[1] *Trevor Ravenscroft, o. cit 6., p. XIV - XV.*

pre-Christian thought that did not in some fashion coincide with Christianity.

The upsurge of nationalism, the Renaissance, and the Reformation unleashed violence in Western Society in an unprecedented scale. Each monarch fought in the name of Christ, the Prince of Peace, who became the spiritual guide of monarchs in war against each other in Western Europe, England, Scotland, Ireland and Wales as well as in the colonial world in the age of colonization.

It must be recalled that with the spread of Christianity from Rome with the collapse of the Greco-Roman Empire, the prime concern of the church was the conversion of the chiefs of northern European and British Island tribes along with the kings of these non-Christian people. In short, with the conversion of the rulers at the apex of the non-Christian tribes, for the most part, little concern was directed to those at the bottom of the social structure of conquered people. The teachings of the church were to trickle down from the top, hopefully, to those at the bottom, both in the urban and rural areas where education was meager, if at all. This was strictly speaking the trickle-down theory where force was often used to get compliance to a religion from the top.

Could it be that these events would produce the revulsion that the Nazi-Fascist movements had against Christianity at the base of their ideology while proclaiming Christianity as Hitler and Mussolini did, consequently having their feet in both camps?

What would lie underneath the top layer of Christianity among the people of urban communities and the growing population of rural areas with the rise of the commercial, mercantile, and industrial age? A graphic account of the psychic conflict in the Germanies is given in "The Crisis of German Ideology, The Intellectual Origins of the Third Reich," by George L. Mosse. [1]

---

[1] *This material runs throughout the book: "The Crisis In German Ideology, Intelectual Origins of The Third Reich", George L. Mosse, Universal Library originals, 1964. "Aftermath, Martin Borman and The Fourth Reich", Ladislas Fargo, Simon Schuster, New York, 1974. This book contains extensive data on the support of the Roman Catholic Church and The Third Reich. "The Life and Death of Adolph Hitler", Robert Payne, Praeger Publishers, New York, 1973. Data on Dietrich Eckart, Alfred Rosenberg, and Church support of Hitler, as well as material on the Teutonic tradition. "The Mind of Adolph Hitler, The Secret Wartime Report", Walter C. Lauger, Basic Books, Inc., New York. "Hitler, A study*

(continued...)

Under the dynamics of social and ideological change to be resisted in the conflict of urban and rural areas, the setting was ripe for Nazism. The cultural-religious framework of Germany, and in many respects the rest of Western Europe, was as Dr. Stein stated, set for "the inevitable reaction to the petrified religious dogmatism and material complacency of the established order in the west."

Perhaps another approach might throw some light on the subject of the emergence of Nazism. As has been previously voiced, Islam is undergoing dynamic changes that have brought the strong upsurge of Islamic fundamentalism that lay below the surface and broke out full force when the challenge within had some external causes from the West. Some leaders, and those aspiring to leadership, reached into Islamic past to produce its reaction to current circumstances. And, in China, despite the success of The People's Republic of China, the force of Confucius and Mencius, more than 2,000 years old, still play an important part in the dynamics of today in that society. Aside from the defeat of Imperial Japan, as was mentioned previously, Shinto is a force to be taken into account today and in the future.

Moreover, in Latin America after some three hundred years of Spanish and Portuguese control and more than one hundred and fifty years of neo-colonial influence, the indigenous Indian culture has not been uprooted as was their conqueror's desire. It is now being made manifest throughout the vast expanse of Latin America. Underneath the upper layer of Christianity there is the uprising to the surface, in many places of the pre-conquest religious forces that are playing an increasing role in Latin American affairs. And, finally, has the United States uprooted its long slavery idea and practice? The British colonial people and early interspersed people of the United States brought thousands of slaves from Africa to the new world. These slaves carried with

---

[1](...continued)
In Tyranny", Allan Bullock, Perennial Library, Harper and Roe, 1971. "The Borman Brotherhood", William Stevenson, Harcourt Brace Jovanovich, Inc., New York, 1973. "Inside The Third Reich", Memoirs by Albert Speer, MacMillan, New York, 1970. "The History of German Resistance, 1933-1945", Peter Hoffman, The M.I.T. Press, Cambridge, Ms, 1977. "The Anatomy of Human Destructiveness", Erich Fromm, Holt Rinehart and Winston, New York, 1973. "The Rise and Fall of The Third Reich", William L. Shirer, 1960. "From Luther To Hitler", McGovern. "Germany, 1866-1945", Gordon A. Craig, Oxford, 1978. "Nuremberg and Vietnam: An American Tragedy", Telford Taylor, New York Times Books, Random House, New York, 1970. "The Bunker", James P. O'Donnell, Bantom Books, 1979.

them their own culture which was preserved for some three hundred years by oral tradition and is now coming to the surface.

In brief, the past is carried into the present and the present flows into the future unless steps are taken to avert these forces. How may this apply to the rise and spread of Nazism? There is considerable evidence that underlying the Christian religion in Western Europe were pre-Christian religions still in vogue as late as some two hundred years ago. This is the thesis of M.A. Murray, University College, London, England, in her book, *The Witch Cult In Western Europe.* [1] Witchcraft has existed for centuries in England, France, and the Germanies. Many writers on the life of Adolph Hitler refer to his interest in the occult. And Murray states in her work that cult practices existed in Western Europe underneath Christianity, that these practices were uniform throughout Europe and the origin of the their practice can be traced to pre-Christian people. The gods of various cults were anthropomorphic; and were worshipped in well-defined rites. Evidence shows these early people to exist in the pre-agriculture age and the practices in. the overall were uniform and modified in accordance with the influence invading tribes in the area previously mentioned. In these cases, changes occurred in their religious practices when one religion was superimposed upon another by a conqueror.

The overall uniformity of religious practices may be found in the documents of trials and confessions derived from the inquisitions held throughout Western Europe. Further examinations of this material shows that the Christian church regarded their cult leaders as Satan, Lucifer, Beelzebub, Foul Fiend, Enemy of Salvation, or the Devil of the Scriptures.

To the followers of the cult the leader was divine and they dedicated themselves and their children to the leader. However, to become a member, one must dedicate one's self, body and soul, to the cause. Upon initiation, a contract was signed, often in blood, with the devil. Consequently, one renounced one's previous faith and a mark was usually found on the body of the believer, often the evidence of a witch, and was incontrovertible proof of membership.

A general meeting of the faithful, called Sabbath, the date for such was generally to coincide with the breeding season. The witches also celebrated all Christian festivals. Cult meetings were held at night and often the ritual called for blood sacrifices, at times a person's own blood or that of a child. In case

---

[1] *"The Witch-Cult in Western Europe"*, M. A. Murray, Oxford University Press, 1921, 1962. *"The Nazis and The Occult"*, D. Sklar, Dorset Press, New york, 1977.

of the latter, it would be an unbaptized child that was not a part of the community of believers. On occasions there was a sacrifice of their cult god, or an animal substitute.

The witch cult is a survival of an ancient religion wherein there is voluntary membership and submission of one's self to another person, god, or god substitute where duty holds one until death. When the time comes for the god or incarnate deity to die, it would often take place in public, where the leader would be brought before a tribunal for execution. This was done in many instances by hanging or burning and the ashes were scattered over the earth. The theory in many cases was that the god, leader, must die. However, the god, the Grand Master of his area, had all matters reported to him from the covens which constituted the membership of a local area. A highly organized system of rewards and punishment was doled out to members of the covens under the Grand Master's control.

These leaders, as Joan of Arc, and their men-at-arms, were drawn from the lower order of the social group and they believed their leader was sent by God and would follow without hesitation.

One cannot say the parallel is exact, but the premise of Nazi philosophy is there. Hitler had his feet in both camps, proclaiming to be a Christian and yet was deep into Satanism, coming from the ninth century. He believed, as did his followers, in his divine mission until his death.

In addition, Hitler and his followers believed he was a Messiah, the personification of the pure Aryan. His organization saw that all activities of the Third Reich were brought to his attention or to that of his subordinates. It was to him that final and complete obedience was given with the appropriate reward and punishment handed out accordingly. All members wore a distinct marking, the swastika. And, finally, when he and his closest associates faced death at their own hands in the bunker, Hitler had himself cremated so his remains might not be located.

The aftermath of the First World War seems to have broken the veneer of Christianity and failed to meet the crisis of the twentieth century when Nazism and Fascism burst upon the scene with widespread support in the western world.

Let us examine what appears to have taken place in Western Society since the 17th century from another angle. As previously stated, the peace of God that prevailed at an earlier period under the Church of Rome had not met the challenge of the rise of the nation-state system and consequent religious wars and revolts of the Reformation and Counter-Reformation.

Quincy Wright, in his *"Study of War"* [1] shows the correlation between the growth of technology and warfare from 1480 to 1940. The acceleration of battles in the West in the 17th century and after is clear.

The increase in battles in the West goes along with nationalism, the conflicts of Christian monarch through to the French Revolution. Science as applied to agriculture, medicine and technology ripped asunder any vestige of western cohesion in the 19th and 20th centuries as was evident in the acceleration of battles and their destructiveness.

Year and number of battles:

1480-1499 = 9 -- 1500-1599 = 81 -- 1600-1699 = 239

1700-1799 = 781 --1800-1899 = 651 --   1900-1940 = 892

The French Revolution had a devastating influence upon religion in France. The ideas of Jefferson challenged the ideas of monarchs to rule by divine right. This attack would be against the clergy, the royalty, the landed aristocracy and the military. When these ideas were expressed by *The Declaration of the Rights of Man* during the French Revolution, not only the social, religious, philosophical promises of Western Society was under siege, but the same was true of Orthodox Czarist Russia. It also challenged the Islamic world. The French Revolution, and the Napoleonic Wars showed the weakness of the Christian monarchical structure in Europe as well as Czarist Russia. The case was made worse by the failure of the so-called Holy Alliance formed by Austria, Prussia, and Russia in 1815. Proposed by Russia, the alliance was based exclusively upon Christian principles to maintain peace and justice after the Napoleonic wars. Castlereagh, the Prime Minister of England, refused to join the agreement. He stated it was "a piece of sublime mysticism and nonsense." Through great trials and failures the system came to a thundering end in the revolutions of Europe in 1848. Furthermore, no philosopher or theories of note dealing with ideas of state power would use the Bible or Christian fathers by direct quotes to support their political theories in the 19th century.

The devastation wrought by David Hume, the French Revolution and the overwhelming failures of the Holy Alliance in not preventing the Revolutions

---

[1] *"Study of War"*, *Quincy Wright, 1965, 2nd ed. Chicago University Press, Chicago, IL.*

of 1848 underscored the febrile character of the restraint of Christian ideals in holding the European scene together. Its role in the colonial conflicts in Africa and India tells it all.

When only 651 battles were fought in the 19th century, it is often argued that this era represented a period of relative peace. In Europe, as compared with the 18th century wherein 781 battles were waged. What must be considered in the 19th century was a period of carving up Africa, India, and southeast Asia, as well as China, including inroads into the Islamic world by European and English powers. The 19th century European scene indeed set the stage for the ravages of the 20th century, particularly when you consider that Hitler filled the role of the German Messiah, the Beast of Revelation who would lead the Aryan race to glory, who best exemplified the nationalists, egomaniacal power who promised to deliver Western society from certain eclipse. The dreadful point is that Hitler accepted this role as an act of faith along with members of the Nazi party. Even though there were those who believed Hitler was a false prophet who would lead Germany to ruin, this prophecy was overlooked because Hitler was at the threshold, ready to take over Germany and the Third Reich.

It must be admitted that there was a high equation of force in the Third Reich, but there also was a large measure of consent. In addition, German disaffection by defeat in the first World War, the imposed treaty of peace, the reparations demanded and extreme inflation provided ample ground upon which the Nazi movement could and did build. These factors only added to hostility toward Jews, rooted in Christian thought and practice in addition to other forces latent in German and Italian thought which began to emerge and to gain ground as Christian morality became weaker from the top down.

The long struggle for German and Italian unification had produced Italian and German awareness of the veneer of Christian morality. This is evident in 19th and 20th century Italian and German political theories. The contending states of Italy were in conflict with each other, as well as with the Papal states. These events since the Congress of Vienna in 1815 at the close of the Napoleonic wars had an influence on political thought in both Italy and Germany, as well as France and Spain, in the conflict of monarchy versus republican thought. In short, all major forces in Europe were undergoing psycho-spiritual turmoil. The old institutions surrounded with traditional religious support were showing, clearly, the wear and stress of time. Christianity and its morals of control of the social-political-moral structure declined and was being replaced with an appeal to the past to mystic superstition to the glories of a romantic yesterday that fed social dissension. These ancient feelings arose from the ranks of the Italian-German, Austrians,

French, Spanish and Czechoslovakians as the morality of the elite declined. The ingredients of Fascism and Nazism —the most violent aspects of Western Society— arose in the major European nations with Christian approval.

It is clear that any Christian ethics of restraint on violence included in the law of nations was no match for the changes underway in Western Society since the Treaty of Westphalia of 1648. From this, it is evident that if the divine monarchs were answerable to God for infractions of His law, insofar as they were not subject to the laws of man, then serious questions could be raised about the viability of Christian morality. It was weak at best, and no stronger than the monarch's willingness to abide by it. Religion was used as a means to gain support for European wars and colonial conflict.

The magnificent primeval churches and cathedrals of Europe, England, Scotland, Ireland, and Wales are lavishly decorated with statues of warriors, with prodigiously engraved plaques hanging from the walls or embedded into the floors, and antiquated tattered flags waving limply from their respective poles, all depicting victories from numerous military campaigns. Continuous prayer offerings for soldiers who fell in the heat of battle give testament to the belief that their efforts were sanctioned, deified by a God who seems to bestow favor only if the combatant represented the interest in question.

Frederick Nietzsche, in nineteenth century Europe, depicted Christianity as weak, without fiber or character, labelling Christian morality "slave morality." He theorized a new heroic morality; a society directed by a class of supermen with the puissance to set them apart from the usual inferior "herd." Nietzsche's thinking, greatly influenced by that of Arthur Schopenhauer, saw world conflicts as a result of the individual's will, causing much frustration and pain.

And then came Houston Stewart Chamberlain, the son-in-law of Richard Wagner. Both men were violent in their views on German purity and that Jews were the root of Christian weakness. This could be rectified only by freeing Germany of its enemy, the Jews, who had also perverted Christianity by claiming Christ to be a Jew. He, to Wagner, was an Aryan. Richard Wagner clearly expressed in his opera the thesis of the Aryan Master Race.

Wagner believed the blood of Christ was shed exclusively for Aryan people. This is Wagner's theory in his opera, Parsival. Wagner believed it had been revealed to him that Jesus Christ was born of pure Aryan stock and not from parents who were Jews. God was looking for "a final solution" to deliver the Fatherland from their corrupting influence.

The theory that the blood of Christ being shed only for Aryan people was widely held by members of the German General Staff in the late 19th and early 20th centuries by such men as Kaiser Wilhelm, Helmuth Von Moltke of the General Staff who believed Hitler to be possessed of fearful black magic carried through from a previous life.

Nazism and Fascism have left a legacy of horror as a result of their brief period of power in this century. Many find it hard to grasp why and how Mussolini and Hitler, the major proponents, could have created and used systems of power/violence as they did. To others, these twins of death are approached by dismissing the evidence of the slaughter of millions of people by state policy. To them the concentration camps did not exist, and still others make their only criticism of Hitler in that he was defeated. In the final analysis Hitler's National Socialism (Nazism), and Mussolini's Fascism (Corporate State) with all its dehumanizing did take place. The roots of each is implanted deeply in the ethos of Western Society. Hitler's purpose was to destroy the entire structure and thought not just of Germany, but of Western Europe and the Soviet Union as well. Our grim monument to the past stood around us at the former Berlin Wall.

However, the legacy of Hitler is yet not over. It has been approximately a half century since the end of World War II, and still that is not enough time to eradicate the deeply ingrained hatred, not only for Jews, but belief in the myth of Aryan supremacy.

How will East and West Germany present their past history to the generations in the remainder of this century and beyond? To be sure, a generation has arisen that took no part in the Third Reich. If the United States history is to serve as a guide, when at this late date there is still deep-seated hostility toward the African Americans, the American Indians, the Hispanics, and the Asian population —after more than a century and a quarter since the end of the Civil War— then what are the prospects for the future? The demonic hatred which existed in Nazi Germany, Austria, France, the Low Countries, and in Poland, still lies beneath the social facade. The churches and cathedrals of Europe still appear to give a greater amount of space and homage to war than to peace.

*W*ith the fall of the Berlin Wall and the collapse of The U.S.S.R., the borders of East and West Germany were finally opened on November 9, 1990, for the flow of citizens in and out of East Germany for the first time since the end of World War Two. Despite the drama of German reunification; the underlying problems of the past have begun to emerge.

How will the Germanie's past legacies join with the issues of the future? How will it be affected domestically and internationally? The following factors should be observed: Germany has a long history of aggressive warfare. It has been threatening and aggressive from the time of Frederick The Great, in the eighteenth century; through Bismarck; through the First World war; and on through to Adolph Hitler in the Second World War. [1]

Presently, Germany appears to play the role of middle-man between the European Community and the struggling Commonwealth of Independent States, formerly the U.S.S.R. Although The European Community promises to stabilize the Western European States, it is still too early to say what the outcome will be.

Currently, German leaders are attempting to alleviate tensions relative to the borders with its neighbors. The flood of refugees from the East, coupled with the cost factor to care for them, presents a great problem for all those concerned. Unemployment, inflation, and a growing hostility against non-Germans, are creating concerns within the Bundesbank which rules the European economy. Germany has a population of eighty million. And it has the largest army in Europe.

Although the current situation in Germany may be stable, this is no forecast for the future. Unified Germany is confronting the ghost of its past. neo-Nazis, "skin heads" and racial groups are attacking foreign "guest workers," some of whom are Turks, Angolan, and Vietnamese. The motivation is to drive out all foreigners. Their hatred is directed toward anyone conceived to be non-German. [2]

The New Hitler groups, in signs of frightening proportions, are attacking those who hold liberal political views. The surge of street violence is increasing, in East Germany; especially since the police force there has been reduced and unemployment continues to mount. Estimates of violence against foreigners has grown from 128 in 1990, to 341 at the end of the first eight months of 1991. The hard core Nazi movement has anywhere from 2,00 to 5,000 sympathizers, and possibly as many as 50,000 who are prepared to support violent action.

The movements are comprised of West German youth in their twenties and are led by West German men in their thirties and forties. The youth of

---

[1] *Financial Times, London, April 6, 1992*
[2] *The New York Times, December 6, 1991. News Week, July 29, 1991. Financial Times, London, April 7, 1992. Los Angeles Times, March 14, 1991.*

West Germany appear to know more of their history than do the youth from East Germany who were held fast under the yoke of Communism. Consequently, the new freedom of unification has created a movement of reaction from the left to the right. The neo-Nazi outbursts have been greater in the area of East Germany where Communist support is greatest.

There were troubling signs of a resurgence of nationalism in Germany as of July, 1991. This resurgence began while trying to determine the honor which should be given to Frederick The Great, who ruled from 1740 until his death in 1786. The conflict arose over the burial place of The Emperor in conformity with his wishes. Neo-Nazi groups in Germany, Great Britain, and the United States are working together to encourage the recurrence of Nazism in Germany. The British National Party, the Ku Klux Klan in the United States, and the Canadian skinheads appear to want a Fourth Reich, comprising Austria, the Sudetenland, Silesia, and South Tyrol. Dennis Mahon, a K.K.K. leader from Oklahoma, went to Germany and openly encouraged "The Empire of The White Knights of The Ku Klux Klan" in Germany to be active in fighting for the Aryan workers there." The aim, he said, is to create "an exclusive Aryan homeland."

Recently, while Mahon was in Germany, he proclaimed, "Every means are justified, I mean every, to rescue the nation." The attacks have been against Africans, Turks, Yugoslavs, Vietnamese, and Rumanian gypsies. [1]

The subjugation of the Communist rule in East Germany since 1945 may be a factor in the recent upsurge of violence among its youth. But the susceptibility of violence in the German psyche is not of recent birth. In many ways, it emerged from the days of the Reformation, the Counter-Reformation, the belief of the Church and State as one by all factors of Christianity, the educational system, and finally, the family structure basically kept subordinate to the state. It is important to remember that Germany's past glory has been based on an authoritarian premise of superiority. And it now is struggling to regain that status.

France and Britain are fearful of a "Greater Central European Co-Prosperity Sphere" positioned in Berlin. They also fear a German sphere in the Balkans. The collapse of Soviet Communism is creating ethnic, border, religious, and nationalist conflicts among the new republics. Germany is giving large sums of money to the Republic of Russia. This factor, combined with

---

[1] *New York Times, November 3, 1991. New York Times, August 21, 1990. New York Times, May 14, 1991.*

Germany's interest in being the broker state of Yugoslavia presents a basis for its dominance in Europe. Neither France nor Britain show an inclination to offset German aspirations. Clearly, *power politics,* and not a New World Order, is the name of the game.

The question central throughout Eastern Europe and the former Soviet Union is how to bring about a pluralistic social order. Much of the area is without a democratic process. And the ethnic, religious, and nationalistic groups which united against the Soviet domination have suddenly broken apart. Religious forces are attempting to fill the void in absence of Communism. [1] Now arising in the area is a dangerous attempt to bridge religious faith with national unity. It would be well to remember that the same combination created complete and utter chaos in the 16th and 17th centuries. Arising from this sort of religious and ethnic upsurge is the growth of anti-semitism.

However, it is important to note that this latest attempt to merge religion and state is being challenged in Poland, in Hungary, in East Germany, and in Czechoslovakia. [2]

One great problem arises with clerics who compromise themselves with the Communist order. There are some church leaders who fear the development of religious backed parties which serve as a means to bring about order from chaos. They also fear these religious backed parties who simply serve to protect their own interest. When religious forces reinforce nationalism; then what about minority groups? Michael Klinger, an orthodox professor of theology in Warsaw, Poland, stated: "For me, personally, this nationalistic influence on the Church and through the Church is very dangerous."

These conflicting groups: United Catholic, Orthodox Catholic, Protestant, Eastern Orthodox, Lutheran, Islam and Judaism are attempting to provide spiritual leadership to the people during a time of critical change.

Nationalism, as a religion, is mounting in Romania. And with it, a resurgence of anti-Semitism. The primary evidence of this was in April of 1991, on the forty fifth anniversary of the execution of 250,000 Jews. Most of the members of the Rumanian Parliament rose in silent tribute to that ex-leader.

---

[1] *New York Times, July 20, 1990. New York Times, July 22, 1990. New York Times, August 28, 1991.*

[2] *The Economist, June 30, 1990. At the time of this writing, this state has ceased to exist. There now are two nations; one is Czech, the other is Slovak.*

Little or no opposition was evidenced in the whole of Romania. [1]

Here, again, is the heritage of the past. From years of repression throughout Eastern Europe, the ethnic, nationalistic, religious hostility is rearing its ugly head. Each nation is striving to drive out foreigners. Each is seeking an unattainable religious purity. The new movement prevails in a large segment of France, Germany, Austria, and Italy, with an underlying contingent of Fascism emerging. When one speaks of a "New World Order," it is difficult to know to what is one referring? One seems to hear an echo coming out of the past: Is it the 'old' "New World Order" from the Third Reich?

For a thousand years the people of the former Soviet Union lived under authoritarian rule. After this period, a drastic move for change was begun. Its leader, Mikhail Gorbachev, started the move from the top, down. This was in reaction to the delay from the bottom, up. And what was once the Soviet Union, a monolithic state covering eleven time zones, is now divided into fifteen states called, The Commonwealth of Independent States. That title, to date, has gone undefined. However, they are supposedly bound by treaties. The same is true for the various factions within the Republic of Russia.

The Republic of Russia is composed of many different ethnic and linguistic groups who have a tradition of hostility toward Moscow, the capitol. Boris Yeltsin, the president of Russia, aside from his conflict with Ukraine over the Army and Navy, is becoming painfully aware of his internal problems with other republics.

The groups known as The Commonwealth of States are praised as republics and equated with fledgling democracies. Historically, a republic is defined as a form of government whose leader is determined by a process other than by blood. This would have included The Third Reich, Italian Fascism, Spain, Portugal, The Soviet Union, and The Peoples Republic of China, just to name a few. Consequently, the term, republic, means little. Nor does the term, election, for all have used treaties and elections to serve ends not associated with democracy.

The events in history show the weakness of elections and constitutions where there are no deep roots adhering to either. The prime factor depends not only upon the content of constitutions and upon treaties and elections;

---

[1] *New York Times, July 27, 1991. The United Nations is attempting to do what Pax Dei did centuries ago; and what the Holy Alliance attempted to do after Napoleon in 1815. It is not new.*

however, it depends upon the willingness of those in power and the people subject to that power to adhere to the result of elections and the constitutions upon which they are predicated.

There is much talk of a "New World Order." Western Europe and Britain, so far, have not formulated the stability of the European Community and are apprehensive of the assurances of a Unified Germany. At this time, Europe is not united. It is almost as fragmented now, if not to the same degree, as it has been for centuries: Yugoslavia is breaking apart and the defunct United Socialist Soviet Republic is now fifteen republics tenuously held together by treaties under the nebulous word: "Commonwealth." The weakness of the United Nations and the United States declaration to operate on its own, if support for the United Nations is not in conformity with the United States policy at any given time, is nothing new. At the end of the Napoleonic Wars, The Holy Alliance was formed to maintain peace in Europe. At the end of The First World War, The League of Nations was inaugurated for the same purpose. The United Nations and The League of Nations were designed to bring peace throughout the world. Neither has been successful in this endeavor. In addition to the geographical territory, which has fractured Europe as well as England and Ireland, are fifteen new republics arising from the former Soviet Union; each insisting on having its own military. How far Yugoslavia will break apart, remains to be seen.

Within the former Soviet Union and Eastern Europe are an estimated forty nuclear power plants (Chernobyls) waiting to happen. Of the sixty nuclear reactors with safety problems in this area, twenty-six are serious. The nations involved do not have the finances to correct the problems, and is a shortage of parts and supplies; the plants cannot be closed for repair with such a weakened economy. And the cost to build new plants far exceeds the ability to pay for them. [1] A vast number of atomic weapons shall be mentioned in the final chapter of this book.

Eastern Europe, the broken Yugoslavian states and the fifteen independent states of the former Soviet Union have elements of conflicting views, and those of Judaism and Islam as well. The roots of ethnic, religious, and nationalistic animosity run deeper than recently formulated treaties, constitutions and elections.

The ethics of each is local —not all embracing. Let us examine the needs of these independent states to make a degree of stability: The motivating force

---

[1] *Financial Times, July 19, 1990.*

of the fifteen independent states was unified as long as they were dominated by communism directed from Moscow. The localized forces now have broken apart. However, under Stalin, they were made economically interdependent. The various Soviets were forced to be interrelated, economically. The purpose was to make all republics of the U.S.S.R. so interdependent that separation would be impossible and all activities of the realm controlled from Moscow. For as strong as these forces were, the forces of nationalism, ethnicity, and divergent religious beliefs were even stronger. They remained unified as long as they had one opponent, but internal and external pressure permitted the opposition to break the bonds of centralized control from Moscow.

Currently, the fifteen new states do not have domestic and foreign trade regulations and treaties; they have no unified currency; nor a standard weights and measures policy. Nor do they have a unified military, either land, sea or air; no command of the nuclear and hydrogen weapons; no uniform structure to enforce the laws and treaties among the republics. Lastly and very importantly, there is no agreement on human rights.

Foreign capital purchasing state property comes from Germany, France, England, Japan, Italy, Canada, Holland, Finland, Sweden, South Korea, Taiwan, Hong Kong, and the United States. The board rooms where policy on property and labor is determined will not be in the new republics. Unless care is exercised by the governments of these new republics, policy will be set in the headquarters of corporations located outside these republics. This is not necessarily equated with democracy.

In the absence of central military forces, how will border conflicts be controlled? Communist leaders and bureaucrats of yesterday are leaders of the so-called democratic movement, today. Should this pattern remain the same? Equating the promise of democracy with "the free market" under current conditions is highly open to question.

It appears there is not enough capital in any republic at this time to purchase state owned plants which are on sale at auction. Neither can private citizens, for lack of funds, purchase the property. Consequently, foreign interests find a profitable market in which to invest their capital.

Not until society as a whole awakens to the stark realization that *violence on the local level* affects the entire world community, and that the use of violence as a method for teaching ethical standards is of itself destructive, can one begin to look toward a secure future.

The world society has undergone both fundamental and drastic changes in the last five hundred years. The fracturing of Western Christianity during the Reformation, the Counter-Reformation, and the wars of religion have merged with the application of modern science, medicine and technology, to produce the sophisticated atomic and hydrogen weapons of today.

The religious fervor of colonial expansion became deeply implanted in the Western Hemisphere, Africa, and India. Those forces made the nation-state, the expansion of Europe, and its colonial world possible.

Contained within the structure of western imperial expansion at the beginning of this century were ideas that challenged the colonial system and the Nation-State system as well. The ethical, moral and religious institutions and their ideas today are being assaulted. Demands to enforce laws to change certain customs have rekindled a move to restore the kind of religious zeal which played so great a part in the beginning of colonization. There is an underlying sense of amorality and religious fundamentalism in the ideological-religious struggles of today. In this chapter, attention will be focused on the changes taking place in society and the forces that resist them.

There is great technological power —both economical and political— along with a widespread breach between those at the top and those at the bottom of the hourglass economy in Western Society and Japan, in Africa, India, South East Asia, and the new republics of the former Soviet Union. Established institutions make the necessary changes in a time of fundamental, moral, ethical, and religious upheaval in a fractured world order. To whom will the present power be imparted? And will that power now be used to increase the destruction and deprivation so prevalent in the whole of society?

The probable use of the atomic and hydrogen bombs is the ultimate terror under which we live. Weapons are made under the assumption that they will be used. The atomic weapons, much like those which were used on the Japanese over forty years ago, now have the increased capability to destroy the world. This prognosis is not of a doomsday sayer; but, it is a present reality.

The moral and spiritual rationale for the eclipse of all life was formulated by two major superpowers: The United States and the former Soviet Union. Each is highly charged with ideology. The United States, representing an undefined Free World, depicts the symbol of the "Cross and the Crown" to exemplify its spiritual values; while the former Soviet Union depicts the "Hammer and Sickle."

The so-called "peacekeepers," which can bring about instantaneous wholesale death, have so far prevented war among the atomic Hydrogen powers. Much to the contrary, they have had no influence on the conflicts of the near East, Africa, South East Asia, or Latin America. There have been forty times as many war related deaths since World War Two as there were prior to that time.

In exploring some of the major dynamics behind the confrontation of the former Soviet Union and the Western World represented by the United States, the nation-state system plays the dominant role. The Church of Rome was the primary unifier of the Latin Christianity until the Reformation. This relative unity was replaced by a fragmented social order in which each nation-state competed to fill the vacuum created by the collapse of the Church of Rome. Colonial rivalry by Europe and England in the expansion of Europe was a consequence which resulted in the conquest of the New World, Africa, India, South East Asia, and an encroachment upon China.

The Peace of God, as explained previously, that gave a high degree of stability to Latin Christendom, failed to adjust to changing events in the latter days of the Church of Rome.

At the end of the Thirty Years War (1618-48) the Law of Nations was incorporated into the Treaty of Westphalia. The Law of Nations had as its purpose the controlling of warfare. Wherever the colonial, nation-state power system expanded throughout the world, the Law of Nations was carried along to make legal the acquired territories of the European and English powers.

Within this century, there has been a swing against Western colonial policies. Wherever independence has been gained, state-hood has been acquired and recognition granted in conformity with the Law of Nations. Even though colonialism has been removed in the main, the legal, moral psychological, and perhaps some spiritual western concepts have remained.

As the conflicts accelerated among the western powers after the collapse of Latin Christendom, only two would come close to reunifying Europe under one power. Napoleon would make France the unifier in the early 19th Century.

And in this century, Germany would try in both the First and Second World wars to reunify Europe.

Spain and Austria, in the 16th century, would try to unify Europe. And France would try, under Louis XIV, in the last half of the 17th century and the first days of the 18th century. England played one European power against the other and consequently controlled the balance of power in Europe. The combination of conflicts encouraged Czarist Russia to play a greater role in European affairs for what it considered defensive reasons. By the end of World War II, the Soviet Union had moved deep into Western Europe as far as East Berlin and Czechoslovakia.

The power of the United States and England during the First World War was the decisive force in defeating Germany. But the eminent power of the British had already begun to slip by the end of the Boer War (1899-1902); its greatness was consummated by the end of the Second World War.

The rise of Japan also worked to change the configuration of world power in the Far East and in Europe as well. The British Empire could no longer cope with events in Europe, the Near East, and Asia. And the United States, a non-European power, superseded England in dominating the power struggle of East and West.

The intensification of conflict under the Christian absolute monarchs of the nation-states, subsequent to the Reformation, added to the historic animosity of Orthodox Christianity of Czarist Russia and Latin Christianity under the papacy. Subsequent to the French Revolution of 1789, Napoleon conquered Europe. With the defeat of Napoleon, Czarist Russia came deep into Europe as far as France. During the First World War, Czarist Russia and Germany were on opposing sides. At the end of the war, European, Japanese and the United States forces invaded the Soviet Union.

The purpose of the joint invasion was to thwart Lenin's new Soviet government. Fear and hostility against the Czarist system was now transferred to the dictatorship of Lenin. In short: the fear and distrust between Russian Orthodox Christians, on one side, and the Roman Catholics, Lutherans, Protestants, and the Church of England on the other side was replaced by fear of the western power of Soviet Communism. The symbol of the hammer and sickle of Marxian-Leninism represented to the West a "Godless Communism."

The same underlying fear and antitrust still existed on each side. Although these conditions were not created by Vladimir Illich (Nikoali) Lenin and Joseph Stalin, they did, however, intensify them. The Soviet Union took over Czarist Orthodox Russia's fear of Latin Christianity and all the fragmentation that arose from the Reformation. Orthodox Russia professed to have the only correct knowledge and destiny of humankind. This declaration was superseded by Soviet Communism and, in the same fashion, it professed to be without error. Its philosophy, based upon scientific socialism, expounded an unerring ability to foresee the correct course for humankind and how it was bound to develop.

There were, in Medieval Latin Christian history, certain subjects in theology that might be discussed by the rule of reason. But others, such as dogma, had to be accepted on faith. The latter was known by divine revelation. The same is true in Marxian-Leninism. Certain issues, those such as the class struggle theory, and the dialectic process were not matters subject to debate; they were accepted as matters beyond question. Where the *Party* makes a declaration, it speaks ex-Cathedra, it is infallible. This hypothesis, notwithstanding other aspects of history, scientific socialism can be applied to any field of knowledge such as Euclidean or non-Euclidean, geometry, physics, biology, music, and art. [1]

The essence of the state was the Party in the Soviet Union. Its purpose was to carry out the pseudo-scientific policy of the state. The primary enemy of the Soviet Union, from its viewpoint, was western capitalism. The policy of the party, hence the state, was to overthrow by revolution the enemies of the Soviet Union and thereby build a worldwide society of the working class. Russian orthodoxy had the same idea toward Latin Christians and all other religions, as well as the fragmentation that emerged from the reformation.

In the early days of the Sixteenth Century when the people began to pour in from the old world, beginning "the expansion of Europe" and the "age of colonization," with their luggage, they brought along their religious, ethical and philosophic views.

The Spanish and the Portuguese, around 1519, began a domination of Latin America which lasted three hundred years. Spain had just ended an eight hundred years struggle with Islam, which resulted in the Spanish re-conquest of Iberia. The re-conquest began a bloody spectacle in 711 with Iberian Christians fighting Muslims, Jews and Moriscos (a people with a mixture of Spanish and Moor from North Africa) and ended in 1492. The Spanish killed one quarter of a million people and at the end of this costly re-conquest there were soldiers and civilians —ready and eager to conquer the new world.

---

[1] *Sabine, Op. cit.*

Under the viceroy of New Spain, centered in Mexico, and the viceroy of Peru, in Latin America, there was in 1519 an estimated twenty five million population. By the end of the colonial period, 1820-21, the population had decreased to some twelve and one half million.

The viceroy derived his authority from the Christian kings of Spain who in turn derived their authority from God. The inquisitors, the clergy, the military, and the landed aristocracy —under the authority of the imperial Spanish crown— placed a Christian veneer over the religion and culture of the Inca world in the Andes mountain range; the Maya and others of Central America; and a multitude of Indians in the Aztec confederation of Central Mexico as well. The deprivation, starvation, excessive overwork, malnutrition, and uprooting of the tribal Indian, has few parallels in recorded history.

The English, with similar aspirations, came to the New World to convert the Indians and take over their land. Of those Indians which they did not kill or exile to the west, they subjugated.

Some of the predecessors of this struggle to evangelize the New World were derived from the Old Testament, the well-known Christian fear of the wilderness. [1] Combined with this fear is an obsession to subdue it and establish dominion over it. An even greater component of this same fear and the obsession to dominate it is to be possessed by the spirits of the wild people of the wilderness. Whereas Christians look upon possession negatively, in a number of other cultures there is a wish to seek out and become one with a power greater than one's self.

A fundamental part of the mission of Christ was to cast out devils. Heavy emphasis is placed upon demonic possession in both the Old and New Testament. The early Christian church held exorcism to be a principle part of Christian faith, and its use was extensive. The Christian venture of the Portuguese, Spanish, French and English into the New World was confronted with horror by the religious practices of the indigenous Indians. Their dances, symbols, drums and incantations were bad enough, but their spiritual leaders wore masks. Assuredly, they thought that Satan had come to the New World in an advance guard to lead the people astray. Consequently, the Christians developed an aversion to the Indians.

Although the Christians were to conquer the Indians and take over their

---

[1] *"Beyond Geography, The Western Spirit Against the Wilderness"*, Frederick Turner, Viking, New York, 1980.

land, marriage with them was not permitted. They believed the Indian religion was false. God had prohibited the Israelites from marrying outside their religion, thereby sustaining tribal purity, and solidarity. The same policy was ascribed to the Christians in the New World. It was not an easy policy to follow, particularly for the English who fervently tried to prevent intermarrying by sending white women to the New World by the shipload; and by enacting stiff penalties on those who married Indians.

With the promotion of black slavery in Spanish and Portuguese America, and among the British colonies as well, the same negative positions were taken toward the African people. They too were considered outside the pale. Uprooted from their African heritage, they were under white domination and subject to Christian conversion; as were the Indians. Conversion was at times made possible through frontier missions.

Parallel with the conquest of the western hemisphere by the British, and later as independent people pushed westward, in the United States there was the massacre of the North American Indians, the slaughter of buffalo, and the expansion of legalized slavery, along with the beginning of industrialization. However, as a result of the government's policy and the white people's hostility toward them, it was feared around the beginning of this century that the Indian population of the United States might be coming to an end.

In the United States, the civil war wreaked havoc on the confederation: destroying its legal system, splintering its political parties and with the exception of the Roman Catholic, created antagonistic disagreements within the Christian church. Each side of the bitter conflict was supported by the Christian religious institutions and the authority of the Holy Bible.

The British colonial people, after gaining their own independence, had conflicts with the Indians and drove them west. Some were restricted to reservations. Treaties were made with the Indians, and repeatedly broken. One need go no further than to read Dee Brown's "*Bury My Heart At Wounded Knee*" to find how true this was. Toward the end of the 19th and the beginning of the 20th century, the Indian population was virtually extinct.

The United States, in the nineteenth and twentieth centuries was flooded with people from England, Ireland, Scotland, Western and Eastern Europe, Russia, Italy, and Greece. Since the Second World War, waves of immigrants from the Near East, India, Vietnam, Laos, Cambodia, China and Japan have joined these people; each group bringing with them their own divergent culture.

There now seems to be a re-evaluation of what is called "our historical values," with the bitterness of the Vietnam War, with the Watergate fiasco, with the acceleration and decline of Soviet power, with desegregation and civil rights laws, in combination with these new people. When the Irish came to the United States, they brought with them the bitterness which existed between them and the British. The same was true for the animosity that existed between the Germans and the Polish in Western Europe. The hostility between the Roman Catholics and the Russian Orthodox in Europe would be fired anew in the United States. The Italian and the Greek newcomers added to the ethnic disputes among the non-English. And the acrimony that the English had for all of them was not to be discounted. Disputes between all ethnic groups that were jockeying for power were found in the market place, the work place, and in the political arena as well. Much of the conflicts were unfortunately hidden under an ethnic religious veneer.

Although Christianity and Islam have spread far and wide, so rooted are the people in their particular erudition that each has failed to incorporate the whole and neither has made successful their goal to adjust to an alien culture into which they have immigrated. Beneath these areas, such as in the New World, in Africa, and elsewhere, indigenous religions thought to have been overcome are breaking through to the surface. For example: in the United States and in Latin America, some of the the cults are intermixed with Christianity. Consequently, at this juncture, neither Christianity nor Islam has become world-wide. However, both profess a separateness and distinction from the other and many wars continue to be fought with religious sanction.

Currently, in some of the major cities and the coastal areas of the United States, and in the poverty war-torn areas of Central America, violent groups are organized to wage a form of war against immigrants from Southeast Asia and China. Protestant fundamentalism in the West is on the rise. It occupies a deep-seated and constant place in colonial independent history.

Symbols such as: "God Bless America," "In God We Trust," "One Nation Under God," and "Manifest Destiny," should give some indication of the degree to which religion plays in the ideology of the United States. Such phrases are embedded much deeper into the ethics of our political activity than one may be aware. The implication in some of the phrases could be construed that God is completely confined to the territory of the United States.

One now can hear that Thomas Jefferson had God as co-author in writing the Declaration of Independence. [1] This hypothesis was perceived by no less an authority than Jerry Falwell, the Evangelical leader, and Jack Kemp, a cabinet member in President George Bush's administration. Both men publicly stated that "God's last hope on earth is Christian America." This hope, they say, is supported by the strongest military force on earth. "God is the author of our liberty." The boldness of these statements also encompass the Declaration of Independence, which established the philosophical ideas of liberty that are etched in the Bill of Rights of The Constitution.

In the New York Times on October 8, 1984, Anthony Lewis stated that the most profound political achievement of President Ronald Reagan could well have been granting political legitimacy and power to religious fundamentalists who want to make the United States into their image as a "Christian Nation."

The American Coalition For Traditional Values, a new organization, was formed by the religious right in June, 1984 and a reception was given in the White House where President Ronald Reagan and Vice President George Bush attended. President Reagan praised the organization for its "potential to speak to the millions of committee Christians."

In the fall of 1985, the ACTV had a seminar in Washington, D.C. The featured speakers were Jack Kemp and Jerry Falwell. The speakers were associated with the Reverends Jimmy Swaggart, James Robinson, Jim Bakker, D. James Kennedy, and Pat Robertson. Reverend Tim LaHaye, Chairman of ACTV took the opportunity to announce that, "We have historically been a religious nation, not a secular one — America has been blessed because it was founded on Biblical principles."

The assertion that America is a Christian nation is a comparatively recent idea which the fundamentalist and the conservative evangelists use to promote political action in the belief that the Bible should be *the guide* for America. If that were the case for example then whose interpretation should one follow, and what would be the status of the Jews and those who are non-believers? And are the latter considered to be against God? From this it would follow that a strong national defense is necessary and this nation is "God's special tool on Earth." Fundamentalist teachings demand that Christians accept the Bible as "revealed, inspired, infallible and inerrant."

The historic position of fundamentalism has been, for the most part, that

---

[1] *The Plain Dealer, December 15, 1985. The New York Times, October, 8, 1984.*

Christians should form their lives outside the main stream of society; to separate their lives from the evils of the world. Since the 1970's, the position has changed. Fundamentalists now have moved into the role of political action; this being looked upon as their duty. Jerry Falwell sees America and its citizens as God's modern day chosen people to be used for His purpose. To Falwell, militarism is glorified as "the means of defending the peace so that law and order may prevail, allowing Christians the freedom to spread the message of Jesus Christ to the world . . .." " . . .to see freedom preserved so that the gospel may go on un-hindered in the generations ahead." There is a striking similarity between Falwell's ideas to promote Christianity with those purposed by the Emperor Constantine and Pope Sylvester (314-335), and subsequent popes from the early days in the 4th century, onward.

There indeed appears to be a correlation between the advent of the technological age and the material and educational demands which are part of a changing society. This connection holds true for Muslims, Jews, and Christians.

When religious practices are in vogue for many years, they often become fixed in people's psyche and gradually acquire an aspect of divinity. But whenever these teachings are confronted by social change, they are often met with strong resistance and confrontation, resulting in hostility and violence. As religious traditions become fixed, they grind against other ideas and philosophies. This confrontation occurs among all practices of social conduct associated with religious teachings. Fundamentalism thrives on confrontation.

A glimpse into the late fifteenth and sixteenth century European and English history gives a considerable insight into the late twentieth century fundamentalism in the United States. Among myriad reasons for the expansion of Europe was the belief that its people were spreading the one true faith to the heathen in order to convert them to Christ. If they become rich in the process there was no conflict since it was believed to be in accordance with God's plan.

The English not only believed in the superiority of their faith, they felt that their values were superior to African and North American darker-skinned people. This served as justification for the English to enslave the Indians and the Africans and was consistent with the Christian doctrine which permitted enslavement of non-Christians.

Virtually all the colonists accepted the concept of God; however, they did not agree on the same approach in understanding God. The Pilgrims and the Puritans were non-conformists and did not support the Church of England as did those who settled in Jamestown. The Quakers settled in Pennsylvania and the Roman Catholics resided in Maryland; whereas the Dutch Reform and the Jews located in New Amsterdam. Although sharp differences existed among them; they all professed to believe in God. Roger Williams, however, welcomed all faiths into his colony, even pagans. [1] The colonists were not as devout as commonly believed. By 1700, less than one in twenty belonged to any church, even in Massachusetts.

Religious differences became sharper in the late 18th Century. Thomas Jefferson supported the Virginia Statute enacted in 1779 to avoid religious favoritism in Virginia. This statute gave unrestricted religious liberty. There was no reference to God, with the drafting of the constitution in 1789. In Article Six of the Constitution, it clearly stated that there shall be no religious qualifications for any office or public trust. The Congress is furthermore prohibited from enacting any laws respecting the establishment of religions, or prohibiting the free exercise thereof. These provisions of the Constitution clearly are not in conformity with the viewpoint of the fundamentalists.

Whatever was omitted from the Constitution of 1789 pertaining to God, the document gave legal recognition for another form of tyranny —*slavery*. The slave was considered to be only three fifths of a person for purposes of determining delegates in the House of Representatives of Congress. This legal status remained in the Constitution until the end of the Civil War in 1865 at which time it was excluded by the provisions in the Thirteenth Amendment.

During and after the Civil War, until late into the 20th Century, Christian churches can be said to have supported slavery and its expansion. Indeed, prior to the Civil War, most Protestant churches split, supporting both sides of the blood conflict and the psychological, social and legal remains are still with us.

After the Civil War, the new amendments afforded little for the former slaves during the remainder of the 19th Century, and the American Indians were pushed further and further back to the point of being almost eradicated from the land by the beginning of the 20th Century. A well founded fear was that the original Americans might die out as a result of western expansion and the numerous wars against them. There were 2,500 African people lynched

---

[1]*"Holy Blood, Holy Terror"*. *"The Fundamentalists War on American Freedoms In Religion"*. *"Politics and Our Private Lives"*, Flo Conway and Jim Siegelman, Doubleday and Company, Inc., Garden City, New York, 1982. *An excellent source.*

from 1884 to 1900, and by 1914, some 1,000 more. A graphic account of this age of violence is given in From slavery To Freedom: A History of Negro Americans [1]

Fundamentalism has now reached into the political arena to gain its ends; not only on a national scale in the United States, but worldwide. Its means are modern technology and salesmanship. The current evangelic fundamentalist is promoting Christianity by means of radio and television, and by establishing foreign missions throughout the world. Although this is primarily Protestant, some charismatic Roman Catholics can also be counted. It is using the free exercise of hatred, violence, and the threat of violence. The growing number of paramilitary organizations and "survival schools," inspired by evangelical ideology, can be seen as an extension of this violence. Much of the mounting hatred for Jews, African Americans, Hispanics, Indians and Southeast Asian immigrants is significant and has its genesis from the same source. Although the fundamentalist may deny the relationship, the weight of evidence would suggest otherwise.

One must remember that with Emperor Constantine, the Christian world began a history of the use of violence upon disbelievers and non-conformists. Currently, there are fundamentalists who are lauding Israel in its conflict with Islam. It is seen as an in-gathering of Jews to the Holy Land, thus a fulfillment of the prophecy of the New Testament. These Christian fundamentalists believe that the second coming of Christ, and the end of the world, depends upon the return of the Jews to their homeland. A great conflict will take place between two nations, believed to be Israel and some Islamic state supported by the former Soviet Union. [2] The Christians who support Zionists on this basis are the same ones who believe "God almighty does not hear the prayer of the Jew." That statement issued in 1980 by the Reverend Bailey Smith, President of the Southern Baptist Convention, concurs with Jerry Falwell's assertion that Jews are "spiritually blind and desperately in need of their Messiah and Savior."

The fundamentalists seem to have a fixation with the Jews and the State of Israel. Jerry Falwell exemplified this position by declaring himself a supporter of the Zionists. Falwell also received a medal from the former Prime

---

[1] *"From Slavery to Freedom: A History of Negro Americans",* John Hope Franklin, Knopf, New York, 1980.

[2] *New York Times Magazine, August 18, 1986. "Are You Running With Me Jesus?",* Tel-evangelist Pat Robertson Goes For the White House, Michael Krainser. *Also, consult Cult Awareness Network, and Citizens Freedom Foundation, P.O. Box 608370, Chicago, Il 60626, Telephone, (312) 267-7777.*

Minister, Manachem Begin, honoring him for his position on Israel.

Christian and Islamic religious beliefs take on a significant role in the imbroglio of Israel and the Near East. To the Zionist, the Muslim, the indigenous Christian, and the Christian fundamentalist of the United States, the interpretation of that role is Armageddon. Also referred to as the Apocalypse, Armageddon is prophesied in the Bible as a violent battle of the final struggle between good and evil.

In the last chapter of the New Testament, in speaking of the final days before the second coming of Christ, and the end of the world, it is written that the tribes of Israel dispersed throughout the world shall return to their ancient homeland. A great war in the area shall then take place and this will be a prelude for the last days of the world —*Days of Violence.*

President Reagan —himself a member of the Moral Majority— supported the idea of "*the final days.*" He used the prophecy of the battle of Armageddon to support his sale of AWAC's to Saudi Arabia, and also for the military build up to support his position in the Near East. He repeatedly described the Soviet Union as the empire of "*evil,*" and depicted the struggle as one of "*good against evil.*" Was this not a striking similarity to the final days conflict?

President Reagan's pratice in foreign policy was to support the most ruthless rulers, as long as they were in opposition to the Soviet Union. The events in Haiti and the Philippine Islands hardly changes the picture; the movement to throw out both dictators came not from his administration but from overwhelming forces within each nation. When President Ferdinand Marcos, of the Phipippines, and President Jean-Claude Duvalier, of Haiti were finally ousted from their respective countries, Reagan's administration assisted both dictator-presidents to points of safety; they took with them a great portion of the wealth from their people. Up to the time when they were overthrown, both Marcos and Duvalier, were considered bastions against the forces of "evil."

Religious fanaticism knows no bounds, and its forces are legion. The literal interpretation of the Bible reaches beyond the evangelical throngs by way of radio and television. Frequently, it finds the proper soil in which to grow by promulgating conflict and fear to all with whom its adherents are in disagreement.

Conflict and fear are indeed the common denominators which unite extreme fundamentalists. Their fears cover a range of rapidly changing social directives: the crisis of the civil rights movement, the backlash of the Vietnam War, the farm crisis, the growing number of people living in poverty, the incursion of Hispanic and Asian people into the U.S., the crisis in the Near East, and the confrontation with the Soviet Union and result of its final collapse. An additional factor which is causing fear and conflict is that in the United States, some 35 million people now are living below the poverty level.

The Watergate ignominy was another shocking discovery which left American citizens desperately struggling with their ideals and religious convictions, social customs, and personal identities in a modern world society where change is the only thing constant. All these conflicts left them with an overwhelming fear.

A drastic increase in the use of drugs is now found in virtually all segments of society. The number of secret youth gangs in the major cities is escalating. Individuals who are not a part of the mainstream, may possess a strong sense of alienation from society. They also may feel threatened by what they consider to be their enemy: [1] the Jew, the African-American, the Hispanic, and the Asian. This is precisely what happened in the developmental years of the Nazi movement under Hitler. Some people have chosen to join forces with those who have similar fears and anxieties as a means by which to diminish their own fears. They hold secret meetings under the theory that there is strength in numbers. Religious ideas are used to support the growing paramilitary and neo-Nazi movements in the United States.

The origin of these immure fundamentalist support groups go back to the Book of Revelations in which its members refer to as the Mark of the Beast. They foresee a war against Satan in the final days and fear that they shall have the mark of the Beast upon them:

Revelations 19: 20:

> And the beast was taken, and with him the false prophet that wrought miracles before him, with which he deceived them that had received the mark of the beast, and them that worshipped his image. These both were cast alive into a lake of fire burning with brimstone.

Revelations 14: 11:

> And the smoke of their torment ascended up forever and ever; and they have no rest day nor night, who worship the beast and

---

[1] *"Hitler", Joachim C. Fest, Vintage Random House, New York, 1973.*

his image, and whosoever receiveth the mark of his name.

The fundamentalist basis for hostility toward the Jews stems from their refusal to accept Christ as the Messiah. They also believe African Americans to be the "Sons of Cain" and without a soul. From these kinds of hypothesizes, the fundamentalists hope, insofar as possible, to create chaos and destruction as a means to serve their own end.

The following is a partial list of destructive organizations:

Church of The Creator

American White Bastion

Ku Klux Klan

Populist Party

National Agricultural Press Association

Committee to Restore the Constitution

Branch Davidian (David Koresh)

Silent Brotherhood (Bruder Schweigen)

American Nazi Party

The Skin Heads

The Way International

Scientology

National State's Rights Party

White Revolutionary Army

Posse Comitatus

Christian Identity Movement

Aryan Nations

Anti- Lawyer Party

Liberty Lobby

National Alliance

White American Political Association

American Forces of National Liberation

Satanic Cults

White Patriot Party

Alamo Christian Church Confederate Knights of the Ku Klux Klan
The Order,The Covenant, The Sword, and The Arm of The Lord Mountain
Church of Jesus Christ Christian   Church of Jesus Christ

The effect of some of the destructive cults was explained in a paper entitled "Destructive Cults In The United States," which the author presented in Chicago in 1987, to the "International Society for the Study of Multiple Personalities and Dissociative States."

Today, there are from 3,500 to 5,000 cults in America. The spread in numbers is that many operate under different names; however, they are the same operation.

Dr. Michael Langone, Director of Research and Education for the American Family Foundation in Massachusetts describes a cult as follows:

> A destructive cult is a group which: a) dictated —sometimes in great detail— how members should think, feel and act; b) claims a special exalted status for example: occult powers or a mission to save humanity for itself, and/or its reader(s) that usually sets it in opposition to the mainline society and/or the family; c)

exploits its members, psychologically, financially or physically; d) utilizes various mind-control techniques, especially those which denigrate independent critical thinking, to recruit prospects and make members loyal, obedient, and subservient; and e) causes considerable psychological harm to many of its members and to members families.

Dr. Langone believes that some people may think a group destructive if it is deviant or heretical. He stresses that one should reserve judgement in labeling groups which may be exploitative, manipulative, or psychologically dangerous or totalitarian. He further explains that according to this perspective, a group could be deviant and heretical without necessarily being destructive.

For this purpose, "unethical social influence" or "mind control" is described as a process of manipulation used to persuade members of a cult to conform to patterns of thought, feeling and action prescribed by a group.

Various means are used to this end, such as control of information and of alternatives, deception, group pressure, indoctrination of a belief system that negates independent thinking, considers outside troops as evil and threatening, use of inadequate diet, and the induction of dissociative states by narrowing attention and independent thinking.

Those who join destructive cults are from all stations of life and can be deemed psychologically healthy or disturbed at the outset of their experience. Clinical data available indicates that a large number of cultists are relatively young adults prior to joining and as many as one-third of the entire group showed significant psychopathology before becoming members.

Some of the common reasons for joining cults include stress and crisis in adolescence and young adulthood. Other factors are dependency, lack of self-confidence, un-assertiveness, lack of critical evaluation, low tolerance for ambiguity, and the desire for meaning.

Of approximately 3,500 known cults, the most widely known include: The Way International, The Unification Church of Reverend Moon, Church of Scientology, Children of God, Love Family, Est, Hare Krishna, Ton & Susan Alamo's Christian Foundation, The Church of Bible Understanding and a vast number of neo-Nazi organizations.

In understanding what specific kinds of mind control are utilized in most of these groups, a good example is The Way International. Those who follow the movement believe it is the most destructive in mind control and the most effective in its indoctrination. The danger of its indigenous influence was corroborated by a number of specialists working in this field including Sandi Galant, Intelligence Division of San Francisco Police Department and Kenneth Laninng, Cult Division of the F.B.I. in Quantico, Virginia.

The Way International has some 40,000 members and in 1980 reported assets of $3,000,000. By 1985 it had accumulated $30,000,000 in assets. Its new world headquarters are in New Knoxville, Ohio and it operates in all 50 states and at least 62 foreign countries.

John G. Clark, Jr., M.D. of the Harvard Medical School has stated in the Journal of the American Medical Association, July, 1979, that as a general principle about cults: "Subjects become so conditioned to destruction that they accept the use of violence as an end on itself."

He goes on to say that the point has been reached where cult members were willing to injure without scruples. Those familiar with the recent indictments against members of the Hare Krishna movement located in the West Virginia mountains will recall not only murder, but murder committed in the most violent way.

Dr. Douglas Stevens, a clinical psychologist in North Little Rock, Arkansas, who developed a specialty in forensic work has interviewed myriad ex-cult members whose experiences precisely corroborates the findings of all other professionals, including those of Dr. Clark, Jr. Dr. Stevens relates in detail his findings after questioning some ex-cult members in preparation for a trial that involved members of The Way:

> The Way operates with both adults and children and the interventions used would be expected to have an effect on the intellectual and the individuals interviewed described the use of love bombing. This refers to a great deal of hugging and kissing, but after a few years the emotion is conditioned out and it simply becomes a repetitive act whereby thought stopping in possible. In this situation when other members see someone getting out of line, such as doing independent thinking, they besiege them with "love" in such a way as to break up the thought patterns. These people say that this results eventually in a somewhat disassociated state.
>
> Related to this is the use of tongues. They report that speaking in tongues is used as a hypnotic induction technique and also for

thought stopping. The individual is taught to speak in tongues whenever they have some type of evil urge, such as independent thinking. They are strongly reinforced by the group for speaking in tongues; therefore, it becomes a conditional stimulus to a feeling of approval and love. anytime the individual is depressed or feels uncomfortable, they can speak in tongues and feel emotional relief.

The Way, like other cults, attempts to block independent reasoning. Individuals are essentially put into an isolated environment with other members, where everything is either right or wrong, no gray area, no questions allowed and the rest of the world is described as adversarial. Terminology of usual words is refrained so that cult members virtually use a code among themselves. They teach social alienation, social paranoia, hostility toward non-believers (including family members not in the cult), suppression of reason, reinforcement of blind obedience and adherence to group conformity.

One lady who gave information had been in The Way for six years, living on the Rome City Indiana campus. She had been in the group's Family Corps and in their leadership training program. She eventually left the group and had very strong feelings, believing that they were subversive and described their hierarchy as being like Hitler's SS troops.

She described the use of milieu or environmental control. Individuals are kept within the group where every behavior is reinforced or punished and they are within this environment twenty-four hours a day. They are trained to obey instantly anything that is asked.

For the first two years they are kept almost completely isolated, not allowed to go to town or to interact with non-cult members. Peer pressure is utilized to keep them in line. They are convinced that outsiders are the enemy and their only salvation is in remaining close to their fellow members.

A second intervention she called mystical manipulation. This involves public humiliation in which the individual is singled out in front of the whole group and questioned about their non-approved behaviors. She states that she has seen both adults and children brought up before 600 people, yelled at, humiliated and made to feel horrible.

A third intervention is the demand for purity. Everything in The Way is good and Godly and everything outside is evil or devilish. Members are given a 'new mind,' which is perfect. A fourth intervention is confession. It is somewhat similar to AA in that they repeatedly tell others how bad their past life was. They are encouraged to exaggerate to the point that they become convinced themselves that their life in the outside world was evil. They reiterate that entering The Way saved their life. Stories are made up to justify group control and increase the polarization between themselves and others.

The fourth intervention is the public confessions of guilt and every member has to write an autobiography in which they admit to their awful life before. These autobiographies are kept on file and then used as a threat against individuals who later leave the cult and may have an urge to tell the world what happens.

The fifth intervention is called lifting the sacred science. By this is meant that the cult has the truth and nothing but the truth and no one else has it. The cult leader gets direct revelations from God; he is infallible and only his logic is absolute. Leadership is never questioned and people are trained to obey instantly.

A sixth point is obedience over person. This means that the group is more important than any individual. Lack of sleep is used as an important mind control intervention. People will go to bed at 3:00 A.M. and get up at 5:00 A.M. They are told that sleep is boring and that if you really believe in God, you don't need sleep. Lack of protein in the diet is also used.

A seventh point is loading the language. They develop their own jargon so that they can only be understood by members. It is a way of limiting the mind and thought in communication by re-framing abstract words in very specific and concrete ways.

The eighth point mentioned was dispensing of existence. This involves the idea that they are the good people, they have the right to live and everyone else is bad and does not have the right to live. References are made to the sheep and the goats -- the goats being the bad ones or outsiders.

Discipline for children is very strict and punitive and they are taught that this is what the Lord wants them to do. No matter how violent the punishment, it is always justified. Children are also taught to speak in tongues and actually attend classes so that tongues becomes a language of the cult. The respondent indicated that she has seen nine month old babies whose very first word was from the cult's tongues. She said that speaking in tongues was mind stilling.

If the child is brought up in the cult, she felt that by age four, they would need deprogramming and would experience withdrawal symptoms as the entire structure of their world collapsed. She stated incidentally that it is easier to program children as there are no competing ideas to first remove. Children are trained to also respond instantly. Otherwise they are repeatedly spanked until the child jumps immediately when told to do so. Children are rarely taken to physicians, for they are taught to believe that 'if I have to go to a doctor, I am not believing that God will heal.' Also, most physicians are non-members and are therefore a part of the evil world. There is little play time for children. They are either in school, studying or working.

It seems the main thing they do is minimize the influence of the parent while maximizing the influence of the cult and its leader. They inhibit self-expression, creativity, spontaneity, emotional expression and heavily indoctrinate to the point that there is not questioning or abstract thinking, only obedience in thought and action.

Weapons training is carried on for adults and adolescents under the cover-up of a hunter safety course. It is not voluntary training and the training involves immediate obedience.

There are numerous other cults; however, these are the most widely known and perhaps the most violent fundamentalist Christian organizations. [1]

---

[1] *For the next several pages, data was obtained from Cult awareness Network, Chicago, referred to above. The Arkansas Gazette, April 28, 1985, Little Rock, Arkansas and The Baxter Bulletin, April 26, 1985. The former paper in Little Rock and the latter Mountain Home, Arkansas carried extensive material on the*
(continued...)

Many of these organizations are joined by a computer link called the "Aryan Liberty Net." This linkup is sponsored by the Aryan Nations, an organization based in Hayden Lake, Idaho. This network keeps the various organizations informed throughout the nations. It has an additional list of informers and traitors, "those who have betrayed their race." These organizations exist in some 33 states. There are various levels of security clearance of the questioner.

The computer link was set up by Louis Beam of Dallas, Texas, a member of the Ku Klux Klan. The link describes itself as "a pro-American, pro-white, anti-communist network of true believers who serve the one and only 'God— Jesus the Christ,' and that it is "for Aryan patriots only."

Their thesis is that Hitler was a man with a mission, but he made too many mistakes. The group states that they are holy warriors of the Lord, guided by God, and if God says shoot it out, they will. Non-white people are servants of whites and there would have been no racial strife with civil rights had it not been for the Jews.

What do these organizations teach and upon what do they rest? Many of the members of all these movements believe "White Christians of European descent are the true children of Israel and that Jews are the evil seed of Satan."

Members of some organizations stand in a circle around a child who symbolizes racial purity and vow to hold no fear of death in a racial Armageddon that proposes "to deliver our people from Jews and achieve total victory for the Aryan race."

The neo-Nazi groups maintain that the government has been taken over by Jews. Some aspire to establish a "racially pure" white supremacy state in the Pacific Northwest called the White American Bastion. The Christian Identity

---

[1](...continued)
Arkansas-Missouri neo-Nazi organization and its national connections. Also, see The New York Times, October 2, 1985 and for March 3, 1989. Also, the Violence of the Howard Beach Affair on Race, The Geta case, as well the Skinheads Cult, as identified with the Klan, the Aryan nations and others, The Plain Dealer, May 7, 1989, Cleveland, Ohio. Also, see New York Times, April 22, and April 28, 1985. The Baxter Bulletin, April 23, 24, 25, 26, and May 13, 1985. See, The Arkansas Gazette, April 20, 21, 22, 23, 24, 25, 28, 1985 and May 1, 1985. See: The Arkansas Democrat, July 26, 1984, and The Arkansas Democrat, April 21, 23, 24, 26, 28, 1985. Twin Lakes Citizen, April 22, 1985, Mountain Home, Arkansas.

Movement teaches "the Jews were the progeny of the devil and it was the responsibility of the white race to destroy the Jew." Important figures of society are to be assassinated as well as Jews, if they were considered to be traitors to the race. Those marked for death are Henry Kissinger, David Rockefeller, Senator Packwood, and the heads of the major television networks.

The CSA —Covenant, the Sword, and Army of the Lord— teaches that the world could enter a time of peace only after a time of war. Its leader, James D. Ellison, now in prison, quotes the Bible about retribution against invading Assyria. "I believe the Assyrian is in the land. I believe he is in the government. I believe he is in the White House. For this they will call me a treasonous person . . ." "I believe in using the sword. If they are going to punch my ticket, I'm going to punch as many of theirs before they get mine."

Among the extremist there are those who propose to overthrow the government. The plot is set forth in a novel entitled "Turner's Diaries." A violent overthrow of the government is planned by a small group of white supremacists. The program is to be financed by bank robbery and counterfeiting. The ultimate purpose is the detonation of a nuclear device over Tel Aviv.

The Silent Brotherhood maintains that the government, which it refers to as "ZOG" (Zionist Occupation Government), has been taken over by Jews who are the descendants of Satan, who should be exterminated.

Federal officials have found literature detailing a "point system" to achieve status by killing "Federal-officials, blacks, or Jews." In line with these ideas is the Christian Identity movement. It propounds that the Lost Tribes of Israel are actually Aryans with blue eyes and that Jews are impostors.

Stated clearly in a 1982 Aryan National newsletter is their position. "We will have a National racial state," and "at whatever price is necessary." "Just as our forbearers purchased their freedom in blood, so must we." "We will have to kill the bastards."

A newsletter was found in possession of a member of the Order advertising, "a convention in which, if you brought your own little black boy for target practice, you got in free . . ." There was a picture of a little black child with a target drawn on him.

One group, Alamo Christian Church, in Arkansas, supported its pastor in the following of the American Association of Non-denominational Christian Schools. Tony Alamo, the pastor claimed that the Communist party is secretly a division of the Vatican, in the same fashion as the Nazi party was a division of the Vatican in World War II. He also included the F.B.I., the C.I.A., all military and police enforcement agencies, terrorist groups (Neo-Nazi) in the United States as being controlled by Pope John Paul II. These forces are being used against Christians who are not Roman Catholic as well as Jews. Alamo maintained that the Nazi party of Hitler, the Gestapo, the Ustachi, were part of the Vatican's army. In the United States he asserts the President, Ronald Reagan, the Congress, the United States Supreme Court and the armed forces are all under the control of the Vatican. The hatred shown toward the Roman Catholic Church in 1985 caused Arkansas Christians and Jews to support the Roman Catholics of that state.

Alamo quotes from the Bible: Revelations, Daniel, Thessalonians, Matthew, I John, II John, Luke and Mark, to support his views that Pope John II is the Anti-Christ and the Church is the beast. He extends the scope of the Vatican to have agents in the Israeli Knesset as Roman Jesuit rabbis. Pastor Alamo spoke of the end of time and the violent destruction spoken of in The Book of Revelation at great length.

In what sort of activities have these cult groups been involved? Some members visit cemeteries in order to obtain false identification, set up "safe houses" around the country and offer salary bonuses for crimes like armored car holdups. Some are responsible for and have had convictions for numerous murders such as that of Alan Berg, a radio talk show host in Denver, Colorado, and Walter E. West, a former member suspected in a number of robberies, as well as a trooper in Missouri. There was also the robbery of a Brinks armored car in Ukiah, California for more than three million dollars. They were also involved in obtaining illegal firearms, semiautomatic rifles, submachine guns, antitank and antiaircraft guns and thousands of rounds of ammunition.

Members of the Order have been charged under a federal racketeering statute with 67 crimes including arson, robberies, and murders that have netted more than four million dollars, and for counterfeiting. Others were involved in a plot to overthrow the government, and to assassinate prominent Jews, such as Norman Lear, the television producer, and Baron Eli de Rothschild, the French banker. Armored tanks were found under construction, dynamite, P.C.B. and cyanide to take if caught by federal or state agents.

In northern Arkansas, April, 1985, a large encampment was found with barracks, buildings, escape tunnels, and an entire silhouette city was found for practice in taking over small rural towns. In California, large amounts of gold and the remains of the Brinks robbery were discovered.

Several children, apparently kidnapped, were taken from a camp by armed forces of the Arkansas, and Missouri state police and federal marshals. In the compound there was an image of a state policeman with the star of David which had been used for target practice. There was also an armored car under construction. The head of the camp was convicted on racketeering charges in connection with bombing a natural gas main pipeline in Arkansas, an attempt to defraud an insurance company, the burning of a homosexual church in Missouri, and the burning of a synagogue in Indiana.

Other groups had plans for the destruction of utilities and communications facilities as well as several dam sites. A textbook entitled "The Road Back" is used for instruction on weapons use and guerrilla warfare. It included twenty chapters on weaponry.

The theology of the Moral Majority, now known as the Liberty Federation, has the same thesis as the extreme fundamentalists. Both parties expound on the theological justification for the use of violence. Their purpose for violence may be differently described; however, there is little question as to its use. If one group uses the Bible to justify its violence, there is no way in which its use can be restricted to just that one group.

If the political leaders of a nation rest their collection and building of arms on theology, there is nothing to prevent the political-fundamental extremists from formulating its base and goals upon the same hypothesis. The Biblical reference for one is no different for one as it is for the other.

Scholars of the American religious scene state that many people in this country are flocking to the ultra-fundamentalist Christian sects. Leaders of these groups are persons who have virtually unlimited control over their members. Dr. Ronald Enroth of Westmont College in Santa Barbara, California —a specialist in the study of this field— said: "They claim they alone are plugged into the Almighty, they practice elitism, authoritarian control that almost always dips into the personal lives of its members, and they try to lead them away, isolate them from the rest of society."

Reginald Alev, the former executive director of Citizens for Freedom, located in Chicago, Illinois, states these groups that split from fundamentalists give almost absolute authority to their leaders.

Former members of the Community Chapel and Bible Training Center, near Seattle, Washington, state that their leader, Donald Alee Barnett has erected "mind control" over his church members, about 3,000 in number. Because of the conduct of the group under Barnett's direction, local King

County Police Department officers are carrying out criminal investigations of the center members and armed guards of the church because of alleged sexual abuse to children as young as 12 years of age.

Many local groups in the United States may operate in privacy and number from as low as a dozen or more; however, the strongly established groups throughout the country number into the thousands.

The Cult Awareness Network of Chicago, Illinois, which studies these organizations, alleges that the side effect of the emergence of Christian fundamentalist in the last decade is the ultra-fundamentalist, its proliferation, and the wide use of evangelist television which promise their followers a solution to their life problems.

Some researchers state that the roots of the organization are staked in Argentina with an Assembly of God pastor, Juan Carlos Ortiz. He organized a highly structured movement in 1970 and the group was brought to the United States in 1972 by Bob Mumford, a Bible teacher from Ft. Lauderdale, Florida. One group is called the Christian Growth Ministries, another large umbrella group is called the Christian Restoration Ministries, located in Wheaton, Maryland. And the movement continues to grow at a rapid pace.

The fundamentalist belief is that the Bible is literally true is the common thread which they share. A special relation to God is shared by their leaders; therefore, they profess divinity for themselves. Their followers are said to be the chosen people; that their leaders have been placed on earth by God to guide them to heaven. These leaders, considered to be shepherds of God, control the life of all members; instructing them what to read; what to watch on television; and with whom to associate. This type of mind control reminds Dr. Enroth of the power structure of the late Reverend Jim Jones, founder and leader of The People's Temple, who in 1978 took his group to Guyana, South America and instructed some 900 members in a mass suicide.[1]

The final measure of alienation and confrontation which may be evolving in the ultra-fundamentalist groups can be seen in the followers of Charles Manson. *Helter Skelter,* which Manson spoke of and acted out was predicated on the New Testament thesis of The Book of Revelation.

A group of black Puerto Ricans, who go by the name of *Move,* had an alienation-confrontation in 1978 with the police in Philadelphia, Pennsylvania.

---

[1] *The New York Times, June, 1986.*

Professor Murray Miran, of Syracuse University, states that "Society continues to reject them because they act out and provoke hostility. This reinforces the isolation they need —there can't be interaction between society and the group, or the group will disintegrate." [1]

A vital point to recognize is that the neo-Nazi groups: the ultra-fundamentalists, the street gangs, and the underworld —regardless of class or personal position— are all in need of confrontation which supports their already established alienation and use of violence. As the younger ultra-fundamentalists begin to age and grow in number, their alienation is enhanced and their psyche becomes fixed. As a result, positive dialogue with the outside becomes hardened and impossible. Alienation arises in direct proportion to whatever people are taught to believe their opponents personify, "evil" as opposed to "good."

The bombing of abortion clinics also is based upon theological grounds. A federal jury returned a verdict on all counts against two twenty-one year old men accused of bombing clinics that performed abortions. The defense lawyer, Paul Shimek, quoted scriptures and presented a fundamentalist preacher. All defendants were active in the Assembly of God Church. The defendants claimed to be following a higher law in opposing abortion. All those who participated in the crime plead not guilty.

In this case, however, God was alleged to be "the thirteenth juror" and "an indicated co-conspirator."

Thomas Dillard, the United States District Attorney for the Northern District of Florida, said that if they committed crimes in the name of religion, they were no different from the terrorist of the Middle East or Northern Ireland. He said: "It's frightening to see what happens when you put religion into a lawsuit like this. We are not the forces of Satan. Satan isn't on trial. God certainly isn't on trial."

The leading defense attorney, T. Patrick Monaghan, cited a letter from President Reagan saying "something must be done" to stop abortions.

The neo-Nazi organizations and their leadership are being pursued under the Racketeering Influenced and Corrupt Organization Act. An interesting corollary presents itself regarding the morality of those engaged in "legitimate" and "illegitimate" enterprises. Russel Mokhiber, staff attorney at

---

[1] *Newsweek, May 27, 1985.*

the Corporate Accountability Research Group, currently preparing a book on Corporate crime, has made the double standard operating in the United States clear.   Attacks of the law have been made that it does not apply to the "legitimate" business such as General Motors, E.F. Hutton, Lloyds of London, Shearson/American Express, Price Waterhouse, and Peat Marwick Mitchell, all of which have been made defendants in civil anti-racketeering lawsuits.

The United States Supreme Court set the record clear. The Court held that Congress wanted to reach both "legitimate" and "illegitimate" enterprises. The former enjoys neither an inherent incapacity for criminal activity nor immunity from its consequences. A strong campaign is under way to change this law as applicable to "legitimate" enterprises. This drive comes at a time when corporate crime is at a high level.

G. Robert Blakey, Professor of Law at Notre Dame and former Chief Counsel of the Senate Subcommittee that drafted the statute, states the case clearly when he said "corporate crime defense lawyers are suggesting that if certain ethnic groups wear black shirts and white ties and engage in criminal conduct, it is all right to call them 'racketeers,' but individuals who wear Brooks Brothers suits and white collars and engage in similar conduct ought to be called by less pejorative names." [1]

The use of and the justification for violence is a common feature in the United States and there appears to be an increasing number of people who are becoming conditioned to it. There are roughly 10,000 people killed by crimes with handguns in the United States each year, accounting for 25 people each day.

More than 50,000 Americans are either murdered or commit suicide each year. In the last decade, handguns were used in the murder of 100,000 Americans. And of this number, 700 were police officers. This is in sharp contrast to those which listed handgun murders reported in 1983, with 4 in England, 92 in Japan and 6 in Canada.

The murder rate appears to be accelerating in the United States. Louis J. West of the University of California at Los Angeles School of Medicine, states that if we had the same death rate from any infectious disease, millions of dollars would be spent for its eradication.

The murder rate in the United States in 1960 was 5 for every 100,000

---

[1] *The New York Times, September 14, 1985.*

individuals. This was five times the rate of 19 other developed countries. The rate doubled in twenty years in the United States. In the other 19 other countries, the rate was about one for every 100,000. In the group from fifteen to twenty four years of age in the United States, the major cause has been violent death and injury. And Louis West concludes, "Here's a country that's having an epidemic . . ." [1] There is considerable evidence to also indicate that in the process, a new generation of poor youth is being dehumanized.

The plight in New York City is an example of what is taking place in most all major cities in the United States, and perhaps in all major cities of the world. New York City has more homeless and hungry people now than at any time since the great depression. One out of four live below the poverty line; of which the federal line is $10,178 a year for a family of four. It is virtually impossible to live on such a low income in New York City. For the wealthy, New York City is a place of prosperity and pleasure; for the poor, the homeless, and the poor elderly; it is a place of despair. Emanuel Tobier, an economist, predicted that by 1990 in New York City, one in three would be living in poverty. And Sidney H. Schomberg, [2] reports that New Yorkers consider crime the worst problem facing the city.

Senator Daniel Patrick Moynihan, recently stated that "The U.S. today is the first society in history where children are much worse off than adults," since some 13.8 million people representative of the population under the age of eighteen live in poverty. Forty eight percent of all black children live in poverty and poor white children outnumber poor black children two to one.

In New York City some 700,000 families live on incomes less than the poverty line. Some fifty percent of the babies born in 1980 will be on welfare before they reach eighteen years of age. And an estimated 3,000 babies in this city are born addicted to drugs each year, 10,000 children live in shelters and hotels for the homeless, 12,000 were abused or neglected so severely they had to be removed from their homes. The problem is made worse by the breakdown of the family. It is estimated that the Special Services Program in the city will have to cope with some 69,000 children this year suffering from abuse and neglect. The rate of such cases increases ten percent each year.

The author, Claude Brown, painted a graphic picture of the

---

[1] *Scientific American, October, 1985.*

[2] *The New York Times Magazine, June 5, 1986, What Kids Who Aren't Wolves Say About Wilding. The New York Times, May 1, 1989. Notebook, Murder He Wrote, Robert Fulford, September, 1986.*

dehumanization of the emerging youth of Harlem. Brown states: "In the streets of my boyhood, today's manchild is now more knowledgeable, more amicable, and more likely to commit murder, than in the 1940's and the 1950's." He further stated that, "Among today's young black men are many who prefer prison and possible death to abject poverty. This poses a challenge that society continues to ignore, with tragic consequences. Manchild is the product of a society so rife with violence that killing, mugging, or robbing a victim is now fashionable."

The following is a dialogue between Brown and a New York youth involved in crime which further illustrates the point:

"That's what they do now," the 16 year old Harlemite said.
"That's what who does now?" I asked, not understanding.
"You know, you take their stuff and you pop' (shoot) em."
"You mean shooting the victims is in style, like wearing a pair of Pony jogging shoes or a Pierre Cardin suit?"
"Yeah, its wrong to kill somebody. But you gotta' have dollars, right?"

"This is the new manchild enigma. He is so deadly," Brown concluded.

The future is bleak for the youths who are in the 35 million people who live below the poverty level. And youth gangs are accelerating and committing crimes in record numbers in nearly all major cities. A major preoccupation for these groups is securing drugs which creates its own dynamics as they openly fight for turf.

A growing alienation among the disadvantaged is complicated by the fact that the social-economic elite are separating themselves from the alienated ranks of society. An increasing number of people are sharing less and less in the economic-social and spiritual benefits of society; therefore, they are becoming more impoverished which results in turn with an escalation of violence.

CHAPTER EIGHT

LATIN AMERICA, SOUTH AFRICA and INDIA

IN THE WORLD SETTING

It has been approximately five hundred years since the Spanish and Portuguese colonized Latin America. Religion played a major role in the conquest and domination of Latin America which lasted about three hundred years. Although Latin American won its independence over 150 years ago, this vast area has been dominated by "the baleful trinity" composed of the Church, the landed aristocracy, and the military.

Only within recent years have an appreciable number of the clergy begun to recognize the deprivation which this prolonged legacy of domination has produced. Throughout the major part of the last five hundred years, the church played a major role in the lives of the faceless millions of this area.

When the Dutch and English expanded into South Africa, along with them went their version of Christianity which helped to play a dominate role in the practice of apartheid for the mass of Black Africans in that area. The Dutch and English were diligent in their quest to reform the indigenous people and have them become Christians; however, they were less than eager to place them in the white man's social-economic order. The same religion brought to these people was, in fact, deemed to have the basis to keep them out of the social order. And this basis remains the crisis there, today.

The religious violence of Hinduism presents another picture, as will be shown. Hinduism has as many faces as there are Hindus in India. Some of the faces are violent, and their history goes back some four to five thousand years.

The long period of the Spanish and Portuguese colonial control of Latin America left a heavy legacy in the wake of independence which is still evident in the authoritarian power of the state. The entrenched landed aristocracy, hand in hand with the clergy, continues to influence virtually every aspect of life there.

Although the ideas of Thomas Jefferson and the French Revolution played a great role in the fires of revolt which covered Latin America, these ideas were not deep-rooted among the leaders or the masses that revolted.

Brazil and Mexico established monarchs patterned on the old European establishment. However remarkably stable the system was in Brazil, it did nothing to prepare the people for self-rule. It did, in fact, continue the ideology of single authoritarian control that has had little concern for its masses.

The remaining area of Latin America fell victim to dictators, all patterned from the viceroys, the military and the clerical role of the colonial period -minus the relative degree of stability provided by the old system. The overwhelming belief in the authority of state, the military, the clergy, and the landed classes, remained. Responsibility ran from the bottom up and relatively none from the top down.

The indigenous Indians maintained, wherever possible, their own customs, traditions, religious practices and beliefs that had been in vogue for centuries. The Roman Church, the landed aristocracy, and the military placed a veneer of Christianity over these traditions through which many aspects of their own older religious practices could be seen and are still today more visible. In many places this merger produced a double loyalty, one to Christianity and the other to their ageless indigenous religions and practices. Mexico has a history of turbulence from the date of its independence from Spain. Only since the early days of the 1930's has it found measured stability which at this very hour is being threatened.

Central America has never been under centralized control since gaining independence, even though many wars have been fought to gain that end. Mexico's geographical location, its variations in climate, and the Indian traditions have been great factors in preventing any form of unification. Central America, which consists of Costa Rica, Nicaragua, Honduras, Guatemala, and El Salvador (named for and dedicated to the Savior), have had internal conflicts and power struggles since its independence from Spain. Violence has been embedded in the area and is part and parcel of the neo-colonial ethic of power. This power structure, until recently, has been the church, the army, and the landed aristocracy.

In South America, La Grande, Columbia broke into three nations at the northern most part of the land mass: Venezuela, Columbia, and Ecuador. In the entire history of independent government, none has had a stable government. On the contrary, they all three have lived with the instability of dictatorships and revolts. However, Venezuela has been slowly moving toward democracy in the last twenty-five or thirty years.

Bolivia has never sustained a stable government nor a military structure.

Paraguay has been ruled by ruthless dictators and Chile has had only short intervals of any semblance of democratic order. Dictators have been in power throughout virtually all of Chile's history. Argentina is an example of government historically known for dictators, revolts, and terrorism. Only in recent days has Argentina had a democratic basis for its government which is yet not yet stable. All the countries, including Cuba and Haiti, have never had the least aspect of a democratic government. The Dominican Republic appears slightly better.

Mexico, Costa Rico, Columbia, Venezuela, and in recent days, Argentina and Brazil, are struggling, at best, with a weak social structure of democracy.

Governments in the colonial period were controlled and ruled by a Viceroy (Vice King). This was done from the crowns of Spain and Portugal by the grace of God. The viceroy was supported by the clergy, the military, and the landed aristocracy. Under the law of Spain and Portugal, the Crown, through the viceroy, claimed all mineral rights in the New World which consisted of gold, silver, copper, platinum, and tin, as well as any other minerals which might be discovered. The best available farm land was given to the aristocracy, brushing aside Indian claims to minerals, land and crops. In Latin America, "The Baleful Trinity", the military, the landed aristocracy, and the clergy truly did leave an indelible mark.

The Conquistadors had an aversion to manual labor and carried it with them into The New World, therefore, the inherent Indians and Blacks were forced to labor on the estates and in the mines throughout the vast area of Latin America. African slave labor was introduced at a later date in the Caribbean Islands and Brazil.

Legalized slavery no longer prevails in Latin America; however, its pattern of labor in industry for the Black and Indian people remains fundamentally the same. Industrial growth has not brought about stability. And throughout Argentina, Brazil, and Chile, the most industrial growth has sustained dictators. Although Mexico is becoming more industrialized, it still depends heavily on the production of petroleum to sustain it —which has thus far been an unstable situation.

Industrialization in Latin America is compounding the social imbalance of the landed aristocracy, the military, and until recently, the vast majority of the clergy. Throughout Latin America, there is a vast movement of peasants evolving from the rural communities into the urban centers. The Indians, with all their racial and ethnic mixtures are being uprooted from their tribal and traditional background. In most Latin American countries, the national debts are disproportionate to the available national income. This in addition to large amounts of flight capital, places a heavy burden on the people. Consequently, the mass of people moving into the urban centers are not being absorbed into the main stream and structure of the urban centers. Thus, rent from their old grounding and moral support, the uprooted migrants are unable to adjust and fit into urban society. Without a moral or spiritual base to hold them, the privations which they suffer become intolerable and their hopes grow dimmer with the unfolding future. The problem is compounded for the burgeoning population by an extremely high infant mortality rate, poor education, and access to adequate nutritional and medical attention.

The poor of the world are indeed being squeezed out in ever increasing degrees by the forces of an industrial, military, economic, and social complex which denies them basic human rights and a modicum of human dignity whether in Latin America, Africa, Asia, or the United States.

In Latin America, in addition to intolerable poverty of its masses, this threat is compounded by the enormous debts which its governments owe to non-Latin countries ——which currently is over some $350 billion. Payments of debts depends on exports which were only $95 billion in 1985, whereas the interest on the principal was $45 billion. As great as Latin America's need is to industrialize, external cash flow leaves little for economic development and improved social programs. The decline of foreign trade, also related to the reduction of exports to Latin America, fell from $38 billion in 1981 to $20 billion in 1983, which was primarily linked to the economy of the United States.

Urban centers are fast becoming areas for the world's population. More than forty percent of the world's population live in urban areas, and by the end of this century this concentration will have reached more than fifty percent.

About seventy percent of the people of Latin America live in urban areas. Within fifty years the urban movement will forever erase the rural population. The disintegration of the family is a great threat to individual identity, often leading to alienation. More than this, however, is the threat to the national society if conditions become widespread. The projected growth of population in Latin America poses a grave threat to the individual, the family, the nation, and possibly the whole region. A report No. 2985/7 of the Universities Field Staff International, Inc., South America (1983-85) entitled, *Population and Development in Latin America and The Caribbean,* by Thomas G. Sanders, states the following:

> Brazil, Mexico, Columbia, and Venezuela include over 250 million of the regions 390 million and of this proportion nearly

two thirds will be maintained in the year 2000, when the population is scheduled to reach 564 million. The total estimated to reach is 801 million by 2020. Of this group, Columbia is the poorest with a per capita income less than one third of Venezuela and about 60 per cent that of Mexico and Brazil.

One must recall that Columbia is the source of great quantities of illegal drugs, as is Bolivia, which is of great concern for the issue of increased violence in the United States. However, these governments are increasingly aware that the population growth rate underlies the issues of unemployment, housing, education, nutrition, and a stable government which they constantly face.

This rapid surge of urbanization is unique in world history. The 1986 World Population Data Sheet of the Population Reference Bureau, Inc., places the estimated population of Brazil at 143, 300,000 in mid - 1986. It is projected to be 194,000,000 by the year 2000. Data obtained from Y.C. Yu, Chief of the United Nations Population Division -*Estimates and Projections Section Population Division, I.E.S.A., August 20, 1986,* show the following for Brazil:

The population for 1950 was 53,444,000; in 1985 it was 135,564,000. The projected figures for the year 2000 is 179,487,000 and the year 2025 the figure will be 245,809,000. The growth from 1950 to 1985 (35 years) was 82,120,000. The projected growth from 1950 to 2025 (75 years) is 192,365,000.

The urban movement reflects a similar growth. In 1950 the urban population of Brazil was 15,430,000, 34.5%; the rural population was 35,014,000 or 65%. In 1985 the urban population was 95,599,000 or 72%; the rural population was 36,966,000 or 27.3%. This is a great shift in just 35 years. By the year 2000 the figure will be 148,397,000 or 82.7% of the population in urban areas, as over against 27,020,000, or 11.0% in the rural areas. The total population will be 218,789,000 or 89.0%, of the largest nation in Latin America.

The ten largest cities of Brazil currently have more than one million each. The largest, greater Sao Paulo, estimated in 1983 to have a population of 12,106,000, and Rio de Janeiro, with 9,154,000; some 29% live in ten areas. Amazoneas and Para Manaus, the capital of Amazones, had 63,659 of the 1,432, 066 people in the state in 1980; Belem had a population of 934, 322.

Urbanization leads to growing demands in housing, education, employment, medical aid, sanitation, police control, transportation, food supply, and the intricate process of bringing the new members of the cities into a common set of social ideals that are often different from those of the deep rural interior from which they came. Growing indications are that many people rural interior from which they came. Growing indications are that many people are unable to make the emotional-psychological transitions from rural to urban life in the growing mega-cities of Latin America. As urbanization augments, it will be an increasing demand for public services, and little evidence exists that the governments of Latin America can supply these needs.

Signs of abandoned and destitute children are common throughout Latin America; however, disintegration of the family is greatest in Brazil than in all of the other countries. Brazil is fast becoming a Tale of Two Nations. [1] One element lives excessively in luxury, while others live in demeaning dire poverty. Should these present trends continue, Brazil may become the world's most destitute "wealthy" nation by the end of the century. This kind of poverty stands in the shadow of what proposes to be the eighth largest economy in the world; by the end of the century its economy is likely to pass that of Canada, Italy, and Britain.

The breach separating the wealthy minority from the poor majority is fast becoming an ongoing crisis. Despite the economic growth of Brazil, it does not appear capable of lifting its poorest citizens out of a mire of misery.

Over the years of industrialization, there has been a flood of peasants from the north and northeast migrating south to Rio de Janeiro and Sao Paulo. These people are illiterate; therefore, unemployable. Thus, alienated from mainstream society, they are forced to survive in ghettoes and on the streets. Though few migrants are reportedly involved in crime, the middle class, nonetheless, perceives them as potential assailants. At present, the government has done little to address the issue.

According to government figures, some 36 million Brazilians are under the age of eighteen and about 60% of this total are "needy." Some seven million have lost most if not all links with their families or are purposely abandoned. One third of the children between the ages of seven and fourteen do not attend school and more than one half of the children under age six suffer from malnutrition. This situation is in sharp contrast to the economic growth rates of over ten percent and billions of dollars which are spent on industrial projects, whereas the social needs have been miserably neglected. Projects initiating education, land reform, labor practices, and health policies have failed to forestall this migration to the cities.

---

[1] *Brazil 2000, Para Un Novo Pacto Social, Helio Jaburaibe (et al). Rio de Janeire, Paz Ferra, 1986.*

Brazil has a history of relative non-violence, although the extreme contrast between the very rich and the very poor gives little assurance that it will continue into the future. Brazil is second only to the United States as a food exporter, yet sixty-five percent of its 135 million people are undernourished, while one per cent of its extremely wealthy earn as much as the poorest fifty percent.

There is nothing new about the problems of Brazil. The military rule of yesterday pursued the trickle-down theory, thinking it would aid the masses. It did not! The hallmark for the future of Brazil is clear: it must reform the way it cares for its children or juvenile crime will begin to mount.

A child has a legitimate right to defend himself against a hostile society. [1] First, the child holds out his hand in innocence. After being rejected, he begins to steal surreptitiously, after which he openly takes what he needs by force. This is the Manchild of Brazil —with all that is in his wake. He is the counterpart of the Manchild of New York.

Mexico is the most populous Spanish speaking nation in the world and second in its number of people. In conformity with other nations, there is a great migration of its people to the principle urban areas with a primary focus into Central Mexico. Lacking economic opportunities elsewhere, the people move to industrial urban areas and to northern border states. Mexico City is currently the largest city in the world with some 18 million people. Other cities with large population concentration are Guadalajara, Monterey, Ciudad, Juarez, Pueblo de Zaragoza and Leon.

Mexico was conquered in 1519-1521, by the Spanish warrior Hernando de Cortes who found a highly advanced culture including the Olmec, the Maya, the Toltec, and the Aztec. This domination lasted some 300 years. Independence was declared in 1810 and a republic was set up in 1822. This was followed by a would be Emperor Augustin de Iturbide, succeeded by General Antonio Lopez de Santa Anna who controlled it from 1833 to 1855.

Mexico lost the war in which Texas proclaimed its independence in 1836. This reverse was followed by a war with the United States (1846-48).

During the presidency of Benito Juarez (1858-71), Napoleon III of France used military force to place Archduke Maximilian of Austria as

---

[1] *The New York Times Magazine, June 5, 1986, What Kids Who Aren't Wolves Say About, Wilding.*

Emperor of Mexico in 1864. President Juarez captured the so-called Emperor and executed him in 1867. Subsequent to the death of Juarez was the dictatorship of General Porfirio Diaz from 1877 to 1910.

The events of social disorder, invasions, and foreign control of much of Mexico's economy resulted in a violent revolt against Diaz in 1910. Although a constitution was set forth in 1917, considerable disorder continued until the presidency of Lazaro Cardenas in 1934. Since the early 1930's, the Institutional Revolutionary Party has been the primary force in Mexico's stability. The world economy and the oil slump combined with excessive inflation, and the enormous foreign debt, have the potential to destroy the social order of Mexico. The psyche of its people is in danger of being shattered. More than some fifty years is required to set up a permanent stable government structure.

These conditions, as grave as they are, were made worse by the earthquake of September, 1985, which caused the death of some 10,000 people and cost about five billion dollars. The focus of the damage in Mexico City makes the problems worse.

Mexico, with its long border to the United States, has a serious problem with which to deal. At the end of World War II, it had a population of some 20 million. According to Y.C. Yu, of the United Nations, which has been previously referred to and cited, the Mexican population of 1950 was 27,376,000 and by 1985 it had grown to 78,996,000; an increase of 51,620,000 in 35 years. The 1986 World Population Data Sheet, of the Population Reference Bureau, Inc., stated that Mexico had by mid-1986 a population of 81,700,000, and projected a growth to 112,800,000 by the year 2000. The estimates vary, as is seen. In the fifteen years to the end of the century, the projected figure is 109,180,000. By the year 2025, Mexico will have increased its population another 44,905,000 to reach a staggering 154,085,000, if these projections are correct.

As great as the population projection is for the future concentration of Brazil, the projection for the future of Mexico seems far greater, especially in the Federal District. Urbanization in 1950 constituted 11,677,000 or 42.7 percent of the population in the rural areas. However, in the past thirty-five years, there has been a dramatic shift with 55,012,000 or 69.3 percent of the population in urban areas as opposed to 23,984,000 or 30 percent in 1985 in the rural communities. By the year 2000, some 84,492,000, or 77.4 percent of the population will be living in the cities and only 24,688,000, or 22.6 percent will be residing in rural areas. The dominating urban areas will be more graphic in the year 2025 when the population of urban areas will reach 45.4 percent of the total population of 154,085,000, whereas rural areas will have been reduced to

14.6 percent, or only 22,557,000.

The figures for the 1980's projected future years must be placed alongside the June, 1986 estimated rate of unemployment and under-employment which was determined to be over 50 percent. Mexio's national debt is overwhelming. Its oil market is faltering, --not to mention the tragic results suffered by their devastating earthquake. And, yet, it can neither ignore its population explosion nor the threat which it poses to its already weak economic situation.

The substance of the psycho-dynamics of Mexico, and its relation to the social-ideological basis of the political structure, may be seriously challenged by the concentration of massive urban migration and the demands of its people. Such a challange could bring about a type of violence which produces the *manchild* of Mexico like that which now exists in New York City.

Urbanization and migration in Mexico is somewhat similar to Brazil. The areas with the greatest convergence are the Northwest, the Southeast, the Federal District, and Mexico City. In ten years, beginning in 1970, Mexico City increased its annual population 3.8% to reach 9,991,000 by 1980.

As late as 1950, Greater Mexico City had an approximate population of 3.1 million. By 1985, it had grown to roughly 18 million. By the year 2000 the figures are projected at near 26 million. Mexico City ranks first in the world in the number of people and is spread over 890 square miles. It is reported that each day some 1,000 people migrate to this city. [1]

From personal observation, this city is vastly overcrowded and its social services extremely neglected. More than two million people are without indoor plumbing and some three million have no sewage facilities. The water level of the city is greatly reduced. In 1984 the city pumped one billion gallons of water per day for its use, and lost 20 percent as a result of faulty plumbing. Problem drainage such as this has caused certain areas of the city to sink from five to thirty feet.

Out of the 14,000 tons of daily waste, only 8,000 tons are processed; the remainder lies in open areas overrun by rodents. Exhaust fumes from diesel fuel operating the millions of automobiles and buses (some three million cars and 7,000 buses) and 130,000 factories is reported to be responsible for the death of some 30,000 children each year. Still, an estimated two thirds of the

---

[1] *Time Magazine, Mexico City, The Population Curse, (August 6, 1984).*

Mexican peasants move off the land and end up in the cities; the other one third move to the United States. While luxury on a lavish scale lives next door to poverty, unemployment, and under-employment, burglary, theft and crime continue to rise, increasing an estimated 35% from 1983 to 1984. Begging for handouts from tourists and other strangers also has become a way of life for many Mexican peasants.

In 1984 the United Nations estimated that the growth of Mexico City would house 26 million people by the year 2000. However, the officials of Mexico City estimate that by the year 2000, some 36 million people will inhabit the area.

From a personal observation, Mexico was found to be comparable to the major cities of Brazil. From Belem, Recife, Rio de Janeiro, to Sao Paulo, thousands of displaced impoverished people —also from personal observation— were found living under appalling circumstances. This factor poses an alarming threat to the overall social order.

The Mexican government is fully aware of its problems: the population explosion, urbanization, the oil and debt crises, health care, and unemployment. If these circumstances are allowed to continue, the current social dilemma will create a far greater strife for its future. Mexico must exert an all-out effort toward social stability.

The drastic conditions —particularly those in Mexico City— should sound a warning to all other major cities in Latin America, Africa, India, and Southeast Asia.

Venezuela and Columbia have the same problem as that of Mexico and Brazil. The population of Venezuela in 1950 was 5,009,000 and 53.2% of this total or 2,667,000 lived in the urban areas; whereas, only 2,313,000 or 46.2% lived in the countryside. By the year 2025, some 94.7% or 35,987,000 people will live in cities and only 2,017,000 or 5.3% will live in rural areas.

Columbia had a population of 11,594,000 in 1950, of which 37.1% or 4,301,000 were in urban areas. Residing in the rural communities were some 7,296,000 or 62.9% people. The population of Columbia reached 28,717,000 in 1985 and 19,375,000, which equal 67.4% were in cities and 9,357,000 or 32.6% lived in the countryside. In the years ahead, the move from the countryside to urban areas will be more dramatic. The population of Columbia will reach 37,999,000 by the year 2000, and 28,557,000 will reside in the cities. This equals 75.2% of the population and leaves 9,441,000 or 24.8% in the countryside. Look at the shift predicted by the year 2025! Out of a population of 51,718,000; 43,407,000 or 83.7% will be residing in the cities and 8,311,000 or only 16.1% will live in the urban areas.

Neither Venezuela nor Columbia has had stable governments in their period of independence from Spain; however, in recent years the former has been moving in that direction.

Having traveled throughout all four nations, as well as the remainder of Latin America —and studied them for more than forty years— the fact, to me, is unmistakingly clear that all four countries are in perilous circumstances, economically, socially, and environmentally.

Robert W. Fox of the Latin Interamerican Development Bank has stated that if half of population growth in Mexico were directed away from the Federal District to the next sixteen largest cities, their population would have to grow 184% during the period from 1980 to the year 2000.

The following is from an unpublished paper, <u>Latin America's Population Growth: Perceptions, Projections, and Issues</u>, presented by Robert W. Fox at the World Demographic Outlook Conference in New York City on September 23, 1982:

> In the United States in 1977, three million jobs were created. This was our best year in this regard since World War II. During the last decades, our yearly average, however, was closer to two million jobs. Latin America, with 20 percent of the economic base of the United States, is facing the requirements of creating four million jobs yearly on average over each of the next 20-40 years simply in order not to fall further behind in its present high unemployment rate; and almost all these jobs must be created in the cities.

Countless now in Latin America are the faceless *"manchildren."* These are the forgotten ones who harbor a deep-seated rejection of the prevailing social order. Sorely lacking in any manner of religion or social ideology, their single motivation is an uncontrollable desire to survive. And, unfortunately, there will be millions more to come in the immediate future.

Apartheid is a dominant factor in The Republic of South Africa. In 1982 the estimated population of this much troubled land was around 30 million. Some 75 percent were non-white, and about 70 percent of its work force were black.

Bantu-speaking black Africans moved into the region from Eastern Central Africa about 1506. However, in 1652, the Dutch East India Company became the first permanent European settlement. Not until 1707, or there about, did the number of freeholders reach 1,780. These European descendants had more than 1,000 slaves. By 1779, a long series of wars broke out between the Xhosa people and the white farmers, the Boers, who moved inland from coastal areas. By 1795, the British had replaced the Dutch at Cape Town, a port city on the southern tip of Africa.

When British rule abolished slavery, some 12,000 Boers began the Great Trek (1835-1843) to Natal which was annexed by the British in 1843. The Orange Free State and the Transvaal were established in the 1850s.

A succession of conflicts led to the Boer War (1899-1902) in which the British conquered the Orange Free State and Transvaal. Independence from Britain would not be gained until 1931.

Throughout all these years, there has been a progressive repression of non-whites by apartheid (complete segregation). White supremacy has been strengthened by such leaders as H. J. Verwoerd (1958-1966), B. J. Vorster (1966-1978), and P. W. Botha (1978-1979). F. W. de Klerk, of the National Party is now the President of the Republic of South Africa.

President de Klerk, in his September, 1989, inaugural address, expressed the view that while white minority domination must come to an end; it should not, however, be replaced and dominated by the black majority. He concluded his speech by saying that "we shall continue to deal with unrest, violence and terrorism with a firm hand." [1]

The day of accountability is now at hand for this South African Republic, a nation governed by a small white minority. The small ruling white minority control the government as to the legislative, judicial, law enforcement, armed police force, and the economy as well. The hypothesis of this arrangement rests on the assumption that white superiority is supported by Biblical scripture. The same thesis brought about the expansion of Europe into North, Central, South America, and India and Asia, as well. It was believed

---

[1] *The New York Times, September 30, 1989.*

that Christianity must be brought to these primitive people who were to be servants: "drawers of water and hewers of wood."

The Republic of South Africa —as a government— holds that black people are beyond the pale. When a parliament was set up in 1984, one house represented five million white people and another represented three million Asians who were mainly Indian. The white people retained all power from which all black people were totally excluded.

Although the government of South Africa has denied any comparison to Nazism, the following points bear consideration:

1. The leaders of the government believe in the basic superiority of one class of people over another.

2. The subject class is to be the servant of the ruling elite.

3. Minority rule prevails under a semblance of law to which subject people have no part in formulating, nor can they take part in any form of protest which could prompt charges of treason, long term confinement without trial, disappearance, death, and the plundering of homes and townships with massive movement of whole communities.

4. The head of state virtually controls the press and all other media, the legislature, and this executive for the most part, is protected from any interference by courts.

5. The former leader, President Botha, claimed his support was by some divine mission. The Nazis found it essential to resurrect Nordic gods and they put great stock in their symbols. Hitler was never excommunicated from the Church of Rome and received its open support against communism.

6. President Botha believed in a divine, Christian mission against external and internal enemies. In both cases the chief enemy was Communism; however, there is another internal one —his name is Nelson Mandela.

The only position where a comparison between the South African government and Nazism may fall short is that South Africa has not set forth a program to exterminate the black people. Since seventy five percent of the population is black, to kill them —as Hitler did the Jews, the Poles, the Slavs, and the Gypsies— would be the same as destroying the work force of the nation and a major portion of its consumers.

When President Botha took the oath of office at his inauguration in 1978, he displayed all the pomp of royalty with heavy overtones of religious fervor. Among other statements, he recounted the following: "The pioneers who came to South Africa heralded the advent of a new civilization here, which decades later met with other communities and their civilizations, thus forming part of God's plan for mankind. We are part of God's great design." The clergyman, a member of Dutch Reform Church, officiated at the occasion and prayed that the new president might remain in office. ". . .that he may have the spiritual courage and grace to follow that divine will." He was, no doubt, referring to the past violence against the government, and the anticipated future of the black majority. This man of the cloth reached far back to St. Paul and continued as follows: "Those who rebel against authority, rebel against what God has ordained."

This position stands against a more recent statement by the Dutch Reform Church, wherein it announced that: "We confess with humility and sorrow the participation of our church in the introduction and legitimization of the ideology of apartheid and subsequent suffering of people." Going further, it declared that ideology was sinful and any attempt to defend it heretical.

The Afrikaners firmly believe that God's divine plan ordained the Anglo Saxons entering South Africa. They believe, also, that *He* ordained the events leading up to and including the inauguration of the new president and all the laws of apartheid. If they accept this hypothesis when countless black South Africans are murdered and their homes destroyed, when they are uprooted and imprisoned by the thousands, and when their supporters are harressed by the army and the police as well; then, they must believe that this is a part of God's plan. Is the latest position of the current Dutch Reform Church correct? Or is the old position correct? And when, if ever, will these old notions and customs be abolished?

It has been so ordained that Apartheid legislation is based upon the belief that their definable groups —white Afrikaners— should be kept apart from other groups. There is a paradox to this thesis which is: that countless dominant Afrikaners inherent seeds have issued forth from mixed bloodlines.

The World Alliance of Reform Churches, reacting to the Afrikaners view on apartheid, suspended the South African Reform Church and declared apartheid a heresy.

Eugene Terre Blanche, leader of The Afrikaner Resistance Movement, an extreme exclusionist organization, recently stated that South Africa was at the beginning of a bloody revolution between whites and blacks, claiming that the land of the republic as their own. The emblem of this resistance movement is taken from the Revelation of St. John the Divine. Sevens are drawn from biblical references, -which stand for the seven angles, seven stars, and seven seals. These symbols, according to Blanche, is the antithesis of the three sixes that evoke the mark of the beast which is also found in the Book of Revelations. Blanche also fears international Zionism and Judaism, believing that they control all of the wealth and resources in South Africa.

Another group of Afrikaners, led by Dr. Andries P. Treurnicht, opposes all concessions or anything that would open the way to majority rule. He further argues that all effort should be taken to implant racial and ethnic separation, as proposed by the original theologians of apartheid.

All of these theological views supporting the tyranny of the South African government are of course opposed by the present outspoken Anglican Archbishop Desmond Tutu and the Reverend Allan Boesak who also place their opposition on Christian thought despite the statements of the clergy supporting the state and its laws.

Those at the head of the South African state who oppose the opening of their order for a pluralized society are using all matters of force to preserve their position. Thousands of people have been uprooted, and put in places of detention, while others have been killed. Basic rights such as freedom of movement, freedom of the press, freedom to assemble, simply do not exist for the millions of black people in South Africa.

The leader of state must fear the debt which they owe for past and present abuses. Meanwhile, they are alienating millions of blacks with the violence that is steeped in uncompromising ideological religious hypothesis.

The white minority of South Africa voted to abolish apartheid in the first days of 1992. It is one thing to abolish apartheid by law; however, it is quite another thing to remove its customs, traditions, and accumulated psychological and institutional practices.

Two references regarding Africa, which were provided by the World Bank, explain the problems of population growth: Egypt had a population of 26 million in 1960; however, by 1984 it had reached 46 million. The population increase for Egypt by the year 2025 is a projected 86 million. Nigeria had only 52 million in 1960; however, its number had swelled to 97 million by 1984. The World Bank also projects that by the year 2025, the world population will climb to 8.297 billion.

India, almost twice the size of Alaska, has monumental problems relative to its increasing population. In 1950 India had some 357.561 million people, by 1985 it had 758.927 million. In the year 2000 there will be 964.072 million and by the year 2025 the estimated figure will be around 1,228.829 billion.

The movement toward urbanization is having a drastic impact on India. In 1950, 17.3%, or only 61.893 million people were in urban centers, whereas 295.866 million, or 82.7% were in rural areas. The balance in 1985 was still in favor of rural areas. There were 231.604 million in the cities, or 25.0% as against 595.548 million,or 72.0% in rural areas. However, by 2025 the shift will be away from the rural communities toward the cities with 568.218 million, or 53.6% residing there. India had a work force in 1985 of 300 million.

The disturbing problem with the population explosion in India is intensified by the tremendous diversity of ethnic groups with differing religious beliefs and diverse languages. The ethnic groups are 75% Indo-Aryan, 25% Dravidian, and 2% Mongolian. The major religions and their percentages are: Hindu, 83%, Muslim, 11%, Christian, 2.6%, Sikh, Jain, Buddhist, and Parsi. Although the two primary languages are English and Hindi, there are some 16 official languages.

India's problems with an escalating population of intermixed cultures, and a shift from rural areas to urban centers, are intensified as the already overcrowded major cities struggle with food shortages, inadequate housing, poor sanitation, insufficient water supply, and poor education.

New Delhi, the capital of India, has a population of seven million. The population of other major urban centers are: Calcutta, 9.7 million; Bombay, 8.6 million; Hyderbad, 2.8 million; and Ahmedabad, 2.3 million. These figures are 1984 estimates.

Having nearly fifteen percent of the world's population —second only to China— the problems of India are compounded by the fact it occupies only 2.4% of the world's land mass. In 1985, some 40% of its people were younger than fifteen years of age. Paralleled with this, about 85 percent in 1984 lived in over 550,000 villages and the remainder resided in more than 200 towns and cities. Eighty-three percent of these people are Hindu. India also has the largest Islamic population in the world. These two groups have always had their graphic differences, especially in the 19th and 20th centuries; however, one must remember the bitter strife between them during the Islamic invasions.

The caste system, deeply rooted in Indian history, reaches centuries back

—prior to the beginning of the Christian era. It continues to play an important role in Indian life in fact, fiction, and myth, despite efforts to reverse it.

India was among the earliest people to develop a higher civilization. Its history reaches further back than 2500 B.C., and it is known to have existed as early as 1500 B.C. The Aryan tribes from Central Asia, foraging their way over the northwest frontier of India, conquered the subcontinent. Only a short while did the Indian people rule themselves in the intervening years after the Aryan conquest, and the Islamic expansion in the 7th and 8th centuries of the Christian era. The Muslims, controlled by the subcontinent mogul empire, directly or otherwise, combined Hinduism with Islam until the British made their first outpost in India in 1619. Gradually, the British gained all the area of present day India, Pakistan, and Bangladesh. This domination continued until India proclaimed its independence in 1947. The second largest number of people in the world have had little opportunity to grapple with the mounting problems confronting them since 1947, problems inherited from the long history prior to their independence.

Extreme violence resulting from centuries old rivalry between Hindus and Muslims brought about the partition of British India in 1947; however, this resulted in bitter disputes regarding Kashmir, and also created hostility and warfare between India and Pakistan in 1947-48 and again in 1965.

There was in 1971 another conflict regarding East Pakistan and the flight of millions of Bengali refugees to India. This dispute produced yet another war and the creation of Bangladesh. After initial good relations between India and China, a border dispute in 1962 led to a conflict; however, since 1981, India and China have had conferences designed to bring about improved relations between them. These dissensions, together with its geo-political location, has resulted in India having the fourth largest armed force in the world.

India's outside altercations, and internal problems as well, have placed the world's largest democracy in a dangerous position. The continuing problems with the exploding population, inadequate housing, poor sanitation, the lack of pure water -inducing typhoid, tetanus, hepatitis, and diphtheria, pose a monumental threat to the future of India.

In their religion, Hinduism teaches non-violence —among other things— based on the Bhagavad-Gita and the Upanishads. Unfortunately, similar to other faiths, the deepest aspects of its teachings have not reached the greatest number of its people.

There are almost as many faces in Hinduism as there are adherents.

While commonly thought to be a religion of many gods, Hinduism is fundamentally monotheistic. In Basham's "*The Wonder That Was India*," states that Hinduism is essentially tolerant and would rather assimilate than rigidly exclude. In Hinduism, "the Divine is a diamond of innumerable facets:" --some brighter and more highly polished than others. The devotee, regardless of his sect, worships the whole diamond which is perfect.

There are three major facets of Hinduism: Brahma the Creator, Vishnu the Preserver, and Shiva the Destroyer. It is with Shiva that complications arise, because   everything is in the process of change: Nothing that is supposedly created with the appearance of preservation is not, at the same time, in the process of disintegration or destruction. Kali, evolving as it did from early Hindu mythology, is the goddess of terror and destruction.   Kali, apparently, was another name for Shiva.

Thugs have their origin at some early point in Hindu mythology and are believed to be worshippers of Kali. Committing outrageous acts of terror and violence, their date of origin is not known, although they have clearly existed for at least six hundred years, and are estimated to have killed one million people in the last three centuries. These thugs, it is said, may have been the most important terror group on record, even though they operated in secret and attacked individuals rather than institutions, and believed their governing rulers to be of divine origin.   Secrecy of operation is the thug's hallmark, distinguishing them from other criminal groups who also worshipped Kali and operated without disguise. When the early 20th century Hindu terrorists used Kali, they threw aside secrecy because their aim was political, they wanted to rid themselves of Britain.

From the earliest days of the Islamic penetration into India, centuries ago, Hinduism as a whole became confronted with Islam and its open approval of violence and the two opposites therefore produced more violence. The conflicts, combined with centuries of foreign domination and the consequent fragmentation of India has served to produce yet another source of crisis for the government. India's independence from Britain has been less than forty years. Therefore, with an unpredictable future, the strife may be too great, for the largest pluralized social order in the world, to overcome.

The Sikh-Hindu turmoil and bloodshed only perpetuate the problems of India. The Sikh faith was organized about five hundred years ago when it split with Hinduism. Its main objective was to incorporate certain features of Islam with Hinduism, thus founding the new religion of Sikhism. Among other things, the faith teaches monotheism. Its followers adhere to strict discipline, practice meditation, propound the virtues of martyrdom, and oppose the caste system.

The Sikh faith is respected by many Hindus who see them as brave and virtuous members of society. Sikhs played a vital role in the armies of India when they were brought into the British armed forces; however, this began a gradual alienation of many Sikhs and Hindus. Although the Sikhs constitute only two percent of India's population, they are highly self-motivated and remarkably successful in business. The government of India, recognizing this positive trait, allowed the Sikhs to take Punjab, in northwest India, as their own state. The immense prosperity which they have gained and come to enjoy has prompted some of its members to turn from the religion, or to not fully adhere to its strict doctrine.

Having gained an obvious prestige derived from their prosperity, a backlash has been created from the extreme fundamentalists within the religion which is turning Sikh against Sikh. This group has also turned with violence against the Indian government, demanding permission to form its own *nation,* called Khalistan.

This movement has been launched with much stimulus, both in India and among the faithful overseas, since they now fear the faith may disappear. The violence directed against the government resulted when Indian troops were ordered to take over the Golden Temple from Sikh radicals at Amritsar, setting Sikh against Hindu and Sikh against Sikh. This outbreak also precipitated violence by some Sikhs in Canada, West Germany, and Great Britain. India's Prime Minister, Indira Gandhi's decision to have the Sikh radicals routed from the Golden Temple resulted in her assassination at the hands of her own Sikh bodyguards. Her death culminated in further anti-Sikh violence and bloodshed throughout India.

Converging from this turbulence are the Sikh youths who seek to return to the historic psychological glories of the past; and this has led to more outbreaks of bloody feuds. The Hindus have formed their own militant forces to oppose the Sikhs. This too springs from historical, economic, religious, demographic, and psychological dissimilarities which the politics of India may not be able to control.

The past is not dead. It dwells in the thinking and emotions of those who are living and carried over into the future through accumulated customs and traditions. Under changed conditions our view of the future becomes distorted with the passing of time and former universal ideals become ethnic, and that is compounded when ethnic ideals become nationalistic.

The Universality of Hinduism in India has locked into nationalism. In Sri Lanka (formerly Ceylon), Theravada Buddhism is the dominate religion.

This aspect of Buddhism is known as Hinayana "the Lesser Vessel" or "Vehicle." It now is also referred to as "Way of the Elders." Emperor Asoka (264-226 B. C.) is historically as important to Buddhism in Asia as Constantine is to Christianity.

Legend has it that King Tissa, the ruler of Ceylon, known in the West at that time, sent Asoka precious pearls from his realm. Asoka, in return sent the gift of Buddhism to the King by way of his missionary son and daughter. The King converted to Buddhism in the middle of the 3rd Century, B.C. [1]

Much of this material was recounted by the *"Mahiavaonsa"* (the Great Chronicle of the 5th Century A.D.) which tells of the early history of Sri Lanka and its relation to India. The Chronicle tells how all the people in the kingdom became Buddhist. It also relates that the people of Sri Lanka were honored by a visit from the Buddha. [2] King Dutthagarmani (ca 101-77 B.C.), the chronicle continues, who desired to expand his domain went to war and consolidated the island in the glory and honor of Buddhism. As time passed he had a feeling of deep sorrow for the destruction and death which he had caused. Eight Buddhist monks were dispatched to the King to reassure that he had acted to fortify Buddhism, this was a justification after the fact. [3]

These facts seem to be a preamble to the current violence which plagues Sri Lanka which constitutes a centuries-old dispute. The Buddhist Sinhalese constitute a majority in a nation of some sixteen million who see themselves in a larger scope as a minority from the Hindu Tamil ethnic group and a smaller Moslem population.

The Sri Lanka Tamil Hindu population seeks a separate state; they have carried out extensive guerrilla warfare, a conflict which has continued for some one thousand years, supported by some fifty million Tamil's in Southern India. This is a case where ethnic spirit overrides the teachings of Theravada Buddhism which is common in all aspects of Buddhism, "To Cherish all Life."

At this particular juncture, the major theological and philosophical

---

[1] *"Terrorism In Three Religious Traditions"*, David C. Rapeport, *University of California, Los Anglees. The American Political Science Review, Vol. 78, p. 658ff.*

[2] *"The Footprint of The Buddha,"* E. F. C. Ludewyk and George Allen, Unwin Ltd., London, (1985), pages 110-111, relate that there is nothing to support the presence of The Buddha in Ceylon.

[3] *Zygon, Journal of Religious and Science, op. cit., p.426-427.*

aspects of violence have been explored. There now is emerging a different kind of ethics of violence: that of individual survival where indiscriminate mugging and murder is beginning to echo throughout the world community, the consequence of the alienation of individuals as well as groups. This has graphically been described in a previous chapter as "Manchild, 1984." The accelerated population growth since the 1950's —especially the unparalleled movement of people from rural communities to the cities— greatly intensifies the already acute problem.

There is little to indicate that the metropolitan governments in any way are prepared to deal with this problem. Among the major powers of the world, national governments have other priorities which not only divert attention away from this issue, but they also draw the human wealth and natural resources away from it.

Not until the early days of the 19th century did the world population reach one billion. The world population had grown as much by the time of the great depression —*within one hundred years*— as it had from the dawn of human activity to the beginning of the nineteenth century. By the year 2000, the world population will be some six billion plus, and by 2025, the number projected around eight billion.

There were in 1950 only seven urban centers in the world that had more than five million people. They were New York, London, Paris, The Rhein-Ruhr area of Germany, Tokyo-Yokohama, Shanghai, and Buenos Aires. The predictions are that by 2025 there will be ninety-three centers, and eighty of them will be emerging nations.

How will the world's social demands be dealt with in the not too distant future? Will there be better housing, cleaner water for human consumption, and sufficient water for industrial use, an improved sanitation system, an up-to-date education system, ample food distribution, equitable medical care, an expanded transportation system, and substantial employment placement, all of which, at this time, are drastically inadequate in the world's metropolitan areas?

The crucial question to humankind is one of priorities. Those in power in the world community have their attention focused on strengthening the arms race. As of 1985, the world was spending *eight hundred billion dollars a year* for military equipment, and the forerunners in this endeavor were the United States and the former Soviet Union. Both powers, however, were far behind in social developments. The United States ranks fourteenth among the nations in infant mortality, and the Soviet Union ranks fifty-one. There was one soldier per forty-five people, as over against one physician per one thousand people. It cost the government $590,000,000 in 1985 to operate one U.S. aircraft carrier, while each day in Africa 14,000 children die of starvation.

World leaders are in the throes of a military crisis, this is confirmed by the number of military bases strategically stationed throughout the earth. The former Soviet Union in 1985 had military bases ranging from Cuba to Vietnam. It had battalions in some 22 foreign countries with troops ranging in the thousands. There were around 115,000 troops engaged in the Afghanistan invasion; and approximately 625,000 troops in the Warsaw Pact countries of Eastern Europe and Mongolia. However, with the collapse of the U.S.S.R., that aspect is no longer true.

The United States, with military bases in forty countries and territories in 1985, had more than twice that of the former Soviet Union. There are 95,000 U. S. forces overseas; it has another 385,000 in the North Atlantic Treaty Organization, stationed in Europe and Japan since 1945.

The stability of any social order depends on its internal security and well-being. The strongest military force in any given society cannot assure peace and order without meeting the basic domestic needs of its poorest and weakest components. In the present world community, military and social organizations are competing for human resources, natural resources, and monetary assistance.

The structural violence, defined as social neglect and the destruction of human life by this process, far exceeds violence which is brought about by war. On an international scale, there were from 1945-83 some fifteen million deaths each year due to social neglect, as against sixteen million brought about by war during the entire period. A careful study of world governmental priorities shows the trend to be slanted toward the military.

Only two nations, France and West Germany struck a near balance on social and military needs. Among the 142 countries listed, the United States was ninth and the former Soviet Union was twenty-fifth.

There were 25 million men in the armed services throughout the world prepared for conflict in 1983 with access to military equipment made by some one-fifth of the world's foremost engineers. This in itself raises an interesting point. It is said that military technology is used for world security, yet, it threatened all life. Not only were one-half of the developing nations in 1985 under military control, there were enough mega-tons of atomic weapons to kill 58 billion people -or enough to kill all living people 12 times over.

The expenditures on the Unites States Air Force alone is greater than the combined sums spent on education for 1.2 billion people in Africa, Latin America, Asia, and Japan. The United States, between 1960-82, spent $3.1 trillion for military arms; this was one-third more than all other super powers combined. These figures prove disturbing when one considers that the population increase was greater than all natural resources and the world-wide distribution needed to meet that increase. The stark reality comes to light when one measures the might of military wealth against the stark contrast of some one-fourth of those in the world whose lives are enervated by poverty.

The escalation of the arms race between the United States and the former Soviet Union did in fact forestall the outbreak of war; however, since the Cuban Crisis of 1961, both powers were the primary suppliers of arms throughout the world in their attempts to overthrow those governments that failed to conform to their own ideological application.

The emerging third world countries now are threatening to gain access to arms from the outside —from superpowers. The major increase of population congesting the urban centers —as discussed previously— is found in Third World countries. One half of the developing nations of the Third World in 1983 were ruled by military forces. Amnesty International reports that of the 114 countries in the Third World, 83 of them are known to use violence against their own people, such as kidnapping, torture, and execution. This means of terror is used frequently in forty-eight of the Third World countries and less frequently in thirty five others. This analysis leads one to conclude that the greater degree of defense seems analogous with the increase in violations of human rights against those whom the arms are supposed to protect. There have been 105 major wars in 66 countries and territories since World War II that have lasted on an average of three and one half years. With urban migration under way throughout the world, especially in the Third World countries, the congestion is creating a situation which arms alone cannot resolve. The Universal Declaration of Human Rights which declares "The will of the people shall be the basis of authority of government" is unfortunately being retracted.

The research and development for war far exceeds that done on malnutrition and care for children and suitable housing. In 1985 there was estimated to be 600 million youth in the world who could neither read nor write. Seven hundred million school age children are not being educated. In the poorest countries, life expectancy is no more than forty years, this is thirty seven years less than those living in developed countries.

Some two billion people in the world live on less than $500 a year and one person in five live in absolute poverty. This is a form of genocide —silent genocide. The flight from wars, brutality, and persecution —both religious and political— is greatest in this modern age. Some three million have escaped from war and persecution in Afghanistan, and another two million in Palestine. In Africa, another two million have been scattered over 20 countries and an equal number have been displaced in their own country.

The people scattered in rural areas do not constitute the kind of threat as do those who are moving into the cities en mass; they increase the number of unemployed and under-employed. This is becoming more aggravated among the working age population which is increasing at the rate of some 60 million a year, and the local youth represents an urban time bomb. If the ills of social, economic, psychological, and spiritual ills are left neglected on a mounting scale, society will become radicalized, and violence for survival will take over as more and more people become *dehumanized.*

Conditions such as these exist alongside a storehouse of missiles which have a range so great as to remove all moral implication from the mind of those who are behind the weapons. In 1945 the world had 3 atomic bombs; however, in 1983 there were 50,000, each with the potential power far exceeding the bombs used on Hiroshima.

It has been said that all is safe so long as sane leaders remain in control. Just what does the word "sane" suggest? Does it have any valid meaning in a world of such powerful and conflicting ideologies?

Throughout this expository study, it is clear that one cannot escape the finality with which Christians have promoted the use of violence, each against the other, in the outgrowth of Latin Christianity, the Reformation, the Counter-Reformation, and among the warring divine monarchs of the west. When they turned to the New World, Africa, India, South East Asia, and China; they did it with the same overwhelming fanatical drive.

In Czarist Russia, those of the Eastern Orthodox Church were also objects of violence; it was returned against all that came from Latin Christianity. These two main segments of Christianity carried out the same violent acts against the Jews, some of whom are now displaying a violent presence.

These three forces joined into conflict with yet a fourth force: Islam. They all had, and continue to have, a common idea. Each believes its own correct theological position excludes all others. The Hindus and Sikhs have their own violent differences among themselves as well as disparities with those of the Islamic faith. China and Japan were opposed to each other regarding Confucius and Shinto, and both were encroached upon by the Christian West. Under the Czar, Orthodox Christendom threatened China and Japan, then Czardom eventually converted to Communism along with China. However, their old fears did not diminish, —they became even greater.

The expansion of the democratic government of the United State in the New World pushed the Indians to the West Coast, to Old Mexico, to the Islands of the Pacific, and to the Philippines. Those who were not enslaved were killed for the sake of spreading democracy. It was Manifest Destiny.

The point being made here is that virtually every ideology has its own ardent leaders who believe that *their one cause is the only cause.* Confrontation is the issue they all face with little room for compromise.

The justification for the use of violence is acceptable, depending on the personal experience and historic data which prejudices the user. The use of long range weapons available today can indiscriminately cause countless loss of lives. By this process, the users project the stigma of *"evil"* as opposed to *"good"* upon their victims. Therefore, it removes from the user the likelihood of suffering some major psychological disorder, as was the case with close encounter combat during the Vietnam war.

The world community faces drastic changes dealing with external\internal social, religious, ethnic, and cultural differences which create negative confrontations and conflicts. Individual societies face internal pressure and opposition brought about by changes in long established beliefs and traditions. The consequence of social upheaval prompts countless disillusioned citizens to adopt a fundamentalist ideology, one which offers a benevolent and lasting stability, especially when similar beliefs are combined. Strength in numbers can have a great impact when the pent-up rage of an individual gains collective acceptance by a group; this kind of power cannot be obtained on a solitary basis. The group, now able to hide individual weaknesses, channels its collective fears and hatreds against the *"evil"* by which it perceives to be threatened. The individual now becomes an integral part of a collective group and sees his/her fears and hatreds in terms of *"good"* against *"evil"* where in their final struggle, *"good will prevail."*

In days long past, The Peace of God, also known as The Truce of God, granted a longer period of relative peace; however, this social structure fell by the way and was replaced by Hugo Grotius' Law of Nations, put into operation in 1648 in the Treaty of Westphalia. This system took root in Europe and from there spread throughout the world. With all the modifications made since 1648, the Law of Nations, as constructed, is falling apart —as did the Peace of God. If the world society faces a continuation of terror in this present age of transition, what will it look to in the future?

Prominent leaders in the world community on whom humanity depends seem to overlook an ancient truth: that the future is fashioned by the present. And the present is an outgrowth of the past. One might hope that the present world society —now aware that it can neither go back in time, nor continue to repeat the misdeeds of the past— will endeavor to learn from the ancients, and perhaps begin to recognize that one of the most inherent human principles is *"To Cherish All Life."*

SUMMARY

W hile there is much talk of a New World Order; the world is more fragmented today than it was prior to the fall of the Berlin Wall. There are those who now believe that the United States is the only super power. This hypothesis obviously ignores The People's Republic of China with the largest armed force in the world, its ever growing arsenal, and a population of over one billion.

What nation is prepared to wage war with The People's Republic of China? And if it were conquered, how would its people be governed? Few people in the United States are able to speak, read, or write the Chinese language with its numerous dialects. Communism is but a flimsy mantle superimposed on Confucianism and will never completely seclude this ancient philosophy which is deeply embedded in Chinese culture.

The collective interest to control warfare is not new. The effort to thwart war has a history of some 1000 years. As early as 989 A.D., French bishops attempted to limit warfare by The Peace of God, or The Truce of God. The European powers in 1648 sought to control war with the Treaty of Westphalia. This treaty, which was made applicable in Europe, introduced the concept of International Law, and thereafter it spread throughout the world. Another effort was made at the Congress of Vienna in 1815, at the end of the Napoleonic Wars. Two more attempts were made in the twentieth century: at the end of the First World War the League of Nations was established at the Treaty of Versailles, and in 1945 when the Second World War ended the United Nations was established. And all these attempts thus far have failed to control war.

As long as humanity ignores the perilous consequence arising from a fragmented view of the world, there is little reason to try to discontinue plans for war. In spite of the psychological and technological innovations which have come about since the dawn of recorded history, humanity continues in what it perceives to be a fractured world. Moving from temple communities to super powers, religion —or some form of social ideology— has played a dominant role in world conflicts. Although numerous attempts have been made to maintain a balance of harmony within religious communities, various religious concepts are so allegorical that they act as catalysts in the continuation of violence.

The current dominant theo-centric religions are Judaism, Christianity, and Islam which arose with Judaism from Mesopotamia, Egypt, and Saudi Arabia. Although they profess to many common beliefs, they engage in bitter confrontations resulting from their different interpretations. These conflicts are spread over a major segment of the earth which encompass millions of people.

Communism is a Judao-Christian heresy, a fact not commonly perceived; although, in Arnold J. Toynbee's classic work, *A Study of History,* it is explained in great length. Communism is a western philosophy; however, it was rejected in major portions of the west, it was sanctioned by the Soviet Union —which was a former Christian society— and The Peoples Republic of China —a former society of Confucianism— some Baltic and Balkan states, and Eastern Europe. Communism, with its own internal conflicts, has created yet another formidable obstacle among the present social orders.

Shinto is the religion of the dominant ruling class of Japan and in many respects it is an ethnic religion. Although it consists chiefly of ancestor worship, nature worship, and a belief in the divinity of the Emperor, its advocates, nonetheless, attempted to force it on Korea, China, and much of Southeast Asia.

Nazism and Fascism sprang from the nucleus of Roman Catholicism and Lutheranism; however, the leaders of each party remained members of the Church of Rome. It may be said that Nazism and Fascism came about when Christianity failed to espouse brotherhood. Ignoring the reign of violence and terror, endorsed by Nazism and Fascism, strong disagreements regarding the different religious practices still exist among national and ethnic organizations.

South Africa advocates apartheid in the name of Christianity. Proclaiming racial superiority —that of white over black— it is not dissimilar from the Nazi concept of Aryan superiority.

The Confederate Christian Churches supported slavery; however, the Northern Churches contested it. In this same fashion, there are those who are on opposite sides in South Africa. Both parties, those who support apartheid, and those who oppose it, use statements from the Bible to confirm their positions. Archbishop Desmond Tutu and other prominent clergy are leading Christian forces in opposition to apartheid.

Hinduism, with its many faces —both violent and peaceful— is almost exclusively confined to India.

In each dominant spiritual realm discussed here, one fact remains: the deepest and most spiritual aspect of these doctrines, and their historical development, is not understood by a vast majority of followers. Consequently, the majority of faithful are simply just that, *"faithful."* They fail to pursue any appreciable knowledge of their own religion. This point confirms that a great number *"faithful"* in all major religions are not necessarily disturbed by the destruction of the world. For many, it is predicted by their faith as the *"the end of time."*

"The end of time" was also a Nazi theory. Hitler sought to bring about "the end", should he fail in his own mission. One should recall that death was the center-point for Nazi blood cults to which Hitler and a number of Germans and other Europeans subscribed.

The prediction of violence and terror in the final judgment consumes a great part of Christian theology. The same is true for Islam, which is found in The Holy Koran. And Shinto followers make extensive use in glorifying death.

Hinduism propounds the idea of the cycles through which the cosmos revolves; these are called kalpa, the basic cycle of some 4,320 million years. Hinduism also speaks of Kali-Yuga as the end in which there is a confusion of classes -a rule of cruel and alien kings. The world is then destroyed by flood and fire. The space of time is not clearly designated in terms of human years or of "years of the Gods." Neither is it clear from Hindu records when the destruction is contemplated. Was the Mahabharata War (circa, 900 B.C.) the date from which destruction was to come?

In *The Wonder That Was India*, A. L. Basham states (on page 321) that the word cycles of the Hindu system is an imperfect synthesis of more than one independent doctrine. Consequently, the measure of time and its outcome are not clear. There are many conflicting views as to the final destruction of all that exists and the creation of a new world.

In Buddhism, the word kalpa is used as a reference to a great expanse of time in the following fashion: One of the sutras defines a kalpa as the period of time it would take a heavenly being descending from heaven once a year and making one sweep of its wings across the top of a mile high mountain to wear it down level with the ground. There are no sutras (sayings attributed to The Buddha) which espouse violence. The same is true of koans and precepts.

Communism justifies violence as a means to overthrow an existing order and establish a new one. The new order would consist of a classless society with a withering away of the state; however, when the forces of Communism overthrew Czarist Russia and the previous regime of China, their respective states remained.

Has Communism really disappeared in the former Soviet Union? It is too early to draw a conclusion. Despite dramatic changes which have taken place in Eastern Europe and within the former Soviet Union, members of the Communist party are still in control of the Russian Parliament, the civil service, the bureaucracy, and the courts —the legal system is controlled by members of the old regime. With a thousand years of a totalitarian state, controlled by a Czarist state and its Communist successor, the creation of a democratic system at this time seems ineffective.

The Empire of Alexander the Great fell into many parts —as did the Greco-Roman Empire. Each was far flung without any available means of adequate transportation and communication where-by authorities could hold onto an area and thus unite divergent people with a common purpose. The Roman Church had to overcome much the same difficulties, yet, today it remains active.

The great empires of the Spanish, the Portuguese, the Dutch, the French and the British lasted for centuries; however, only fragments now remain. In each case, the expanse of oceans, the lack of transportation, and the lack of communication were vital factors in their demise.

There have been periods in the history of the United States when it appeared as though it might collapse. The Articles of Confederation were so haphazardly put together that a new constitution had to be established in 1789. There were many who believed the expanse of the west was too great for one government to hold together. Some of those from New England proposed to withdraw from the Union and go back to England. The growth of sectionalism and the problem of slavery became so great a problem that the result was civil war. The beginning of railroads and industrial growth —with freedom from the strife of Europe— kept the United States from breaking apart.

In light of the breakup of the former Soviet Union, what might this suggest? Its territorial expanse far exceeds any other land mass in the world. What major power is prepared to take over its problems with its lack of railways and highways for transportation, with ethnic unrest, the changing configuration of Eastern Europe, and the Balkans? China is the only major power geographically close; however, there is little indication that it could add millions of people to its already overburdened population. No power bordering the former Soviet Union could either sustain a confrontation with it, or could they absorb it. The former Soviet Union is presently undergoing drastic changes, and it may possibly consolidate, as did the United States after the civil war.

Although the super powers are not openly at war, they still engage in covert acts against each other. Violence in all its myriad forms is increasing throughout the world, prompted by numerous divergent religious and philosophic and ethnic ideals. The increase in the sale and use of drugs heightens violence as does the vast hidden wealth in the international marketing of illegal money. The deplorable acts of today are obvious indications that the social order is failing throughout the world.

The impoverished under-developed world population is accelerating at a pace never before witnessed. As of today, no organization has set forth a plan to employ, house, educate, and provide health care for the population we now have, let alone provide for growth in the immediate future. This was evidenced by the studies of what is happening in Mexico City, Rio de Janeiro, Sao Paula, Cairo, and Calcutta. The current migration into the metropolitan areas is accelerating, creating untold physical violence and destroying the environment.

As the world society moves onward, today becomes tomorrow and all past deeds —great and small— shall be listed in the pages of history. What awaits the youth who shall inherit tomorrow's world? It is hoped that they will have the courage to denounce all acts of violence and terror which continues to shatter today's world.

Since the manuscript of *The Ethics of Violence* was completed more than two years ago, the United States has engaged in war in the Persian Gulf. This brief postscript is necessary to complete the book.

The Saud family conquered Arabia early in this century —with the aid of the Wahabi division of Islam— to bring about a pure form of Islam to the area.

Saudi Arabia is understandably sensitive to the fact that infidels from the West were invited to play a major role in taking part in an Arabian dispute. The consequence of foreign —non-Muslim— intervention in the Persian Gulf War remains to be seen.

To identify a policy of war with a religious theme is as old as recorded history, if not older. Even today, some leaders of state merge Christian Theology with the moral pledge of war. To identify the success of this operation with Christ, to the exclusion of Allah, will be remembered far into the future. The fear, the mistrust, and the doubt that the Islamic world has toward the West has been indicated in previous chapters of this manuscript.

President Bush, on January 28, 1991 cited the teachings of Jesus Christ as the moral force behind the Persian Gulf War (The New York Times, January 28, 1992). Speaking before the National Religious Broadcasters, the President commended them for their support in helping to drive Iraq from Kuwait: "I want to thank you for helping America, as Christ ordained, to be a light unto the world."

An outstanding observation into Islamic thought regarding the foreign intervention in the Gulf War is made by Dr. Safar al-Hawali, Dean of Islamic Studies at Umm al-Qwa University in Mecca. He is a respected scholar, theologian, and spokesman for the Wahabi sect on whom the House of Saud depends. In United States documents from former President Nixon and former President Carter, Dr. Hawali finds a plan to establish military bases in the Near East and he points to the history of the British and French in that area which he asserts now is being taken up by the United States. When he quoted Mohammed, The Prophet —and warned against relying upon the West— it created fear in the House of Saud. He further stated that it is contrary to

Islamic law to use non-Moslem forces in a struggle with Muslims. He sees the West as the primary enemy of Saudi Arabia (the New York Times, November 24, 1990). His cassette tape speeches are distributed throughout Saudi Arabia. With his command of respect within the Wahabi sect, the House of Saud can ill afford to ignore his assertions.

It has been proposed from somewhere within the government —perhaps, as a trial balloon— that since the United States is the last of the super powers, it must work to see that no other arises. This was no sooner stated than a White House spokes-person denied it.

The United States government has agreed to work with the United Nations as long as its purposes are in agreement. If its purposes are not in agreement, the United States asserts that it will work alone.

Throughout the ages, countless leaders have aspired to fashion human society into whatever mold they deemed appropriate; and their tombstones are as legion as were their delusions.

Another shocking act of violence is the final inclusion to this study. A special televised report from Waco, Texas has vividly described the horrifying climax to the critical situation in the standoff of the Branch Davidian cult and its leader, David Koresh. The entire compound was enveloped in a blazing inferno, housing some 87 to 90 men, women, and children. It is not surprising that David Koresh and his followers would obviously choose to die as martyrs in a flaming holocaust, rather than submit to government authority. The anguish comes from the thought that they also chose to sacrifice the lives of innocent children.

From an historical and psychological approach, those who have studied cults know that the leaders and their followers thrive on confrontation —a fundamental fact too often overlooked by the Justice Department and the Federal Bureau of Investigation. This same kind of pattern is followed by authoritarian states where stability —both internally and externally— is at variance with their continued existence. Internal cohesion is gained by searching out enemies from within their ranks; however, when wide acceptance is obtained internally, they must find an enemy on the outside. Cult leaders operate on the same principle as do the dictators who must create foes in order to forestall an appraisal of their own leadership.

The government officials have stated that one primary purpose for an investigation into the Davidian cult was knowledge that David Koresh had procured a large collection of illegal weapons and stored them inside the compound. Another reason —and most important— was the belief that the children inside the compound were being abused.

When David Koresh was reported to have provoked the FBI, and they decided to implant tear gas into the walls of the compound, it only served to confirm his Biblical apocalyptic belief that: according to Koresh's teachings from The Book of Revelations, he and his followers would be caught up in the final day of destruction. It also would prove to his followers that he was, *the Messiah,* their true and unfailing leader.

Patience, however costly and painstakingly drawn out, would have been a better part of valor on the part of the government officials. One shall never know if the children could have been saved; however, their fate would not have hinged upon what action the government officials decided to take. As questions pour in from all across the country, the responsibility of that decision must rest with those who gave the order. To reiterate that from an historical and psychological perspective —*given time*— in all probability, the Branch Davidian organization would have deteriorated and collapsed from within.

BIBLIOGRAPHY

Abe, Masao. 1985. *Zen and Western Thought.* Honolulu: University of Hawaii Press.

Abdiati, Hamonndah. 1975. *Islam In Focus.* Indianapolis: American Trust Publications.

Asprey, Robert B. 1975. *War In The Shadows.* New York: Doubleday.

Baigent, Michael; Richard Leigh, and Henry Lincoln. 1983. *Holy Blood, Holy Grail.* New York: Dell Publishing Company.
____. 1986. *The Messianic Legacy.* New York: Henry Holt.

Basham, A.L. 1954. *The Wonder That Was India.* New York: The Grove Press.

Bergamini, David. 1971. *Japan's Imperial Conspiracy.* New York: William Morrow.

Bloc, Marc. 1961. *Feudal Society, (Vol. 2), translated by L. A. Manyon.* Chicago: University of Chicago Press.

Bohm, David. 1980. *Wholeness and The Implicate Order.* New York: Arc Paperback.

Brown, Raymond Edward. (ed.). 1968. *The Jerome Bible Commentary.* New York: Prentice Hall Press.

Beuger, Morrow. 1962. *The Arab world Today.* New York: Doubleday.

Buttrich, G. Arthur. (ed). 1951. *The Interpretors Bible, (Vols. 3,7,8,9).* Nashville: Abingdon Press.

Carlyle, R.W., and A.J. Carlyle. 1903-1936. *A History of Medieval Political Thought In The West, (Vols. 1-6).* London: W. Blackwood and Sons.

Chacour, Elias. 1984. *Blood Brothers.* Old Tappan, NJ: Chosen Books.

Chen, Kenneth K.S. 1968. *Buddhism, The Light of Asia.* Woodbury, NY: Education Series, Inc.
____. 1964. *Buddhism In China, An Historical Survey.* Princeton: Princeton University Press.

Commager, Henry Steele. 1985. *Academic.* Chicago: University of Chicago Press.

Cook, Francis H. 1977. *Hau-Yen Buddhism, The Jewel Net of India.* University Park: The Pennsylvania State University Press.

Conway, Flo, and Jim Seigelman. 1982. *Holy Blood, Holy Terror.* New York: Doubleday.

Crell, H.G. 1950. *Chinese Thought, From Confucius to Mao-Tse-tung.* New York: Mentor Books.

Dunn, Richard S. 1970. *The Age of Religious Wars, 1559-1689.* New York: Norton.

Durant, Will. 1944. *Caesar and Christ.* New York: Simon and Schuster.

Edwards, Charles S. 1981. *Hugo Grotius, The Miracle of Holland.* Chicago: Nelson Hall.

Encyclopaedia Britannica, Inc. Great Books of The Western World. 1952. *Locke, Berkley, Hume, (Vol. 35).* Chicago: William Benton.
____. 1952. *Karl Marx, The Communist Manifest and Capital, Vol. 50).*
____. 1952. *The Prince, The Levithan, (Vol. 23).*
____. 1952. *Augustine, (Vol. 35).*

Fairbanks, John K. 1986. *The Great Chinese Revolution, 1800-1985.* New York: Harper and Row.

Fargo, Ladiolas. 1974. *Aftermath, Martin Borman and The Fourth Reich.* New York: Simon and Schuster.

Fest, Joachim. 1973. *Hitler.* New York. Vintage Random House.

Franklin, John Hope. 1980. *From Slavery to Freedom.* New York: Alfred Knopf.

Hawking, Stephen. 1988. *A Brief History of Time.* New York: Bantam Books.

Hitler, Adolph. 1971. *Mein Kampf.* Boston: Houghton Mifflin.

Hobhouse, L.T. 1918. *The Metaphysical Theory of The State.* London: Allen and Unwin.

Hoffman, Peter. 1977. *The History of German Resistance.* Cambridge: MIT Press.

Karris, O.F.M., and George H. Spoltz. 1982. *Collegeville Bible Commentary.* Collegeville, MN: Liturgical Press.

Kapleau, Roshi Philip. 1978. *Zen: Dawn In the West.* New York: Doubleday.

Ludewky, E.F.C. 1985. *The Footprints of The Buddha.* London: Unwin Press, Ltd.

MacMullem, Ramsey. 1964. *The Christianization of The Roman Empire.* New Haven: Yale University Press.

Mc Ilwain, C.H. 1932. *The Growth of Political Thought in the West from the Greeks to the Middle Ages.* New York: Macmillan Company.

Mc Neill, William H. 1963. *The Rise of The West.* Chicago: University of Chicago Press.

Mortimer, Edward. 1982. *Faith and Power, The Politics of Islam.* New York: Random House.

Mosse, George L. 1964. *The Crisis of German Ideology, Intellectual Origins of The Third Reich.* New York: Grosset and Dunlap.

Murphy, Paul I., and Rene R. Arlington. 1983. *La Popessa.* New York: Warner Books.

Murray, M.A. 1962. *The Witch Cult in Western Europe.* Oxford, England: Clarendon Press.

Needham, Joseph. 1954. *Science and Civilization In China.* Cambridge, England: Cambridge University Press.

Noss, John B. 1963. *Man's Religions.* New York: Macmillan Company.

Ozmet, Steven. 1980. *The Age of Reform, 1250-1550.* New Haven: Yale University Press.

Pares, Sir Bernard. 1973. *A History of Russia.* New York: Alfred Knopf.

Payne, Robert. 1973. *Adolph Hitler.* New York: Praeger Publishers.

Ravenscroft, Trevor. 1973. *The Spear of Destiny.* New York: Putnam's Sons.

Riding, Alan. 1986. *Distant Neighbors.* New York: Vintage Press.

Sabine, George. 1958. *A History of Political Theory.* New York: Henry Holt.

Sansone, G.B. 1938. *The National Faith of Japan, A Study of Modern Shinto.* New York: E.P. Dutton.

Sanders, George. 1963. *The High Walls of Jerusalem.* New York: Holt Rinehart.

Sarton, George. 1952. *History of Science, (Vol. 1).* New York: The Norton Press Library.

Shipler, David K. 1986. *Arab and Jew, Wounded Spirit In A Promised Land.* New York: Times Books.

Shirer, William L. 1960. *The Rise and Fall of The Third Reich.* New York: Simon and Schuster.

Sklar, D. 1977. *The Nazis and The Occult.* New York: Dorset Press.

Smith, Huston. 1965. *The Religions of Man.* New York: Harper and Row.

Spengler, Oswald. 1926. *The Decline of The West, (Vols. 1-2).* New York: Alfred Knopf.

Stein, Walter Johannes. 1988. *The Nineth Century and The Holy Grail.* London: Temple Lodge.

Toynbee, Arnold J. 1955. *A Study of History, (10 Vols.).* New York: Oxford University Press.
____. 1957. *Christianity Among The Religions of The World.* New York: Scribner's Sons.
____. 1961. *America and The World Revolution.* New York: Oxford University Press.
____. 1966. *Change and Habit.* New York: Oxford University Press.

____. 1969. *Experiences.* New York: Oxford University Press.

____. 1971. *Surviving The Future.* New York: Oxford University Press.

____. 1978. *An Historian's Approach To Religion.* New York: Oxford University Press.

Trevor-Roper, Hugh. 1964. *The Rise of Christian Europe.* New York: Harcourt Brace.

Williams, George Huston. 1974. *Four Modalities of Violence, Journal of Church and State, (Vol. 16).* Waco, TX: Baylor University Press.

INDEX

About the author

GEORGE FAUST was born in Eureka Springs, Arkansas. He earned a MA degree in Political Science from the University of Arkansas, a PhD in Latin American History from the University of Chicago, and a JD from John Marshall School of Law, Cleveland State University.

Professor Emeritus, History, Cuyahoga Community College, Cleveland, Ohio where he taught history for 23 years. He is also legal counsel with Lustig, Icove, and Lustig legal firm.

He was an investigative reporter on special assignment in 1963 for WHK Radio and traveled throughout the Caribbean Islands and Latin America to areas of revolution in Venezuela, Brazil, Peru, Ecuador, Columbia and Guatemala. As result of trip he delivered a White House Special Report to President John F. Kennedy.

A member of the International Society for Study of Multiple Personalities and Dissociation, sponsored by The Department of Psychiatry, Rush Presbyterian, St. Luke's Medical Center, Chicago, and chairperson of the Law and Ethics task force.

Appeared on local radio and television as an historian and lawyer versed in the dynamics of rapid social change, resulting in stress on individuals and institutions.

Cleo Heron Award in History and Charles R. Walgreen Award in History - The University of Chicago.

Special recognition from State Legislature, State of Ohio. Meritorious award for service to Cuyahoga Community College. Special Service award from president of ISSMP&D, 1991. Current study in urban guerrilla warfare in conjunction with international terrorism. Taught special courses which aim to make clear the social, psychological, cultural, and religious dynamics of terrorism in its historical and modern context.